China Assignment

CHINA

ASSIGNMENT

By Karl Lott Rankin

★★★

Seattle: UNIVERSITY OF WASHINGTON PRESS

TO MY WIFE

☆☆☆

Preface

THIS ESSAY sketches the development of United States relations with China from the middle of 1949 to the beginning of 1958, as seen from Canton, Hong Kong, Taipei, and during short trips to the United States. It was written abroad, in spare moments, where documentary material often was unavailable. Moreover, I could not know all that was happening behind the scenes in Washington, particularly outside the Department of State. I venture to say, however, that my position during this period of eight and one-half years permitted me to see as much of the whole picture as any American dealing with Chinese affairs.

It will be noted that quotations are very largely from correspondence that I prepared. This need not imply claims to originality for the ideas presented. Many persons in and outside the United States government were thinking, speaking, and writing along similar lines. Still others, no less conscientiously, were developing quite different approaches to the China problem. However, extensive inclusion of material written at the time is the most convenient way of describing the unfolding scene as it appeared to me at successive posts abroad, and without the benefit of hindsight. Some of these excerpts may sound unwarrantedly alarming, or seem to support unduly the side of Nationalist China. This was done deliberately, for my pervading purpose was to assist those in Washington who shared my own sense of urgency about China and the Far East in general and who believed that a positive and active American strategy was indispensable. The milder presentation of so grave a situation could have given comfort in quarters favoring disengagement. With American responsibilities so heavy and widespread, I could not place those with whom I agreed in a position to be told, "What are you worrying about? Our man on the spot doesn't seem alarmed."

A major responsibility of the diplomatist is to interpret to his government the policies and opinions of the country where he is stationed. In so doing he often appears to favor that country more strongly than would be expected from a dispassionate observer. Today, however, the United States is no longer a neutral observer in world affairs. Rather, the task is to determine how a given situation can be exploited in our national interest, which we hope and believe coincides with the best interests of friendly nations everywhere. Particularly in a region where peace is under constant threat, the question is not whether we should support those on our side, but how we can do so most effectively. One of the oldest communist techniques is to discredit our friends in the hope that we may grow weary of supporting them. In this they count on the aid of many Americans, well meaning and otherwise. Unfortunately, even today a substantial minority of our fellow citizens seem not to have progressed in their thinking since the days when isolationism and neutrality were in vogue.

The shortcomings of the government of the Republic of China, now established on Taiwan, are an open book. They have been elaborated, admitted, exaggerated, or belabored by a host of Americans, Chinese, and others. I felt no compulsion to add to these indictments, except as the practical application of our aid programs, or an overriding American interest, might be involved. On balance, the Republic of China was and remains a very great asset to the United States and the free world. A substantial portion of the cream of China is on Taiwan, laboring intelligently and devotedly. They are as keenly aware of their shortcomings, past and present, as any American. Criticizing them needlessly only invites quotations out of context to the detriment of both American and Chinese interests. We cannot be "neutral" in any case.

Our practical task is to keep Nationalist Chinese strategy in harmony with our own to the largest extent possible. Views that seem widely divergent as to the offensive capabilities desirable in

their military establishment usually give way to reasonable compromise after careful and sympathetic discussion. In the economic
field, short-term and long-term considerations, as well as the degree
of self-sufficiency warranted for the island of Taiwan, also can be
harmonized by the exercise of patient effort and good will on both
sides. Even on the great issue of mainland China's future, we can
share the hope of its eventual liberation from the communists.
Meanwhile, American firmness and consistency provide the best hope
for preventing the outbreak of large-scale open conflict and for
fostering the evolution that will some day bring a united China back
into the family of nations.

I take full responsibility for the opinions expressed, although
they represent an interpretation of what I believe to have been basic
policy under two administrations. Differences between the Department of State and its representatives abroad usually and naturally
stem from the greater importance attached to domestic political
factors in one case, and to the situation where the diplomat is
stationed in the other. In practice, such differences usually relate to
tactics, notably timing and emphasis. It is the duty of an official
representative in the field to report frankly on the situation in his
territory and to make recommendations accordingly. Whether these
recommendations can or should be adopted is a matter for higher
decision in the light of circumstances at home, and within the limits
of political possibilities. The man in the field must try to accept such
decisions with good grace.

A popular notion today is that American diplomatic and consular
officers abroad simply carry out orders received by teletype or
otherwise, which leave them no discretion and no possibility of influencing policy. Yet we also are told that on occasion one or two
comparatively junior Foreign Service officers at a critical post have
been able to sabotage official Washington policy and redirect it
along entirely different lines. The truth, of course, lies in between.
An unwritten law in the Foreign Service is: Never ask for instructions from Washington if you can help it. It is presumed that the
officer in the field is familiar with official policy; in most cases he
is in a better position than anyone else to decide how a given problem should be handled in the light of that policy, and whether
circumstances demand that he ask for instructions. His responsibility

sometimes is very great. A mistake is not impossible, and on the rare occasions when damage results, it may be assumed either that the officer stationed abroad had been inadequately informed of recent policy developments, or that those in charge of personnel assignments made an error in selecting him for the post. Despite these risks, our system works far better than that usually followed by authoritarian states, whose representatives dare not take action without specific instructions and are not encouraged to have opinions or to make recommendations.

The officer in charge of a Foreign Service post has wide latitude and freedom in expressing his frank opinions on policy and other matters to the Department of State. I have heard of instances in which ambassadors and others were told to cease and desist, but never having experienced this myself during thirty-four years of foreign service, I must conclude that it rarely happens. There is, of course, a wide difference between expressing one's self confidentially to the Department of State and letting down one's hair before representatives of the press, particularly on a delicate issue at a crucial moment. Under several administrations, I always have felt encouraged to express myself freely on policy in addressing the Department, whether or not my views seemed to diverge from the accepted position.

The following pages doubtless would make more interesting reading if they featured direct quotations from prominent persons on controversial subjects. In so doing, of course, I should be liable to charges of quoting out of context. More important, attention would be diverted from issues to personalities. My effort in this book, as at the time events were taking place, was to present pertinent facts as they were known to me, and to discuss issues frankly but impersonally.

Some repetition is inevitable, even essential, in emphasizing points of particular importance over a period of years. I have tried to reduce iteration to the minimum needed for clarity by including only the more significant passages from despatches, letters, and telegrams, selected in a manner to make footnotes unnecessary. Progressively fewer details have been included in the later chapters, again to minimize tedious repetition. In consequence, the narrative becomes less continuous. Official visits and conferences inevitably covered much the same ground over and over again. Many different individuals were involved, particularly on the American side, and it was desirable to stimulate everyone's interest in China's problems. But the basic character of these problems did not change. New and significant developments, of course, required interpretation and handling as they occurred. Later chapters deal with such developments, and no pretense is made of presenting anything approaching a complete account. Several volumes would be required to do so.

My hope in preparing this book is that it may contribute in a modest way to a better understanding of China in relation to the national interests of the United States, and thereby help to justify a continuing strategy of active support for our Far Eastern friends in general. A secondary purpose is to portray the magnitude and complexity of the task confronting us today in coordinating United States operations abroad. The steadily increasing scope and dimensions of government in the United States continue to be reflected, unfortunately but perhaps almost inevitably, in the number of American agencies and personnel working abroad. Nevertheless, gratifying progress has been made during recent years in coordinating these activities. I should like to think that my efforts made some small contribution to this result, and hence that the strictures that I directed to Washington over the years may be regarded with tolerance. Despite the incubus of a large and complicated organization, the coordination of American activities on Taiwan and with the various interested agencies in Washington had reached a most satisfactory state during my last years in Taipei. There and elsewhere, our foreign program of political, economic, and military aid had come of age.

Over six years have passed since the end of my China assignment. On a visit to Taiwan in 1962, I was gratified to see that many of the economic, military, and social projects started in earlier years had been brought to completion or were advancing commendably. With a population rapidly approaching twelve million, the island was enjoying an ever rising standard of living. I was glad to find President Chiang in evident good health and spirits. He was as confident as ever in China's future. But basic problems evidently remained. For all the successes of our cooperative effort on Taiwan, the sheer magnitude of Red-held China, and its growing strength, despite setbacks, served to perpetuate the vital question whether the free world was indeed holding its own in East Asia.

Increasing troubles for the free world in Southeast Asia have underlined anew the vital role of the strong Chinese Nationalist forces in being on Taiwan and other islands. Unquestionably, they have been a major factor in discouraging open and large-scale intervention by Peiping in Vietnam and elsewhere. Had it not been for this potent threat to their flank, the Red Chinese might well have taken over most or all of Southeast Asia, in the absence of intervention by United States forces on a scale approaching that of the Korean War. In contrast to 1950-53, the Chinese Nationalist forces today are well armed and combat ready.

One of the most extensively publicized developments of the past several years has been the increasing friction between Red China and the Soviet Union. Eventual trouble between the two communist giants was not unexpected, although it reached a stage of public altercation rather earlier than had been generally anticipated. Historically, Russia has been China's chief enemy. The Great Wall was built more than 2,000 years ago as a defense against attack from the north and west. Since the end of the sixteenth century, the Russian empire has been expanding eastward, adding territory at China's expense. Outer Mongolia was detached from China and proclaimed a "Peoples' Republic" as recently as 1924. It was inevitable that even a communist China would not relish taking orders from Moscow forever.

Following the usual communist technique, differences between the Soviet Union and Red China have been portrayed as an ideological conflict, whereas in fact they represent a power struggle. Ironically enough, Moscow's intensive military and economic aid to Peiping during the 1950's undoubtedly exacerbated mutual relations. As the Chinese Reds found themselves growing stronger, militarily and industrially, their actions became more independent. At the same time, the Soviets realized that they were creating a Frankenstein, which some day could be a serious rival, and meanwhile might involve them in dangerous and unwanted adventures. No doubt the virtual stoppage of Soviet aid programs has slowed the economic and military progress of communist China, to the relative advantage of its neighbors and the free world in general.

☆ *Preface* ☆

Have the troubles between Moscow and Peiping altered the Far Eastern situation fundamentally? I think not. Red China carries the flag of communist conspiracy and aggression in Asia at least as avidly and perhaps more recklessly than Russia. So far from not being "real" communists, the leaders in Peiping are at pains to prove that the mantle of Marx now rests on their shoulders rather than on the Russians. And despite grave internal weaknesses, Red China is still the mightiest Asian power, other than the Soviet Union itself. It remains true that there can be no peace in Asia while mainland China is ruled by a predatory regime, particularly a communist one. Moreover, Moscow and Peiping are quite capable of patching up their differences, for a time at least, as have other communist states after similarly acrimonious wrangles. They are most likely to do so when they see an opportunity to discomfit their common and chief antagonist, the United States. And let no one suppose that the Soviet Union has yet abandoned its purpose to dominate the communist world, while proceeding to bury the rest of us.

For the time being, however, important cracks are evident in the formerly monolithic communist conspiracy. Evidently these were not started by any United States efforts to wean satellites away from Moscow. Rather they are due in large part to strong American action in Greece, in Korea, in the Formosa Strait, in Vietnam, and elsewhere, which forestalled new communist successes and promoted dissension among the Red aggressors. But monolithic or not, communism as it has proved itself internationally, rather than as an internal politico-economic system, remains the capital enemy. It promises to remain so while propagated by such colossi as Red Russia and Red China, together or separately.

How, then, should the apparent schism between Moscow and Peiping affect United States policy? If we use the word "policy" in its traditional sense, there can be no change whatsoever. The foreign policy of the United States is well stated by the Preamble to the United Nations Charter. In support of the continuing purposes and principles of the Charter, American strategy must maintain a global confrontation of the communist menace until, in God's own time, our enemies have proved by word and deed that they are enemies no longer. So much for policy and strategy.

☆ *Preface* ☆

In the field of tactics, however, even temporary disunity among communist states can provide opportunities for flexible action by the United States in its own interest and that of the entire free world. Commodity and cultural exchanges, transport, credit, and other features of international life may be encouraged or discouraged as circumstances warrant. To date, Red China qualifies only for negative treatment, in contrast to certain countries in Eastern Europe. In all of this, however, the criteria of relative benefit must be continuously and rigorously applied, both on behalf of American interests, and of our friends and allies most directly concerned. In this process, no opportunity should be missed to build up bargaining positions, a field in which the United States has been habitually negligent.

Under no circumstances must the employment of flexible tactics be allowed to erode basic policy and strategy, or to undermine the confidence of either friend or foe in our determination to persist until that policy and strategy have triumphed. We must continue steadfastly until the would-be aggressors have been convinced that aggression in any form no longer pays, and that the peaceful principles and purposes of the United Nations set forth a policy which all nations must accept without reserve. "Aggression" and "peaceful," of course, are understood to mean what they do to reasonable men everywhere. Communists, whether of the Moscow or the Peiping strain, try unceasingly to insinuate acceptance in men's minds that aggression is anything which interferes with communist expansion, and that peace results quite simply from the absence of such interference. We must keep these issues clear as we go forward.

K. L. R.

Athens, March, 1964

ABBREVIATIONS

a.i.	Ad Interim
ANZUS	Australia, New Zealand, United States
APO	Army Post Office
CBS	Columbia Broadcasting System
CINCPAC	Commander-in-Chief, Pacific
* ECA	Economic Cooperation Administration
FE	Bureau of Far Eastern Affairs, Department of State
* FOA	Foreign Operations Administration
FY	Fiscal Year
GRC	Government of the Republic of China
* ICA	International Cooperation Administration
JCRR	Joint Commission on Rural Reconstruction (U.S.–Chinese)
JCS	Joint Chiefs of Staff (U.S.)
KMT	Kuomintang (Chinese National Party)
MAAG	Military Assistance Advisory Group
* MDAP (MDA)	Mutual Defense Assistance Program
* MSA	Mutual Security Administration
NATO	North Atlantic Treaty Organization
POL	Petroleum Products (Petroleums, Oils, Lubricants)
PX	Post Exchange
SCAP	Supreme Commander Allied Powers
UN (UNO)	United Nations Organization
UNRRA	United Nations Relief and Rehabilitation Administration
UPI	United Press International
USAF	United States Air Force
USIA	United States Information Agency

* Successive names of organizations and programs for U.S. foreign aid.

USIS	United States Information Service (USIA operations abroad)
USN	United States Navy
USO	United Service Organizations
U.S.S.R.	Union of Soviet Socialist Republics
USTDC	United States Taiwan Defense Command

Contents

☆☆☆

Illustrations

China Assignment

China Coast and Taiwan

1: China

THE NEXT post was to be in China after all, and the date was July 9, 1949.

Returning from a fishing trip in northern Maine to our summer home in South Bridgton I found a letter from the Department of State. Instead of going to Jerusalem after home leave, as my earlier orders read, I was to relieve Jack Cabot as consul general in Shanghai. Two years earlier I had been slated for Shanghai, but the serious illness of our ambassador to Greece and the imminent transfer of his deputy had led the Department to send me back for a third tour of duty in Athens. Cabot had gone to Shanghai instead. Now it was my turn.

The Department's letter admitted that conditions in China were rather unsettled, but spoke hopefully of the future. In fact, it was suggested that the situation probably would be stabilized shortly after my arrival, although no compliment to me seems to have been intended. The Chinese communist armies had occupied Shanghai not long before, and our consular staff had been besieged for some time in their office building by disgruntled former employees of the Navy. One consular officer had been imprisoned and beaten. All of this and much more had been featured in the American press.

But the immediate point was that the Department wanted me to leave my wife behind in the United States. I was annoyed at the prospect of having to fight this out for the third time in eight years. There are circumstances, of course, where wives should not accompany their husbands. In the Foreign Service these are indeed few and far between, and long experience has shown that it is a matter for the persons concerned to decide in all but the most exceptional cases. The place for a Foreign Service wife is with her husband unless they themselves decide that the welfare of children or other pressing family problems require a temporary exception. Pauline and I talked it over; my reply to the Department was that I would return to Washington immediately and expected to find a way for my wife to accompany me to the Far East.

This solicitude for families reminded me of a letter I had received some months earlier from a storage and forwarding company in Washington. I had been expecting transfer orders, but nothing definite had come through. The storage company informed me that I was about to be moved and offered the use of their lift vans. Some days later a second letter arrived stating that the company had just learned my new post was to be Jerusalem; it was regretted that a valuable lift van could not be risked in such a move. This was the first definite word I had received of my new post, and the Department's later confirmation failed to indicate a solicitude corresponding to that of the forwarders for their lift vans.

In Washington there was more concern than decision as to what the United States should do about China. The unhappy White Paper dealing with recent Chinese-American relations was in the printer's hands, and I was given a typescript to read en route to the Far East. Ambassador John Leighton Stuart was to leave Nanking and return to the United States shortly. Consul General Cabot was ill and would accompany him. Meanwhile our embassy was being set up on a skeleton basis in Canton, where the Chinese government had established its temporary capital after evacuating Nanking. The position of consul general in Canton, our oldest consular or diplomatic post in the Far East, was vacant. My passport would show that I was assigned there; I was to await the arrival of the communists in Canton and persuade them to let me go on to Shanghai.

Our flight across the United States and the Pacific was uneventful. The extent of reconstruction in Tokyo was a revelation after seeing war-damaged cities in Europe. Our next stop was Okinawa. Typhoon Gloria of 1949 had just passed over the island, causing great destruction. Ambassador Stuart and Consul General Cabot were expected to fly in any day from Nanking, but weather and exit formalities were upsetting all plans, and there was no certainty as to when their plane might get through. They landed in Okinawa the day after we took off in a vain attempt to reach Hong Kong. We wound up in Manila instead, and arrived in the British Crown Colony a day later, in a rainstorm.

II

Except for the midsummer heat, humidity, and torrential rains, Hong Kong was wonderful. A political anachronism, it was nevertheless an outstanding example of what Chinese intelligence and hard work could accomplish under a capable government pursuing sound economic policies and dispensing justice of a high order. Of course, we had no idea at the time that we would soon be returning to Hong Kong to spend a pleasant if strenuous year.

My first call in Hong Kong was at the American Consulate General, which for more than twenty years had been located in an upper floor of the Colony's most imposing business structure, the Hong Kong and Shanghai Bank Building. A small crowd was waiting to go up in the elevators, but my chances of being included in the first trip seemed rather good. The door opened and the descending passengers were disgorged. Suddenly the elevator was full and I was still outside. No one had pushed me or stepped on my toes; I simply had not made it. Next time I wormed my way to within three feet of the elevator; by means of a little pushing, I fear, the door closed behind me instead of in my face.

It was my first experience in a Chinese crowd. The individuals were mostly short and slight, as is usual among the so-called Cantonese of South China, and their average weight was little more than half of mine. How, then, had I been pushed aside without realizing it? Later I learned something of both the philosophy and technique involved. China has suffered from overpopulation for centuries, and a Chinese who allows himself habitually to be overtaken or crowded out should expect to starve. Yet the Chinese are essentially a polite people, even if few of them can afford the luxury of saying, "After you, my dear Alphonse!" So they use a light but steady pressure with their backs, which is both impersonal and effective in a crowd. In my little adventure with the elevator I noticed also how clean and neat everyone was about his person, no matter how simply dressed. There was nothing of the odor one experiences in a crowd in many warm regions, only a slight mustiness from clothing which a damp climate rarely allows to become perfectly dry.

Consul General George Hopper gave me a cordial welcome and was most helpful. Nothing startling had occurred since my departure from Washington a few days earlier. Communications with Canton were normal and the communist army had made no further advance to the south along the Hankow-Canton railroad. They were reported to be at least three hundred miles north of Canton. Hong Kong itself was jammed with refugees, mostly Chinese but also including many Americans and others, all fleeing from the doubtful delights of communism. The Consulate General in Hong Kong was still a comparatively small office; that in Canton was considerably larger. Mr. Hopper and his staff were hard pressed to assist Americans coming out of China. Hotels were overflowing and accommodations of any kind were difficult to obtain. The entrance hall and main corridor of the Consulate General were piled with the baggage of Americans who had no other place to leave it.

After calling on the Consul General and several leading American businessmen in Hong Kong, I obtained reservations on the river steamer for Canton. The distance is about ninety miles, a night's run. The vessel was simple in its appointments, but clean and comfortable. I was intrigued by the elaborate iron grill which shut off the forward part of the steamer, including the bridge and wheel house. This seems to have been a common feature along the China coast where, in the past at least, a gang among the passengers might attempt to take over the ship for purposes of their own.

At daybreak we had left the wide Pearl River estuary and were moving slowly up a muddy channel bordered by low, flat land. In the distance were weirdly shaped hills springing abruptly from the great plain. Mist rising here and there against this background recalled typical Chinese paintings. And why not, since this was indeed China, improbable landscape and all?

III

By midmorning, August 6, 1949, our steamer was moored in Canton, near the great steel bridge that was to be blown up only a few weeks later. On shore some American faces could be seen in the teeming crowd, which justified that adjective as only Asian crowds can. There was much shouting as numerous coolies swarmed on board, by regular and irregular routes. At least one fell in the river, but he came to no harm. In due course we went ashore and were greeted by Lewis Clark, who was in charge of our refugee embassy, and Robert Folsom, the senior consul, with other members of their staffs. A short drive brought us to one of the foot bridges which provided the only access to the island of Shameen.

Built on a bank of mud and sand in the river nearly a century earlier, Shameen was a bit of Europe with its substantial buildings, broad lawns, magnificent trees, and wide avenues where no wheeled traffic was allowed. After World War II the island ceased to be an international concession and came under full Chinese control. However, it remained the site of foreign consulates and business houses. The American Consulate General occupied a large rented compound, including a spacious but rather shabby residence and a somewhat larger building containing offices and staff apartments. We moved into the residence, where Clark and Bradley Connors, the senior representative of the United States Information Service, also were living.

Although the communist armies had advanced no further, thinking in Washington had developed rapidly in a matter of days, according to the telegrams awaiting me in Canton. My continuing on to Shanghai, and the earlier assumption that Consul General Edmund Clubb in Peiping would soon establish some kind of *de facto* relations with the communist regime in that city, apparently had been shelved.

Everyone expected the Red troops to occupy Canton very soon, without serious fighting and within perhaps a week after resuming their southward march. The immediate question was whether both the Embassy and Consulate General in Canton should be closed and the American staffs and records evacuated before the communists took over. The Department had asked Clark's opinion. He had replied in the affirmative just the day before I arrived, adding that my views would be telegraphed subsequently.

As a new arrival in China, I made the only comment that seemed appropriate. I telegraphed that the decision should be based on broad policy. The United States could choose among at least three courses of action. One of these would foresee hampering the Chinese communist conquest by such means as encouraging resistance movements and tacitly acquiescing in the "port closure" or modified blockade of a portion of the Chinese coast, which had been announced by the Nationalist government of the Republic of China. A second course for the United States would be a complete hands-off policy in China for the foreseeable future. Either of these alternatives suggested the desirability of announcing that all or nearly all United States government establishments in China should be closed, including Canton in any case. This would help to clarify our position and hasten decisions by missionary and other American organizations on withdrawing their personnel. As for routine consular functions in the Canton district, I observed that they could be assumed conveniently by the American Consulate General in Hong Kong.

In the same telegram I mentioned a third policy alternative, in which the United States might envisage the eventual recognition of the Chinese communist regime. In that case, I assumed that skeleton staffs would be maintained at certain American consular establishments in China to provide continuity.

IV

Pending a decision from Washington, tentative plans were made either to close the Consulate General entirely or to keep it open with a skeleton staff. After considerable inquiry I determined that ten Americans would be sufficient to carry on the prospective volume of work. Several rented buildings could be given up and all United States operations concentrated in two government-owned buildings on Shameen, which would provide office space and also house the greatly reduced American staff. Personnel were interviewed individually; ten were selected who had the necessary qualifications and were prepared to remain under communist occupation.

I reported my findings to Washington and commended the staff for its devotion to duty.

There was also the larger problem of the American community as a whole. Businessmen nearly all had left for Hong Kong or points beyond. Our records showed several hundred American missionaries as residents of the Canton consular district, but the true figure evidently was smaller. United States citizens living abroad are traditionally lax in registering at the nearest consulate. Missionaries are more careful than most, and usually had registered in Canton on arrival. But with the threat of communist occupation, and the frustration inseparable from still another evacuation, it was not surprising that many had failed to notify the Consulate General of their departure.

We therefore based our figures on the usual assumption as to numbers of Americans: when the colony in a given area is increasing, consular figures are too low; when the actual total is declining, they are too high. Although it seemed unlikely, considerable numbers of American citizens might possibly appear in Canton, seeking help of various kinds, if it were announced that the Consulate General was closing. The probabilities were assessed as far as possible pending a decision from Washington. Meanwhile no action could be undertaken that would attract public notice.

As chargé d'affaires, Lewis Clark was maintaining close contact with the refugee Chinese government in Canton. I was in touch with Chinese officials only incidentally, but among others I met for the first time the Acting Foreign Minister, George K. C. Yeh. Later, on Taiwan, he was to contribute spectacularly in reviving the prestige and influence of the Nationalist government. But in Canton the outlook was calamitous. The publication of the American White Paper at that critical moment seemed almost a *coup de grâce* for his government. Nevertheless, Yeh refused to issue a public reply other than a simple, noncontroversial statement: desperate as its position was, the Republic of China was not yet burning all of its bridges, whatever the United States might do.

The bulky White Paper, consisting largely of selected official documents dealing with Chinese-American relations in 1944-49, was a mixture of fact and opinion as expressed in confidential correspondence by various American officials. The chief criticisms of the paper related inevitably to the inclusion of certain documents and the omission of others, together with the fact that it was published so soon after the events had taken place. It had been a fairly general custom among friendly countries that official publications dealing with important and controversial subjects, such as the war period in China, would be issued only after a considerable lapse of time. The Vatican is said to regard one hundred years as an appropriate interval, although ten to twenty years would be more usual, except perhaps during a war. But the White Paper on Chinese-American relations dealt with recent, almost current, events, making public confidential material touching upon many persons still in high office. I feel that the most valid position is that it should never have been published at all.

▼

In a few spare moments during the time we were awaiting Washington's decision, Pauline and I saw a little of Canton. It has been described as the most Chinese of the great seaports of China. Certainly there was not much to suggest Western influence outside the island of Shameen. Yet Canton had been somewhat modernized in the preceding generation. The maze of narrow lanes, which made it impossible to find an address without a guide, had been supplemented by wide, straight streets cut through the old city at considerable intervals on a gridiron pattern. Along these streets seemingly endless rows of monotonous structures had been built of reinforced concrete, the wide balconies on every story providing shelter for pedestrians on the sidewalks and for countless thousands living on the floors above. Color was supplied by great signs in Chinese characters, many in neon lights, which advertised the shops on the street floor, and by the ever-present washing stretched to dry on bamboo poles from the balconies above.

On one occasion I stood by the river bank with an elderly Englishman of long China experience, watching some of the thousands of Cantonese who live their entire lives on the water. Some members of the family might work on land, while others earned a few *yuan* with their sampans in transporting persons or goods. But most of the small craft seemed to move only rarely. Many families kept ducks, who swam about in the daytime but were trained to return to the proper boat every night, on the double, by the simple custom of spanking the last duck to get aboard. With nearly every ordinary activity of human life unfolding before us, my English friend observed, "One can't expect these people to come ashore and pay a nickel."

A week after our arrival in Canton instructions came from Washington to close all United States government establishments in the city. Clark and I were allowed to use our judgment as to the schedule. In size of staff and physical property his problem was simpler than mine, and a public announcement was made on August 19, that, in view of the communist threat to Canton, the American Embassy staff was being evacuated to Hong Kong. The Consulate General was closed for regular business on the same day, but continued to function on an emergency basis until August 24, when the records and more valuable movable government property were loaded on a steamer for Hong Kong and the remaining furniture placed in one of the American-owned buildings for storage. Three Chinese custodians were appointed to stay in the buildings; other members of our Chinese staff who wished to leave Canton were sent to Hong Kong or Taipei. The British Consulate General assumed general charge of our interests; a few months later their staff would leave too.

During the final ten days, meetings were held with representatives of United States philanthropic groups. Although all American businessmen had left, it was only natural that missionary organizations were reluctant to abandon their churches, their schools, and their many Christian Chinese friends. I discussed the problem frankly with several of them, remarking that I sympathized with their desire to stay but predicted that all of them would be out of China within a few months. And so it happened.

VI

In view of the relatively small number of Americans to be evacuated, an aircraft supplied by Vice Admiral Oscar C. Badger, Commander of United States Naval Forces in the Western Pacific, was able to handle nearly the entire movement by a series of daily flights from Hong Kong. August 23 was to see the evacuation of the last official American except for two who were to leave by river steamer with the last shipment of furniture and vehicles two days later. Our bags were packed and the plane came in on schedule—with an unannounced load of American correspondents who nearly filled the aircraft on the return trip as well. In consequence, five of us unpacked, found some beds, and spent another sweltering night in Canton.

On my last walk, alone, in the city I wondered what the Cantonese people thought about the Westerners who were leaving them and the communist armies who were expected shortly. I saw no other Americans or Europeans on my walk, and felt somewhat conspicuous in consequence. But there was no sign of hostility toward the lone foreign devil and not infrequently he received a pleasant smile. Was it right for us to run out on them? Under the circumstances it seemed the sensible thing to do, but in a larger context our withdrawal was an admission of failure. Could we have done better in developing and implementing a policy toward China, and what should we do in the future? I had been in China only seventeen days and answers to these questions were not apparent. I felt a profound sense of frustration and foreboding.

My last duty was to issue a final press release stating that the oldest American consular office in China, first opened in 1786, was closed on August 24, 1949. The Navy plane returned from Hong Kong and our little group, including the last American correspondent, Art Goul of the United Press, flew to Hong Kong.

☆☆☆

2: Hong Kong

I

THE CROWN Colony was becoming more crowded every day with the continuing influx of refugees from China, and no hotel accommodations could be found for the staff from Canton. The Navy came to the rescue. In the harbor was a large destroyer tender, the U.S.S. *Dixie*, which had quarters for an admiral and his staff. A flag officer was not on board, and Pauline and I moved into his comfortable quarters. Other members of our staff occupied nearby cabins, and office space was provided where final reports on the closing of the Consulate General at Canton could be prepared.

Hong Kong was sultry, as usual in August, and my first night on the *Dixie* was spent on deck. The breeze was pleasant and my cot was quite comfortable, but the ship swung slowly at its moorings in mid-harbor amid a continuous kaleidoscope of varicolored fluorescent lights on the island and in Kowloon opposite. The events of recent weeks followed by this sudden transition to fairyland left me sleepless but enjoying the extraordinary beauty on all sides. Behind Victoria, the little-known name of the Colony's principal center of population, The Peak towered 1,800 feet above us, the highest point of the island. To the north I could see the outline of hills marking the Colony's frontier with China. How soon would the communist armies be there, less than twenty miles from our mooring?

Before leaving Canton a message from the Department had said that my assignment as consul general in Hong Kong was being con-

13

sidered. It was a fascinating prospect. Traditionally Hong Kong was a much smaller establishment than our Consulate General in Shanghai and less important than the office in Canton, which I had just closed. In effect, however, Hong Kong would now combine its former functions with most of Canton's, whose records we had brought out. Moreover, with the prospective closing of our office in Shanghai, the only remaining American consular establishment on the China coast would be that in Hong Kong. For how long, of course, no one could say.

One aspect of my prospective assignment bothered me. Consul General George Hopper already had served longer than the normal tour of duty in Hong Kong. But he would reach the statutory retirement age in barely a year's time and had expected to remain in Hong Kong until then. Moreover, in the short time since we first met, I had gained a most favorable impression of Hopper, both officially and personally. Fortunately for us both, he and his attractive wife received the news, when it became official, with the utmost graciousness. They understood that the initiative had not been mine.

II

The *Dixie* remained in port long enough for us to clear up our Canton reports and find quarters in various hotels and private houses for our staff. While awaiting the date on which I was to assume charge in Hong Kong, Pauline and I made a short trip to Macao. After sailing nearly forty miles across the mouth of the Pearl River estuary in a small river steamer, we approached the oldest European outpost on the China coast. We docked on the west side of the one-by-three-mile peninsula which holds the city, and crossed by cab to the famous Praia Grande on the east side, where the Governor's Palace and other public and business buildings, including our hotel, were located.

Macao was not at all what I had expected. Writers and travelers have taken great pains to portray this tiny Portuguese colony as devoted primarily to gambling, opium, and sin in general. These are, indeed, important in Macao, as in Hong Kong and many other cities, but during my two visits, including extensive walks, I saw no evidence of such activities, perhaps because I was not particularly looking

14

for them. But I did see a most picturesque city, with sixteenth-century buildings such as one finds in Portugal, with clean streets, with a fifteen-story hotel, with impressive schools, hospitals, and churches. What one sees often seems to depend on what one is looking for. A call on the Governor, Rodriguez de Oliveira, and, later, on P. J. Lobo, the Director of Economics and a native of Timor, served further to convince me that the colony was governed by men of intelligence.

Portugal has not retained Macao for four hundred years without the exercise of imagination and flexibility. Military strength was a minor factor during most of that period. Japan left Portugal in possession of Macao throughout World War II, and communist China did not disturb the colony despite Portugal's refusal to recognize the Peiping regime. I was told of a Macao method to get rid of an undesirable visitor from abroad. Police would arrive at his address with a great deal of noise and search the house without going to the room where they knew the person to be. After loud threats as to his fate when they could lay hands on him, the police would leave their potential quarry with the impression that they had overlooked his whereabouts by pure chance. He usually left voluntarily the same night.

Before returning to Hong Kong, Pauline and I visited the famous Protestant Cemetery in Macao. Until Hong Kong became British in 1842, Macao was the only place on the China coast where a European or American was allowed to be buried. There were many interesting names and inscriptions, British, American, and other, including the grave of the first American consul in Hong Kong. I was not inclined to be defeatist, but with the communist threat coming nearer every day I could not resist observing that there was room beside his grave for the last American consul.

In Macao we experienced our first typhoon, which was no different from the "big wind" which we call a hurricane on the corresponding southeastern coast of the United States. The path of the typhoon was only a few miles from the colony. Many trees were uprooted and our old but substantial two-story hotel shuddered again and again. It was quite a climax to our first visit. We returned again when I had been assigned concurrently as consul general at Macao and came officially to renew acquaintances and enjoy the rather splendid hospitality of the Governor's handsome eighteenth-century palace.

III

Back in Hong Kong, the Hoppers invited us to occupy the guest room of the tiny but attractive house overlooking Deepwater Bay, on the south side of Hong Kong Island, where we were to live for a few months after their departure. The location was called Shouson Hill, after our next door neighbor, Sir Shouson Chow. Some forty years before, he had retired to Hong Kong after an active military and business career in China. Sir Shouson had been one of the early Chinese students in the United States. A favorite joke of his, on meeting an American, was to remark that he had once shaken hands with the President of the United States—President Grant! Nearing ninety, Sir Shouson had many business interests in Hong Kong, where his civic activities had earned him a knighthood. He was a charming person, with a white beard and sparkling eyes, making him the perfect image of a Chinese sage.

At the Consulate General we had many problems, aggravated by shortage of space and of staff, and the demands upon us mounted daily. Office space was our greatest lack, and not only the entrance hall and corridor but all available storerooms were choked with the baggage of official Americans who had come out of China and departed for other destinations, leaving trunks or packages for us to forward. Eventually this mess was cleared up and every foot of available space utilized by rearranging temporary partitions, using the main corridor for office purposes, and ordering midget desks to squeeze in the absolute minimum number of personnel needed to carry on.

For a time we had no political officer, no economic officer, and no administrative officer, but I was fortunate in my capable deputy, Consul Paul H. Pearson, and in gaining the services of Vice Consul James T. Rousseau, who had been evacuated from Canton with typhoid but had since recovered. His knowledge of the Cantonese dialect was particularly useful. Not long afterward we were joined by Alfred Jenkins, a most capable political officer who had a good

16

command of Mandarin. Another valuable political officer was Fred Schultheiss.

Meanwhile, with Lewis Clark's departure for the United States, First Secretary Robert C. Strong became chargé d'affaires of our embassy to China, whose seat was no less mobile than that of the Chinese government itself. Using Hong Kong as headquarters, Strong commuted to Canton periodically, for a few hours' stay each time, as long as British commercial air service was available. Communist armies reached Canton on October 15, the Chinese government having evacuated its erstwhile capital at Chungking a few days earlier. Strong made one brief trip by air to Chungking. He returned to Hong Kong until ordered to Taipei in December, where the Chinese government was establishing itself.

The occupation of Canton passed off as peacefully as could have been expected, in the absence of military resistance, and developments along the Hong Kong frontier were unexpectedly gratifying to the British authorities. Only a handful of Chinese national soldiers took refuge in the Colony, and for some time regular communist troops apparently did not approach closer than twenty-five miles to the border. Hopefully, a British railway official went to Canton in an effort to arrange the re-establishment of services between the two cities. He returned unsuccessful.

The arrival in Hong Kong on October 21 of no less than eight foreign ambassadors from Nanking, via Shanghai, inevitably started a new crop of rumors regarding Chinese communist intentions and, more particularly, the possibilities of early recognition by the Western powers of the communist regime. In conversation with me, both the British ambassador (whom I knew in Belgrade in 1945) and the Australian ambassador were noncommittal, but others quoted them as having admitted that they were recommending recognition as soon as possible. Neither gave any comfort to the personal representative in Hong Kong of Nationalist China's Acting President Li Tsung-jen, who had been instructed to interview them privately. He (General S. K. Yee) informed me subsequently, however, that Sir Ralph Stevenson did not expect the British government to act favorably on his recommendations as to recognition for some weeks at least.

17

☆ *China Assignment* ☆

A diplomat whose opinion on the political situation was not sought arrived from Canton on October 12; the Soviet chargé d'affaires had remained until the last moment with the legal Chinese government to which he was accredited and which the Soviet government was bound to support without interference in its internal affairs by a thirty-year Treaty of Friendship and Alliance, concluded in 1945. In the succeeding years that treaty had been flagrantly violated by giving large-scale support to the Chinese communists. Without that support, the legal government of China could not have been driven from its homeland. Nevertheless, most of the Western diplomats coming out of Nanking seemed to believe that the communist regime recently established in Peiping and recognized by the Soviet government should be given *de jure* recognition by other countries, on the assumption that it would never remain subservient to Moscow.

IV

At this time the Department of State took a step to which no one could seriously object, although old timers noted it with some regret: the traditional form of "despatch" was abolished. For many years our official correspondence had been addressed to The Honorable The Secretary of State, Washington, who was then saluted as "Sir." The text began, "I have the honor," and the communication was closed with, "Respectfully yours." Many years earlier "obedient servant" had disappeared from the closing; now the rest must go. Only the tradition remained that when a Foreign Service officer felt inspired to place facts or opinions before the Department of State, and wished to state the obvious, he should refer to the fact that he was "reporting" to rather than "informing" the Department. For who was he to inform the very fount of knowledge? In any case, my political report for November, 1949, began quite simply and included the following:

British opinion in Hong Kong, both in official and commercial circles, underwent no basic change during November on the question of recognizing the Chinese communist regime. This step was regarded as rather distasteful but inevitable, and therefore one that might better be taken as soon as possible. The Red conquerors of South China continued to behave as well or better than expected toward British nationals and direct British interests. However, reports from nearby Canton and other points on the mainland of actual communist practices in hampering business, as well as their frequent inability to maintain public order, served to disillusion various Hong Kong elements who had believed that, with recognition, relations between the Colony and the mainland would speedily return to normal. Such self-deception was not uncommon among both British and American businessmen, and continues fairly general among the Chinese in Hong Kong, particularly the refugees from Shanghai and other important commercial centers now in communist hands.

On the military side, Admiral Sir Patrick Brind, Commander-in-Chief Far East, visited Hong Kong and expressed to me his concern over the prospect of Taiwan falling into communist hands. He had been influenced in some degree by press stories from Washington which quoted "authoritative sources" to the effect that the United States had written off Taiwan definitively and expected the Chinese communists to take over. The Admiral stressed the possible effects on Hong Kong if its nearby island neighbor, Taiwan, were taken from the Republic of China, particularly if this should result in any important part of the Chinese Air Force becoming available to the communists. Hong Kong's vulnerability from the air is obvious, with its small area, concentrated targets, and absence of secure bases from which a defending air force might operate. Its strength in 1949 rested upon the availability of substantial British land and naval forces, with no communist air power in opposition. In fact, British policy toward Peiping in early 1950 appeared to envisage Hong Kong continuing as a position of strength until the Chinese Reds should beat their swords into plowshares in the not-too-distant future.

Hong Kong was a favorite liberty post for the United States Navy, and officers from ensigns to admirals called at the Consulate General. I returned all calls in person, which involved everything from the formality of boarding a carrier or cruiser to scrambling on the deck of a small auxiliary vessel or climbing down into a submarine. I thoroughly enjoyed these frequent contacts with the Navy, and we were proud of the excellent behavior of our naval personnel ashore. Imagine, then, my consternation one morning to learn that American sailors on the eighth floor of the Gloucester Hotel were throwing furniture into the street below. I sent an officer to investigate at once; they were British sailors! But in all fairness I should add that, with rare exceptions, British servicemen in Hong Kong conducted themselves in exemplary fashion.

Meanwhile a minor crisis occurred when a few personnel of the two civil airlines controlled through stock ownership by the legal Chinese government suddenly took off from Hong Kong for communist territory in twelve aircraft belonging to the two companies. They had suspended regular operations some weeks earlier and approximately eighty of their planes were laid up in Hong Kong. These organizations and their equipment had considerable military significance; most of the aircraft were of American origin and had been acquired on very favorable terms from the United States government. Neither Americans nor British wanted to see them fall into communist hands, and an American civil airline company held a substantial minority interest in one of the Chinese companies. Moreover, no less than thirty-seven American citizens in Hong Kong were among the pilots of the two companies, most of whom held reserve commissions in the armed forces of the United States.

With British recognition of Peiping in early prospect fast footwork was required, and the unexpected departure of twelve planes for Red China provided the necessary impetus. The Republic of China, whose seat was moving from Chungking to Chengtu, sold the assets of the two airlines to an American corporation. Representatives of both Chinese regimes started legal action and the British authorities impounded the aircraft pending a court decision. A couple of years later the American corporation was able to remove the greatly depreciated aircraft and other equipment from Hong Kong. Our major objective of denying them to the communists, who would have found them most useful in the Korean War a few months later, had been achieved. The American pilots of the two Chinese companies refused attractive offers from Red China and sought positions elsewhere.

While the shortage of hotel accommodations was at its peak no less than a dozen members of our Congress arrived at one time in Hong Kong for a visit. We were glad to see them personally and their stay was useful officially, but most of them had to be accommodated in the private quarters of American consular officers. Senators Theodore H. Green and Allen J. Ellender shared our tiny guest room. Transportation was a serious problem and we were concerned lest the visit should end unhappily on this and other counts. Fortunately everything went well and the visitors seemed to appreciate our informal hospitality. Tokyo was their next stop, and the press reported that one of them had noted the absence of soap in his room at the United States Army's hotel, the famous Imperial. We in Hong Kong could not hope to compete with the Army's facilities, but we did supply our visitors with soap!

v

Some time before I arrived in Hong Kong the United States had purchased a residence on The Peak for its consul general. We obtained possession late in 1949 and Pauline and I moved in. The location is spectacular, with the business center of Victoria 1100 feet below on one side and the South China Sea on the other. The address also was rather fashionable: 507 The Peak. This, it may be noted, is a lot number which happens to be located on Barker Road. The highest building lot on The Peak is No. 1, and so on down the ridge toward the east, in an area where only a few privileged Chinese were allowed to have homes in the old days. It was an almost purely European residential community in a colony where over 90 per cent of the population was and is Chinese. Before the days of automobiles, residents could reach their homes with ease only by the Peak Tram, a funicular railway bisecting The Peak area. From its stations paths lead everywhere, along which the homing businessman or official could walk or be carried in a sedan chair. This latter facility was particularly appreciated by those who had just consumed several pink gins at the Hong Kong Club.

Our next important American visitor was Ambassador-at-large Philip C. Jessup, who was making stops of a few days each in several Far Eastern cities en route to Bangkok. A conference of American chiefs of diplomatic missions in the Far East was scheduled for that city the following month, February, 1950, and Dr. Jessup was to

21

preside. In Hong Kong he and Mrs. Jessup were our house guests, and the remaining two members of his party were put up elsewhere.

Considerable interest centered about the Jessup visit. He had been primarily responsible for the preparation of the recent White Paper on China and was widely believed to favor United States recognition of the communist regime in China, which Britain had just recognized. I heard nothing from Washington or from Jessup himself to substantiate this assumption. As so often happens, however, what people believe may be more significant than the facts, particularly if a degree of official secrecy surrounds the case.

British opinion in Hong Kong was by no means unanimous on the wisdom of recognizing Red China. Those in favor would have welcomed parallel United States action as support for their side, and others at least would have found some comfort in having us in the same boat with the United Kingdom. All were glad to have Ambassador Jessup in Hong Kong. Arrangements were made for him to see the Governor and various prominent American, British, and Chinese residents. To me the most interesting meeting was that with the General Committee of the Hong Kong Chamber of Commerce, which included the Colony's leading British *taipans.* We reported to Washington:

This Committee is composed of the leading British businessmen of Hong Kong; the names of those in attendance and their principal affiliations are listed in enclosure 3. After introductory remarks by the Chairman, the Hon. P. S. Cassidy, the Ambassador gave a brief outline of the purposes of his mission. The Committee members expressed themselves as approving of the British recognition of the Chinese communist regime. They agreed that recognition had made little difference to the business world to date, but felt that the step was necessary and appropriate in view of the communists' actual control of China; also, they regarded the resumption of normal diplomatic and trade relations as the most effective way to forestall increasing Soviet influence in China. They indicated that their opinion had changed in the past six months with respect to the nature of the Chinese communists; they were now convinced that Chinese communists are "real communists." They felt, however, that

☆ Hong Kong ☆

China eventually would get out from under Soviet Russian influence, admitting frankly that if this did not happen there was no future for Hong Kong or for British business in China. They still hoped and believed that the failure of the Chinese communists to respond suitably to British recognition could be ascribed to ignorance of the normal procedures of diplomatic representation. In general, these gentlemen were pessimistic about the China scene in the short-run, but reasonably optimistic for the long-run.

It may be noted that five years was mentioned as a maximum for Hong Kong's economic survival in the absence of normal relations with the mainland. Yet fourteen years after that meeting Hong Kong was more prosperous than ever despite the continued lack of anything like normal relations with Red China. The remarkable flexibility of a free economy worked miracles, but at no time did Hong Kong businessmen in general plan ahead with assurance for more than five years. This period of time, although continuously moved forward, remained a basic conception.

The general belief that Ambassador Jessup represented a policy of appeasement toward Red China was illustrated by an incident at our house. We gave a reception in his honor during which the wife of an American colonel upbraided the Ambassador for his supposed attitude toward the communist threat. Perhaps she had taken a cocktail too many, but there was no doubt of her sincerity. She charged him with leading us toward war. Jessup showed admirable restraint in talking to her; neither of them could have known that the Korean War was only five months away.

Before his departure Ambassador Jessup gave a statement to the press which stressed our unchanging opposition to communist theory and practice as well as our traditional support of a policy of equality and independence for China. Doubtless he went as far as the state of our official stand toward China permitted at that time. In any case, his visit did not alter the general assumption in Hong Kong, both in official circles and outside, that the United States was about to extend formal recognition to the Chinese communist regime. Meanwhile, however, the Reds themselves had taken steps which seemingly proved decisive. Their mistreatment of the American consul general at Mukden and their seizure of a United States consular building in Peiping made early American recognition a political impossibility.

Pauline and I were enjoying a quiet evening at home when the police telephoned that an employee of the American Consulate General had just been arrested for breaking into the main office of the Hong Kong and Shanghai Banking Corporation. A few questions and I understood what had happened. The employee, a clerk, had been working late at our office in the same building. He was a good worker but prone to console himself from a bottle, and among the personal effects still stored at the office he had noted some *eau-de-vie*. After polishing off most of a bottle he had started for home by the rear entrance of the building, which was closed at night. Annoyed at finding the various glass doors in the entrance lobby carefully locked, he had smashed one with his fist. It happened to lead into the bank, and the night watchman had picked him up. The next day he was reprimanded, ordered to pay for the damage, and the case was closed except for the cuts on his hand, which healed more slowly.

VI

At the conference in Bangkok fourteen of our Foreign Service establishments in the Far East and South Asia were represented. They ranged from Japan and Korea to Australia and New Zealand, and to India in the west. Major consular offices such as Hong Kong and Singapore were included, although most of those present were chiefs of diplomatic missions. A wide range of subjects was discussed and some extremely frank exchanges took place. I believe that all of us were convinced of the extreme gravity of the situation that confronted the United States in East Asia. Our differences were in sense of urgency; those stationed farthest from the China coast understandably showed less immediate concern. At one point Ambassador Jessup called for a show of hands on whether the United States should attempt to stop any further communist advance in Southeast Asia, even at the risk of war. Seven of us voted "yes"; several of the remaining seven agreed in principle but were not satisfied with the phrasing of the question.

Our conference was concerned with communist aggression in general, but the most immediate threat seemed to be that directed toward Southeast Asia. It was logical that the Chinese armies, which had been advancing steadily southward and had recently reached the frontier of Indochina, should sweep on over the rich rice lands that offered China so much. As I recall, no one thought of Korea as the probable next field for aggression. In retrospect, we may well have been right in terms of Red China's own ambitions. Their subsequent Korean adventure seemed less in China's interest than in that of international communism and its aims in Japan, to which Korea was the historic bridge.

The conference at Bangkok ended with agreement that our discussions had been most helpful to us as individuals. We hoped that the minutes of our meetings would be useful in Washington. To what extent they received attention I never learned; the minutes, which had been most carefully recorded, were never circulated to the field. I am sure we all agreed that Ambassador Jessup was an extraordinarily capable presiding officer with an exceptional grasp of foreign affairs and a most engaging personality.

Operations at the office were now proceeding as smoothly as inadequate space would permit. We were handling the normal duties of the Hong Kong Consulate General plus those of Canton in addition to a large volume of emergency activities resulting from the continued evacuation of Americans from mainland China. Altogether our work load was certainly no less than the level of several years later, when office space and staff had been multiplied two or three times. I was reasonably satisfied with our political, economic, and sundry consular activities, but passport and visa operations left much to be desired. We needed a substantial increase in staff in these fields, but the limiting factor was office space. A few rooms were found in another building and rented on a temporary basis, but they were far from adequate.

VII

I urged the Department of State to buy an office building, and succeeded in finding one or two that were available and suitable. Plans had been made earlier to erect new quarters for the Consulate General, but they were unlikely to be ready for several years and our needs were urgent. My proposal to buy an existing building with "counterpart sterling," which had accumulated in London as a result of our economic aid programs, was rejected. Instead, we were authorized to put up a temporary structure to meet immediate requirements. This was erected as quickly as circumstances permitted, but a full year elapsed between the closing of Canton and the completion of the temporary building. This structure accommodated the greater part of the office staff until it was demolished and a new building completed in 1957.

The Department of State has improved in recent years in its understanding of problems in the field, and usually is both sympathetic and helpful. Occasionally, however, some minor bureaucrat seeks a minor triumph. At the time, we had been given wide latitude in settling the relatively unimportant financial claims that arose in connection with closing the Consulate General in Canton. The landlord of one rented building had asked for a little less than $1000 to restore alterations we had made. I thought his claim justified, but we persuaded him to accept $370. Many weeks afterward someone in the Department questioned this payment and the correspondence began to grow. The objection finally was dropped after I wrote to Washington:

> The dossier grows steadily in this case, but the fact remains that the Department ought to find some means of paying an obligation of $370 incurred in good faith under the stress of closing an office in the face of an advancing enemy force. Moreover, I am convinced that not only did the government owe this amount in equity but an additional sum as well.
>
> This reminds me of the old story of a consular officer who made certain expenditures on behalf of some shipwrecked seamen, who might otherwise have perished from exposure. In due course these expenditures were disapproved, because they had not been authorized in advance. The consul then wrote asking for the name of the official who was responsible for the disapproval, so that if he "ever saw him struggling in the water after a shipwreck, a telegram could be sent immediately to the Department asking for instructions."

Hong Kong had the three traditional essentials of a colony: a church, a race track, and a club where no natives were allowed.

But Hong Kong also had a rapidly developing social sense which was reflected in good schools, social services, and many other attractions that continuously drew thousands of refugees from Red China. A major problem of the Hong Kong government for generations had been to make life in the Colony better than in China, but not too much better. Otherwise, a deluge would come in. Now the attraction was heightened by a factor common to refugees from communism: in Hong Kong they could sleep at night. I had great admiration for several British colonial officials, notably Governor Sir Alexander Grantham, for the successful balance they maintained among political, economic, and social influences of the most complex character. Hong Kong was no democracy—it could not be under the circumstances—but there was freedom; there was good government.

Pauline and I saw the Granthams frequently in Hong Kong and have visited them on various occasions since we left the Colony. Lady Grantham was American-born and an exceptionally charming and able hostess. I always found Sir Alexander extremely well informed, ready to appreciate both sides of a question but also to make a quick decision when needed, and having a good sense of humor. This last was particularly necessary in his position. I recall accompanying Secretary of the Treasury John W. Snyder and Ambassador Myron Cowen in a call on the Governor. In the entrance hall of his residence, Government House, we were greeted effusively by a Chinese-American from San Francisco, whom I had seen before. When we took our departure the Chinese-American was still there, seemingly very much in charge. Sir Alexander saw us to the front door and I could not resist asking him what the score was. "I never saw him before," he replied with a chuckle. Our Chinese-American friend had chosen an impressive background for himself in greeting the Secretary of the Treasury.

VIII

Our quarters at 507 The Peak yielded to Pauline's efforts and, despite the uninspired furniture and room arrangement, became an attractive home. It was the third government-owned or leased residence that she had "done over" in as many years—an occupational hazard of the Foreign Service which is not always appreciated in

Washington. Most wives are delighted with an opportunity to choose colors and materials, but that is the pleasant side. Our rather pretentious house in Hong Kong had nothing worthy to be called a kitchen, and laundry facilities were extremely primitive. On foggy days, water condensed on the inside walls and ran down in streams, with inevitable damage to paint, pictures, hangings, and floors. Mould and fungus attacked clothing, bedding, and human beings as well. Electrical and water supplies were uncertain, and the long incoming telephone wire often vibrated in the wind until the entire house hummed. In the course of several months, these difficulties were partly or fully overcome, but not without a great deal of determined exertion.

In our efforts to get acquainted we sought a degree of balance among Americans, British, Chinese, and others. The line of least resistance socially was to fall in with British officialdom, the consular corps, and a few leading American and British businessmen. This would leave out of account the many foreigners, Americans and others, engaged in educational, missionary, and other activities, as well as the Chinese in every walk of life who represented all but a tiny fraction of Hong Kong's population. As our first year in the Colony drew to a close, Pauline and I felt that we were making progress along a reasonable line. This involved more social activity than we cared for, but it was a part of the job. A series of luncheons, dinners, and receptions at our residence, now attractively arranged, led up to preparations for Independence Day, July 4, 1950. A guest list was drawn up for a reception at the Hong Kong Hotel, which included eight hundred persons. The size of the American colony and the need to strike a balance among other nationalities seemed to rule out a shorter list. As the invitations were being mailed, war broke out in Korea, but we saw no reason to alter our plans for the Fourth of July. In fact, it was more important than ever to put on a bold front in the cosmopolitan but predominantly oriental city of Hong Kong.

IX

As the heat of May and June descended upon us Pauline and I planned a short vacation in Japan. A comfortable Dutch ship was scheduled to sail from Hong Kong to Kobe in mid-July, and to return after spending about one week in various Japanese ports. The Consulate General was now functioning as well as could be expected until the new temporary building could be completed, and Hong Kong was quiet. The war in Korea made the visit to Tokyo an even more important project than when we had first planned it.

When our ship docked at Kobe, I heard from the American consul general that Tokyo wanted me on the telephone. A highly classified telegram had arrived, which would be held for my arrival in the Japanese capital. We took the night train to Tokyo, where I learned that the Department of State was proposing my immediate transfer to Taipei as "Minister and Chargé d'Affaires." The telegram described this designation as raising the rank of the position in Taipei, following the President's statement of June 27 that American protection was being extended to Formosa, and added that the Department regarded the job as "extremely important."

Of course I was prepared to go, I replied, but the reference to my designation was puzzling. Dr. Stuart was still ambassador to China, although he had been in the United States for a year, seriously ill. Strong was chargé d'affaires in Taipei; he was junior to me in the Foreign Service, but I could not see that the Chinese on Formosa would be reassured simply by the assignment of a new chargé who happened to have the in-service rank of career minister. If the intention was to raise the rank of this position for political effect, then I thought that I should be given the personal rank of ambassador. This would not affect Dr. Stuart's status, but would encourage the Chinese and facilitate my relations with them, as well as with the high-ranking Americans, military and others, who could be expected to visit Formosa. The Department's reply was negative, adding that the President's statement of June 27 was based on military factors, without prejudice to political considerations.

In Tokyo I first met William J. Sebald, whom the Department of State had assigned to General MacArthur's headquarters as political adviser. I quickly gained a high opinion of Sebald's abilities; he has served subsequently as ambassador to Burma and Australia. We called together on General MacArthur, whom I had seen when we were both living in the Manila Hotel at the time of the Japanese attack on December 8, 1941, but whom I had never met. Busy as he was directing our military effort in Korea, where the situation was as yet far from satisfactory, General MacArthur gave us nearly an hour of his time. He seemed confident and relaxed. His discussion of Far Eastern problems in general, and of China and Taiwan in particular, showed a breadth of view which few statesmen could equal. I came away convinced that if in World War II the United States had failed to produce a prophet of the stature of Churchill, MacArthur came closest to qualifying.

We paid brief visits to three of Japan's most famous and historic beauty spots, Nikko, Kyoto, and Nara, before rejoining our ship at Kobe. After five days at sea and a strenuous round of regretful good-byes and packing in Hong Kong, I flew to Taipei on August 10. Pauline followed at the end of the month.

X

This chapter has dealt largely with the "operational" side of my year in Hong Kong. During that period the Consulate General submitted a substantial volume of political and economic reports, many of them concerning policy. The following section gives excerpts from a few such reports and letters, written before and after British recognition of Red China in early 1950. References to matters of purely local or passing interest, or which would require explanation by footnote or otherwise, have been deleted for the sake of clarity. Variations in style are explained by the fact that verbatim excerpts from informal letters to individual officials in the Department are interspersed with paraphrased quotations from telegrams and portions of more formal despatches. "Taiwan" and "Formosa," as well as "Peiping" and "Peking," were used interchangeably to conform with current usage in the Department, or by the individual addressed. I felt that the situation was too serious to risk confusion as among Taiwan, Taipei, Tainan, and Hainan, for example. Later, as the names became more familiar, we were able to standardize on "Taiwan."

XI

September 30, 1949

To the Department of State:

I had not intended to get into the political field so soon after

30

arriving in a new part of the world, but I find that we are right up against it in connection with the organization of the office. Apparently reliable information reaching here from Washington through private channels suggests that not only have our Armed Services "written off" China but that at least one officer of the Department has predicted that we in Hong Kong "won't be here long." If such reports reflect the current policy trend at home, then my recommendations for staffing this office should be very different from what I had planned. From my limited knowledge of the Far Eastern problem, I had assumed that we admitted only to losing the first round in China and that we were prepared to support the peripheral areas against communist aggression. In the case of Hong Kong this presumably would mean only our moral support; without even that, perhaps we won't be here very long!

October 10, 1949

To the Department of State:

The one continuing and clear British policy on which most of Hong Kong felt it could count was that the Colony would be defended with determination against military attack. Every few days brought new contingents of British troops from overseas; it was expected that the total would approximate 33,000 before the communist armies reached the Colony's frontier. No attempt was made to conceal these preparations. On the contrary, considerable publicity was attached to the arrival of reinforcements and to their modern equipment. British officers pointed out repeatedly that the communists have had no experience with such firepower as would face them. Some estimated that they would suffer a million casualties in taking Hong Kong. In any event, such opinions were given currency, not only to inspire confidence among the noncommunist population of the Colony, but also for their effect on the communists themselves.

Despite public confidence in British military preparations, furthered by many evidences of active training and good troop morale, the civilian population of Hong Kong is aware that their immediate fate is more likely to be determined by policy decisions reached in London, Washington, or Moscow, than by trial of arms on the Colony's frontier. The more serious students of international affairs have now had time to study the White Paper with care. In particular, they would like to know whether the warning to the communists contained in the Letter of Transmittal, not to "engage in aggression against China's neighbors," contains the promise of active American support in the event of a communist attack on Hong Kong. Presumably the only immediate support required would be of a moral character, but without an assurance of the full and clear approval of the United States, the British Labor Government might find itself under pressure to curtail its financial and other commitments and to give up the idea of defending Hong Kong. Press reports to the effect that the United States may let Taiwan go to the communists by default, and the seeming absence of an effective agreement among the British, French, and Americans on the problem of Indochina, raise further doubts among the inhabitants of Hong Kong as to their own future. Most reassuring of all would be an agreement between the United States and the United Kingdom on a joint approach to the Chinese problem in all of its major aspects.

The primary purpose of Hong Kong's defense preparations is, of course, to discourage a communist attack rather than to meet one. Most of the local British do not anticipate actual fighting in the near future. They expect border incidents, the unilateral repudiation by the communists of such treaties as that of Nanking, and a fluctuating barrage of propaganda against the continued existence of the Colony. In recent months the tone of such propaganda has been remarkably restrained, by communist standards, which is widely interpreted as indicating the absence of any intention to mount a military attack on Hong Kong in the near future. General opinion seems to be that the communists will wish to consolidate their position in South China, and to gain control of Taiwan and perhaps Hainan and Szechuan, before venturing against Hong Kong. This view also was expressed to me by General Chennault.

The topic receiving the most space in the press during September was the continued effort of the Chinese Nationalists to blockade communist-held ports. In Hong Kong one cannot generalize regarding a British as opposed to an American attitude toward the blockade issue. All shades of opinion may be found among each nationality. In general, of course, the large British firms with extensive investments in Shanghai, and which depend for their continued existence on the China trade, oppose the blockade and hope for a revival of something at least distantly approaching normal commerce. Similar views are held by certain Americans. On the other hand, leading British military and civilian officials, in private conversations, have expressed personal sympathy for the Nationalist blockade effort and the greatest repugnance toward recognition of the Chinese communist regime. Some irritation also is evident over American criticism of the supposed British "shopkeeper" attitude, particularly since American ships plying from the West Coast to Taku Bar, and lately the success of the Isbrandtsen Line in flouting the blockade off Shanghai, have contributed largely to undermining these Nationalist operations.

On the subject of recognizing the Chinese communists, British officials here have admitted to me quite frankly that they do not see how such action can be squared with the conception of the United Nations. Even if Russia considers itself free to promote revolution within the territory of another member, the Western democracies would inevitably face embarrassment in finding a formula to justify the transfer of recognition from a government simply because it has fallen a victim in this process. Of course, the British in Hong Kong are not unaware that the current disintegration of the Chinese government may facilitate the eventual withdrawal of recognition. But the external causes which have promoted this disintegration must remain an unhappy precedent.

November 16, 1949

To the Department of State:

At least two fundamental misconceptions about China, which have undermined American policy formation during a long period of years, seem at last to be disappearing. These are (1) that the Chinese communists are not "real" communists but simply agrarian reformers, and (2) that there exists in China a "liberal" element sufficiently numerous and influential to make possible a program of social reform along Western lines. Unfortunately, however, other old and stubborn misconceptions persist, and new ones have sprung up, all continuing to reflect a state of mind dominated by wishful thinking on the part of Americans and others. Among these are the beliefs that China under the communists will settle down in the near future so that something approaching normal business and cultural relations can be resumed with the West, all without any action on the part of the United States other than extending formal recognition to the new regime. Another common hope is that a communist government will be unable to cope with China's social and economic problems, and will collapse in consequence. . . .

Waiting until the "dust settles" has been a useful formula for American policy in China during an interim period until a new course of action could be developed in recognition of the communist conquest. In actual fact, however, the "dust" may not settle completely for a very long time to come. China has been in the throes of social revolution for a century, since the Taiping rebellion broke out in 1850, and the basic problems which fostered this revolution seem as far from solution as ever. Among these problems are overpopulation and hence insufficient food, the lack of a written language upon which a broad system of education could be built, and so acute a shortage of competent administrators as to render impossible the creation of a modern state capable of meeting effectively its internal and external obligations. Except in so far as the communists may succeed in repressing disorders by usual police-state methods, it seems only prudent to expect that China will continue in ferment for a prolonged period of time. Nor are there substantial grounds for assuming that normal intercourse will be resumed with the West to any greater degree than in the case of Soviet Russia.

While there would seem no good reason to suppose that the communists are capable of finding early solutions for China's basic problems, it is unwise to assume that their regime will collapse in consequence of such failure. The outstanding feature of the communist technique, as developed in Russia, is the ability to remain in power no matter what else may happen. Chinese communists are following the Russian pattern meticulously. Detestable though this pattern of a state may be, it is better adapted to maintaining effective control of a country such as present-day China than any form of Western parliamentary democracy. The similarities between the conditions under which communist governmental techniques were developed in Russia after 1917 and those obtaining in China today are too striking to be overlooked. In each case a vast territory, relatively self-sufficient economically at a very low living standard, contains an enormous population of which all but a minute fraction are ignorant and politically inert. A great expanse of country with widely divergent conditions in various regions is conveniently divided into provinces or "republics," each with a semblance of autonomy, while the real power is highly centralized. With minor modifications, the communist pattern of government may prove no less successful in China than in Russia.

Now that communist control of China proper is all but assured, it may be taken for granted that efforts will be redoubled to place communist regimes in power elsewhere in Asia. With China as a springboard, the ability of communism to continue its conquests should not be underestimated. China may be considered weak and backward by Western standards, but the Chinese are the most numerous and in some respects the most capable people of Asia. In Eastern terms, communist China is a great power, economically, militarily, and politically. Supported by communist dynamism, China might well be able to dominate not only Indochina, Siam, and Burma, but eventually the Philippines, Indonesia, Pakistan, and India itself. Individually or even collectively, these countries would be no match in the long run for a reawakened China unless they were supported actively and consistently by the Western powers.

The preceding paragraph is not intended as a prediction that communist China will undertake, in the near future, the military conquest of any of the countries mentioned, although this possibility should not be dismissed entirely. It appears more likely, however, that the communist techniques of infiltration, sabotage, propaganda, and support of guerrilla or other seditious movements will constitute the chief dangers to the independence of the minor countries of Southeastern Asia. Communist China should serve admirably as a base for such operations, not only due to its geographic location but because it is the most natural sponsor of "Asia for the Asiatics" and can utilize as many agents as may be needed among the millions of Chinese scattered throughout the nearby countries and islands. All of this seems more than likely, irrespective of the relative success or failure of the Chinese communists in bringing order and prosperity to their own country.

In summary, the only expectations upon which the United States is warranted in basing its Far Eastern policy are that the communists will control China for a long time to come, that they will follow Russian direction at least in foreign relations, and that they will constitute a highly dangerous influence in the affairs of their neighbors to the east and south. If future events should happen to take a course more favorable to the interests of the West, no opportunity should be missed to exploit it to the full. But to base a policy primarily on the hopeful assumption that Chinese communism will somehow be better than communism elsewhere can best be described as folly.

In planning a course of action in the Far East, the United States will do well to look first to the security of its bases. As the paramount world power, with its unequaled Navy and Air Force and its world-wide moral and material commitments, America's Pacific ramparts obviously are not on the Sacramento River nor are they confined to such vital staging points as Hawaii and Guam. In present circumstances the most critical points are in the regions of the Japan, Yellow, and China Seas. They are in Korea, Japan, the Ryukyus, Taiwan, Hong Kong, and Indochina. These points are important not only in a strict military sense but also economically and psychologically. The latter term is used advisedly to suggest the grave undermining of public confidence which would ensue in other communist-threatened regions should any of these strongholds be lost, and, equally important, the actual and political value of these bases for maintaining contact with the Chinese people. Such vital factors must be borne constantly in mind whenever it is decided by military leaders that, in the light of equipment and men available to them at a given moment, some given spot is not strategically important. The West cannot afford to yield further ground. . . .

November 26, 1949

To an officer of the Department of State:

In trying to inform myself on our Far Eastern policy I have been collecting a file of recent documents, classified and otherwise, to supplement the White Paper. . . . I had written to you more in detail about Taiwan and its relationship to Hong Kong, etc., but while my letter was in process of being typed the enclosed UP story appeared in the local press under a Washington dateline of November 22. ("Well-informed official sources said today the United States had virtually written off any chance of saving the strategic island of Formosa from the Chinese Communists. . . .") If this story is substantially correct, then my further remarks on Taiwan may be out of place. Irrespective of the intrinsic merits of the case as presented by UP, however, it is inevitable that press stories of this general tenor, which have been published from time to time as portraying the official American position, should be construed by our remaining friends in this part of the world as an admission of our defeat, and by the communists as an invitation to further aggression.

March 29, 1950

To a United States Senator:

I have heard much the same reports about Formosa that you mention in your letter of March 7, but I have no direct knowledge of recent developments there.

Things are relatively quiet in Hong Kong just now. Local

labor difficulties produced a crisis at the end of January, as you doubtless read, when swift government action put down a riot of striking tram workers and their sympathizers by occupation of their union headquarters and the deportation of twelve of their leaders. Agitation for increased pay among the workers of numerous industries in the Colony is still going on, but it is believed that the unions will be hesitant to resort to force again in the near future. In fact, there is a temptation to believe that communist influence here is on the wane, especially among the labor unions.

A closer view, however, indicates that the present lull probably should not be interpreted as indicating any lessening of communist influence in the Colony. They still have a strong underground in Hong Kong and considerable support among labor elements; they have simply been less vociferous in the past few weeks. Moreover, communist influences are bolstered by a growing feeling of identification with the new mainland regime on the part of many Hong Kong Chinese, if only because China is their native country. British recognition has given a measure of legitimacy to the expression of pro-Chinese communist sentiments. Too, many who have no genuine communist sympathies nevertheless feel that they must follow the course of events in order to safeguard their livelihood. The motion picture industry in Hong Kong is an example which could be cited; producers who certainly are not in sympathy with communism find that they must follow the communist line in order to maintain their positions in the industry, since the chief outlet for their products is on the mainland.

Recognition of the Chinese communist regime by the British has so far had little effect on local conditions. Hong Kong commercial circles are still faced with the difficulties imposed by the Nationalist coastal closure and by the economic policies of the communists. Immediately after British recognition, some Americans here showed concern lest British commercial interests gain a monopoly on trade with the mainland. At that time certain American businessmen in Hong Kong expressed the hope that our government would see fit to recognize the communist regime at an early date. At the present time, however, they are almost unanimously of the opinion that recognition would be inadvisable for the foreseeable future.

At the present time the attention of the Colony is turned primarily toward the mainland, where famine and unrest seem to be working up to a crisis for the communist regime. The latter's most reasonable course would be that of coming to some sort of terms with the West, with at least partial resumption of commercial and cultural ties, but so far there is no evidence of action along these lines. Present indications suggest rather the likelihood of purges within the communist camp, leading to closer cooperation with the Soviet Union in an attempt to solve internal difficulties, and/or the possibility of foreign adventures to divert attention from internal problems.

April 14, 1950

To an officer of the Department of State:

Lest it seem presumptuous for anyone to express positive opinions on the Far East after only eight months in Hong Kong, let me assure you that I am not yet posing as an expert on China. But I have spent two and a half years in Soviet Russia, plus a much longer period of time along the Iron Curtain. I believe that I may claim to have some feeling for the Red pattern, based upon experience extending back more than 25 years. And one of the most striking aspects of the Far Eastern situation is the close similarity between communist methods here and elsewhere.

On leaving Greece a year ago I felt that the chances against a general war within the next few years were of the order of 60 to 40. Since arriving in the Far East, and in view of the developments of recent months, I have revised my estimate to 50 to 50. I still believe that the Russians do not intend to provoke an open war, but the policies they are pursuing may produce one at almost any time. When Ambassador Jessup was in Hong Kong I expressed to him the opinions just mentioned, and added my fear that we were in danger of stumbling into war out here in the Far East. He seemed to disagree in that he thought there were now too many influences in existence which would serve to prevent such a development. Perhaps "stumbling" is not the best word, but as long as the other side retains the initiative in creating situations which may involve us in war, at a time and under circumstances for which we have not prepared, just so long will the danger I have in mind continue.

The Russians and their Chinese satellite are unlikely to undertake anything so clear-cut as an attack on Japan or the Philippines, although they evidently are not without means to make trouble in both countries. What seems more probable is an intensification of the techniques they have used successfully to date, plus perhaps certain methods copied from Hitler and others. The British admiral in command here in Hong Kong told me the other night of his conviction that the Russian jet aircraft recently reported in China will be tried out in the same manner adopted by Germany during the Spanish Civil War. Moreover, the possibilities of communism utilizing the large Chinese populations in countries to the south have only begun to be explored. In these and other prospects it is not difficult to imagine situations developing somewhat similar to what might have happened in 1941 and 1942 had the Japanese undertaken their push to the south without actually attacking American territory. Sooner or later we would have become involved, but neither time nor place would have been predictable.

I can see no logical line of demarcation between the "hot" and "cold" wars now going on in the Far East. It is all a part of the same picture, and the methods we adopt to deal with a cold war quite evidently should be calculated to further our policies no matter how much the temperature may rise. Our experience in Europe seems to have established the general pattern of extending economic, military, and technical assistance to countries we wish to save from communism. It is a logical pattern, based upon elements in which our greatest strength lies, but our Far Eastern experience to date, plus the fact that we can expect only relatively modest funds from Congress in the future, emphasize the outstanding importance of selecting and timing our courses of action.

I believe that it may prove an actual benefit in our Far Eastern operations not to have unlimited funds available. It should force the delivery on time of, say, a shipload of food to a given point where it is currently needed, rather than the arrival of fifty million dollars' worth six months later. It should suggest the importance of getting a supply of 3-inch shells to a friendly army before it runs out of ammunition, rather than forwarding thirty million dollars' worth of assorted surplus war material after a critical campaign is lost. It should indicate the desirability of sending out a relatively small number of highly qualified technicians to assist in projects promising comparatively quick results in improved production, health, or defense, rather than the inauguration of elaborate long-range development schemes which will require support from the American taxpayer for an indefinite period. It should exclude the setting up of large and pretentious missions staffed by numerous Americans who, whatever their individual qualifications, may by their very numbers convey an impression of "American imperialism" and thus defeat our purpose.

. . . Certainly our present position in the Far East is not such as to justify overlooking any possibility of furthering our interests. The weakness of our remaining friends, and the prospect of having only modest funds at our disposal, make it all the more important that we should step up our efforts in every promising direction. "Total diplomacy" includes many things. Certainly it includes economic and psychological warfare, although I would gladly substitute another word for "warfare" if it left no doubt as to my meaning. Russia has won China largely by psychological warfare in the fullest sense.

Strategic materials, armaments, money, and other forms of assistance, much of it indirectly of American origin, continue to reach the Chinese communists. You are familiar with the rearguard action we have been fighting to keep them from getting the planes and aviation equipment of the two former Nationalist airlines. Last week at least one shipment of aviation gasoline appears to have slipped through to Tientsin. Today I learn that a Philippine firm is offering communist China twenty-five Mustangs and a large quantity of rifles and ammunition, with an assurance of safe delivery in communist territory. Unfortunately certain Americans, as well as others, appear to be involved in this disgraceful business. We in Hong Kong are doing what we can, with four Armed Services liaison officers and two economic officers on duty, to report on and interfere with these operations, and with some success.

. . . The Seventh Fleet made a useful visit to Saigon not long ago. Such visits, timed to promote our policies, should take place more frequently and with greater boldness. We have tended to be too cautious lest someone might be offended—perhaps Russia! The result again is to leave the initiative with the enemy and to persuade him that we are afraid. I hope that he would be mistaken in any such belief, but the danger is rather in allowing our adversaries any basis for entertaining erroneous opinions of this kind. We should seek means of persuading them that such adventures as they seem to be contemplating in the Far East will bring positive reaction from us in a matter of hours. If Russia really wants to avoid a general war, quick action on our part in a crisis seems the best way to prevent it. Delay and uncertainty as to what we would do under a given set of circumstances may well allow the situation to get out of hand, while public opinion at home and elsewhere is becoming so aroused as to make war unavoidable.

Perhaps most important of all, we should intensify our efforts to find, with the United Kingdom and the Commonwealth, a common basis for joint and positive action in Southeast Asia. France, the Netherlands, and the United Nations should not be forgotten in the process, but if we wait for unanimity or for others to take the initiative, it may well be too late.

April 30, 1950

To the Department of State:

American opinion, both public and official, appears to have made substantial progress during the past two or three months in its appreciation of the Southeast Asian situation. My letter of February 5 closed with a promise to forward certain suggestions as to our future course of action. Most of the proposals which I had in mind at that time have now been accepted in principle as representing American policy. They include:

1. Encouraging the remaining free states of Southeast Asia to cooperate with each other in every practicable way to resist communist aggression.
2. Seeking a joint, or at least parallel, program with the British Commonwealth in dealing with this area.
3. Providing arms and technical and economic assistance to the threatened areas of Southeast Asia.
4. Intensifying American informational and educational programs calculated to further our policies.

I believe that only a small minority of Americans would disapprove of the four aims just outlined, but many will ask whether in implementing them there is not a grave danger of our effort being "too little and too late." As it appears to me, the United States has about a 50 to 50 chance of denying the remainder of Southeast Asia to the communists, on condition that we exploit our every advantage to the full. Anything short of such an effort may be expected to permit continued communist expansion and the eventual domination by Russia of the entire continent of Asia. Someone used the old saying recently in this connection to the effect that we must "fish or cut bait." Actually, we are cutting some bait but we must start fishing as well. . . .

For better or worse, we have assumed a large responsibility in insisting that other colonial powers should follow our lead in granting independence to the Philippines. Fortunately, most of the new countries of South Asia are potentially sound economic units. Politically and militarily, however, a majority of them are woefully weak. We cannot put them on their feet and aid them in resisting communism simply by pouring out money, as our Far Eastern experience to date has amply demonstrated. What will be required is a combination of quick action, patience, firmness, and tact such as Americans have rarely demonstrated in their dealings with foreign countries. The margin in favor of our success is too narrow to entrust the job to any but the most highly qualified individuals, with unity of command in the field and at home. . . .

The American position in the Far East today is not such as to permit overlooking any possible means of furthering our policies: military, economic, psychological. It is a sad commentary that our thinking on Far Eastern affairs seems to be fully three years behind our attitude toward Western Europe and the Near East. Three years ago we were weak in Europe and strong in the Far East. The Truman Doctrine was the turning point in Europe, but in taking the initiative there we allowed our attention to wander from Asia. The time for decision is passing: whether we are ready to implement a Truman Doctrine with our remaining friends in Asia, or simply to stand by while others stir up dust which is unlikely to settle in our time.

Perhaps most important of all would be the psychological effect on our remaining friends of convincing evidence that the United States was again taking the initiative.

June 30, 1950

To an officer of the Department of State:

Your remarks were so outstandingly good that I have hesitated to mention the one clause that disturbed me on first reading. But the more I have thought about it the more I have felt impelled to write to you.

The point in question is in your listing of "realities," where you emphasize the earnest and repeated warnings of our representatives which the Chinese government ignored, and then suggest that there was nothing more our government could have done to influence or alter the basic course of events in China.

As a comparative newcomer to this area, I certainly lay no claim to being a Far Eastern expert, and I have no desire to blame anyone for the loss of China to the communists. But I am impressed by the following apparent facts:

1. There has been serious disagreement among American officials, both diplomatic and military, throughout the past several years as to the most effective ways and means of dealing with China. Several highly competent individuals among such officials have expressed to me the firm opinion that China need not have been lost had a different course been followed.

44

2. Apparently as late as the communist crossing of the Yangtze, various highly placed American officials still refused to admit that Mao and his tribe were "real" (i.e., Moscow-directed) communists and still used the term "agrarian reformers" in all seriousness.

. . . In attempting to analyze the influences responsible for the above, it is impossible to overlook two large sections of opinion among the "Old China Hands." One of these groups believed that China needed "reforms" above all else, and was prepared to make its peace with any political group which seemed capable of implementing such reforms. The second section of opinion held that the Chinese people were hopeless in any case, except as hewers and drawers under the White Man's direction. Far apart as these two views may appear, the two groups had one fatal point in common: an almost total lack of appreciation of the menace of Soviet imperialism and its communist tools.

Now all of the foregoing is by no means conclusive, but it seems at least to raise a reasonable doubt as to whether our efforts in China might not have been more effectively planned and executed. And here we come to what strikes me as the heart of the matter. In our justifiable efforts to absolve sincere and able officials from blame for the China debacle, we are in danger of convincing ourselves that they made no mistakes and that we have no alternative but to follow substantially the same course in our endeavors to save the remainder of Asia. Now, I should like to think that we did make honest mistakes in China, and that we are capable of recognizing those mistakes and benefiting by them as we resume the initiative in the Far East. Otherwise, what reason is there to suppose that we can succeed in saving . . . Korea or Vietnam, after losing China?

It is beyond the scope of this letter to detail the reasons for our loss of China, even if I were competent to do so. One of our ablest Foreign Service officers summed it up thus in conversation with me recently: "We lost because our hearts were not in it." Now that we are so deeply committed in Korea and elsewhere, let us hope that we shall not lack a singleness of purpose and a determination to win through.

Personally, I am not prepared to admit that the other side is better than we, and I see no good reason why we should not win in Asia as we are winning in Western Europe. Not if our hearts are in it.

☆☆☆

3: Taipei

I

A LITTLE group waited in the broiling August sun when I arrived at Taipei Airport. Robert C. Strong, whom I was relieving, Rear Admiral Harry B. Jarrett, the Naval attaché, and Raymond T. Moyer, director of our economic mission, were there with a few members of their staffs. An official from the Protocol Department of the Chinese Foreign Ministry also was on hand to meet me. We drove to the Embassy and reviewed the situation. Strong was to stay on long enough to introduce me to leading Chinese officials and then return to the United States. Admiral Jarrett and I had been assigned to Taipei at the same time. He had arrived about ten days earlier and, as senior military attaché, was to serve as our principal military representative with the Chinese in coordinating the joint defense of Taiwan by the United States Seventh Fleet and the Chinese Armed Forces. Washington policy prevented the assignment of a military advisory group. Moyer had been in Taiwan for several months, and I had heard from various sources that he was doing an outstanding job, with limited resources, in the economic field.

The dilapidated state of our Embassy chancery, coupled with the heat of Taipei and an absence of air-conditioning, did not help my first impressions. After World War II, apparently someone had sold the chancery building to Uncle Sam when he was not looking. It was across the street from the main railroad line whose locomotives burned soft coal, and was located on the wrong side of the tracks

47

at that. The building itself was in worse condition than otherwise might have been the case; for more than a year our staff had been sitting on their suitcases, waiting for orders to evacuate on short notice. At least half of the chancery grounds were occupied by squatters, including a ramshackle automobile repair shop, a shoe-string taxicab business, and a bicycle shop built of bamboo, all constituting serious fire hazards. Our windows looked out on one of the most impressive junk piles I can recall. It was perhaps fifteen feet high, located between the garage and the bicycle shop. Two years of effort were required subsequently to get rid of these squatters so that we could clean up after them.

Strong and I called on China's brilliant Foreign Minister George K. C. Yeh, whom I count among my best friends, and obtained an appointment to see President Chiang Kai-shek. The President received us in his office at the principal government building in Taipei, which was occupied chiefly by the Ministry of National Defense. Having heard so much about the great man and seen his photograph so frequently, I still was unprepared to find him so youthful in appearance, so simple and friendly in manner. I had expected him to be taller, stern, and even formidable, as he often appears in pictures taken at military reviews. He is about average in height for a Chinese, spare but well proportioned, and with an engaging smile which appears easily and frequently. Later, of course, I came to know him well and this highly favorable first impression remained with me.

Chiang Kai-shek is all Chinese. He is a Christian, but has had no formal Western education and has never traveled to America or Western Europe. He is a Chinese gentleman, to whom truth, modesty, loyalty, and magnanimity are among the greatest of virtues. No less important from the American point of view, Chiang is a man of broad comprehension and deep convictions. He is sure of China's future and of his own mission to help mould that future. Although a politician who can be flexible under certain circumstances, he believes that by placing honor before expediency he can await with confidence the judgment of history.

As Strong accompanied me on various official calls I was glad to note that he had been able to maintain friendly personal and working relationships with Chinese officials at all levels, despite the grave handicaps of his position in Taipei. His comparative youth and the fact that he had only recently become a first secretary made it all the more difficult to carry out his responsibilities under an American policy that seemed to have written off the government on Taiwan. Traditional Chinese politeness sometimes misleads a foreigner into assuming that they have so far forgotten the days of the Son of Heaven as to become indifferent to matters of protocol. However, the Chinese today are no less rank conscious than Americans. Strong replaced a senior ambassador as our representative to the government of a major wartime ally after the United States had virtually abandoned that government as a hopeless cause. I gave him full marks for the job he had done in representing our country.

II

A week after my arrival in Taipei we received a policy guidance telegram from Washington. I was invited to comment. As far as it went the statement seemed unexceptionable, but it was based primarily on short-term considerations and was unsuitable for early publication. I have long felt that policy statements that cannot be made public, except perhaps long afterward when they have become history, are of strictly limited significance. In a democracy such as the United States, a course of action in foreign relations must be understood and supported by public opinion to deserve the name of policy. When friendly foreign countries are involved, there must be a degree of public understanding in those countries also if a policy is to be effective.

My reply in a telegram of August 18 questioned whether in the absence of a firm and durable commitment by the United States to assist in the defense of Taiwan we could count on the national forces there to deal effectively with a large-scale communist landing on the island. With no American ground forces available, our position was largely dependent on the behavior of the Chinese. I suggested that a policy of avoiding long-term commitments could be interpreted by the Chinese government as indicating our intention to continue support only until the Korean War was over and a treaty concluded with Japan. Then we might be expected to recognize the Chinese communists, who would be free to cut the throats of the political and military leaders who had collaborated with us on Tai-

49

wan. A more comprehensive and positive policy for the longer term was essential, in my opinion. I also said that I would welcome an opportunity to comment in advance on any important official public statements to be made on China.

As to American official responsibilities on Taiwan, my telegram suggested that a directive be issued requiring the heads of the various civilian and military groups to keep one another currently and fully informed of all United States activities on the island. Although they should not burden each other with unnecessary details, I maintained that in principle there should be no secrets among them. The need for such instructions was emphasized by the presence of a military survey group of some forty American officers from Tokyo, who understood that they were to have no more than social relations with the Embassy. I followed up this telegram with a letter, which I reproduce here in part:

August 25, 1950

To an officer of the Department of State:

Chinese officials have been distinctly friendly in receiving me, but without any of the effusiveness from certain quarters which appears to have been bestowed upon General MacArthur and his principal subordinates. The Generalissimo, who appeared younger than I had expected, greeted me in his office with considerable cordiality and said he would invite us to his house as soon as my wife arrives from Hong Kong (about August 31). As far as it is possible to estimate at present, all of this strikes approximately the balance which I had hoped for.

I trust that you have not gained an impression from recent telegrams of any friction between the Embassy staff and MacArthur's Liaison (now "Survey") Group. Our only complaint is one of principle, that the Embassy cannot carry out its mission effectively unless it is kept fully and currently informed of their activities and plans, and that they have not made appreciable use of our service attachés. Apparently the explanation is that the group was instructed to submit its findings first to MacArthur, that their personnel have been working very hard and for long hours, and, quite likely, that they believed the Chinese would give them fuller information if the Embassy and its denizens were kept out of sight. I am not prepared to deny that there may have been some foundation for this belief, if indeed they held it.

Without actually having seen any of the Liaison Group's reports, Admiral Jarrett and I have been able to gain a general idea of what has been accomplished. They began their work on August 5, and within forty-eight hours had telegraphed to Tokyo listing the most urgent ammunition requirements of the Chinese forces. An August 12 a more general preliminary review was forwarded, and the complete report is being finished today. What I have seen of General Fox and his staff gives me considerable confidence that they have done a first-class job. I have been able to obtain a rather clearer insight into the group's operations than would otherwise have been possible due to the fact that Colonel L. J. Fortier, the Deputy Chief, happens to be an old personal friend of mine.

I shall not presume to put forward a definitive solution for the problem of Formosa after so short a stay on the island. Nevertheless, I venture to suggest that we include the following tactics in our efforts to arrive at a more satisfactory *modus vivendi* with the Chinese government:

1. Our military and economic aid to be accompanied by a more positive, comprehensive—even hardboiled—policy to insure not only the most effective possible use of such aid but also compliance with our desires in other important courses of action.

2. While leaving no doubt in the minds of the Chinese officials concerned as to the firmness of our intentions, any and all criticism, direct or implied, to be conveyed privately to the appropriate persons and not made the subject of public statements or press interviews, except under the most exceptional circumstances and after the fullest consideration by all concerned.

3. Communications from the American to the Chinese government to be conveyed through normal channels, with approaches to the Generalissimo to be held to an absolute minimum. This would not only avoid giving unnecessary affront to him in the matter of protocol—as when a message from anyone less than the President of the United States is concerned—but, perhaps

more importantly, would permit initial steps with the appropriate cabinet minister or other officials.

. . . Since telegraphing to you on August 18, in response to your request for comments on various policy matters, I have been trying to think of some step which might augment local confidence in our intentions toward Formosa and thereby improve morale. Probably the same idea has occurred to various persons in the Department, but it seems to me that further clarification of our policy on recognition would be particularly helpful at this time. For example, we could find an early occasion to restate and amplify the conditions under which we would consider recognizing a foreign government. You will note that I said "amplify," because I believe we should make it our firm policy to extend no recognition to additional satellites of the Soviet Union. A formal declaration perhaps need not be in such bald terms; we could make recognition contingent upon the fulfillment of our long established conditions and, additionally, upon demonstrated willingness and ability to support the purposes and principles of the United Nations. Obviously, no Soviet satellite, including the Peiping regime, could meet such requirements; nor would it ever be able to meet them as long as it remained in Stalin's orbit. . . .

I was dissatisfied with what I could learn about preparations for the defense of Taiwan in case of an amphibious attack by the communists. The Seventh Fleet was maintaining a task force of two or three cruisers and several destroyers in the vicinity. We were reasonably confident that presence of this force would have sufficient deterrent effect to prevent an assault by the enemy, but various practical points were far from clear. I sent the following memorandum to our naval attaché, requesting that he consult the senior Seventh Fleet officer in the Taiwan area:

August 29, 1950

To Admiral Jarrett:

I believe that you and I should be kept currently and fully informed of various military policies, decisions, and other factors if we are to carry out our duties effectively. I refer not only to such vital matters as the prospective date of arrival of military supplies (notably ammunition) most urgently needed by the Chinese Armed Forces, but also to certain questions with far-reaching political implications. Examples of the latter, in the event of developments indicating the beginning of an actual assault on Formosa, include:

1. At what point will the U.S. Seventh Fleet go into action? When the communist ships leave their own three-mile limit and/or when their aircraft bomb Formosa?
2. At what point will the invasion ports of the mainland be bombed and by whom? The Chinese (Nationalist) Air Force? If so, how will its activities be coordinated with those of the Seventh Fleet (including the 13th Air Force)?
3. What will be the mission of the Chinese Navy and how will its operations be coordinated with those of the Seventh Fleet?
4. Will an American officer become commander-in-chief of the joint U.S.–Chinese effort, and will he be afloat or ashore?
5. What will be the mission of the U.S. Survey Group and will they continue to report direct to SCAP (Tokyo) or will they be subject to the Commander of the Seventh Fleet?

III

Pauline arrived from Hong Kong at the end of August and we started looking for a place to live. What had been the Consul General's residence was being used for offices by our military representatives. We stayed at the chancery for a few nights, where the heat and noise were equally oppressive, and then moved up to a little Japanese-style house on the side of Grass Mountain, twelve miles distant from and 1100 feet above the city of Taipei, which had been bought by our government some years earlier for summer use. This was to be our home for more than seven years—longer than we had ever lived in one house before. We left it with great regret, but initially the prospect was not encouraging. The view across the valley to the south was magnificent, and the temperature several degrees cooler than in the city, but the house was in a sad state. We counted

twenty-six leaks in the roof. The kitchen was in a lean-to, apparently
built of packing cases. Plumbing consisted of two bamboo and lead
pipes bringing in water by gravity, when it flowed at all, from hot
and cold springs on the extinct volcano above us. There was no flush
toilet, only the usual Japanese affair in the floor; furniture consisted
of a few battered wicker chairs and tables. We moved in at once.

Less than two weeks after my initial telegram on policy, Taiwan
was rocked by press reports of the reply by President Truman to a
correspondent's question. He was quoted as agreeing, in effect, that
if the Korean affair were settled there would be no need for the
Seventh Fleet to protect Taiwan. Following is a part of my report
by radio, in paraphrase:

September 2, 1950

To the Department of State:

We must expect (the President's reported remarks at his August 31 press conference) to confirm the fears described in my
telegram of August 18.

If we cannot establish greater mutual confidence with the
(Chinese) government on Taiwan, it would be no more than prudent to question the prospects either of holding this island
against military attack or successfully carrying out the program of economic aid now envisaged. Lack of confidence on both
sides, it seems to me, lies close to the root of our troubles with
China in recent years. I trust therefore, that an early opportunity may be found to allay the fears mentioned above, which the
President doubtless had no intention of arousing.

Pauline and I had been looking forward with great interest to our
first meeting with Madame Chiang Kai-shek. We were familiar with
her background, her American education, and the vital part she had
played in China's recent history. But no one can appreciate her
without a personal meeting. Undoubtedly she is one of the world's
most fascinating, talented, and beautiful women. The fascination
stems from her other characteristics, but most of all from that in-
definable something which, for lack of a better word, we call charm.
Always exquisitely dressed and erect in carriage, she is the domi-

nant figure in any group. Madame Chiang received us cordially. We were to share many trials later and to remain good friends throughout.

IV

In one of our early talks, Foreign Minister Yeh expressed the hope that the United States recognized Taiwan as one of the most stable and peaceful parts of Asia, with law and order in a better state even than Hong Kong; also that significant progress had been recorded in promoting governmental efficiency, military capabilities, economic development, and democratic processes. He believed it would be helpful if the United States government could acknowledge these facts publicly. The Minister thought that such action would help to quiet the alarm on Taiwan caused by repeated references abroad to the island's uncertain fate. He had in mind vague statements by officials and others that the future of Taiwan would depend upon the "negotiation of a peace treaty with Japan," or be subject to "consideration by the United Nations" or to other "international action" of some kind.

Since I had been thinking along somewhat the same lines as the Foreign Minister, I reported his remarks by telegram and added the observation that such phrases as he had quoted from official quarters abroad were believed by many people in Taiwan to indicate that any morning they might wake up to learn that the island had been turned over to some international body, with every likelihood that in the resulting confusion the real take-over would be by the communists. This telegram was followed up by a letter summarizing my impressions after almost one month in Taipei:

September 4, 1950

To an officer of the Department of State:

We used to say at the Embassy in Athens that if Greece could be kept off the front pages it was an indication that things were going pretty well. Judged by that standard things are not going well for Formosa. This situation prompts me to take a step now which I should have preferred to postpone until further clarification of policy had been received from the Department, and until I had opportunity to study the position here in more detail. The step I mention leads from the discussion of tactics to that of strategy.

At the present tempo it appears that decisions may be reached in the near future which would commit us to a definite course of action in regard to Formosa over a considerable period of time. Perhaps this will occur at the meeting of the three foreign ministers next week.

. . . First, let me say that I am now inclined to share the opinion that there will be no major attack on Formosa this year, assuming that the Seventh Fleet's mission remains unaltered during that period. The Chinese communist build-up against this island continues at a steady pace, and it is only prudent to assume that they are capable of mounting an attack within a comparatively short time after the order has come from Peiping or Moscow. Certainly, there is plenty of evidence that they intend to make the attempt eventually; but the date now seems more likely to be postponed until early spring. This would be fortunate for us, since there is no evidence here of any tangible progress on our part subsequent to June 27 in preparing to ward off an assault on the island. We have as yet furnished none of the urgently needed ammunition and other critical items required by the Chinese forces, the Seventh Fleet has no comprehensive plan of action that is known to its officers around Formosa, while the 13th Air Force has little notion as to how it may fit into the picture. The flights of jet aircraft over Taipei are being carried out for psychological and "familiarization" purposes; admittedly jets would be of almost no use against a fleet of junks, and the 13th has no napalm on hand, although it is generally agreed that this would be one of the most effective weapons. . . .

To pass on to the field of political strategy, however, it seems that we may be faced again with the necessity of choosing [whether to]:

1. Continue to extend just enough aid to keep Formosa afloat, in the hope that the Chinese communists will not attack until we have reached some kind of settlement in Korea and, perhaps, in Japan.

2. Try to improve our relations with the Chinese government

as a basis for more effective economic and military aid programs, meanwhile endeavoring to work out a longer range political solution for the island which would take into account our own larger interests, those of the "Formosans," and those of the million and a half refugees from the mainland.

In my opinion the first numbered course of action is not responsive to the situation which has existed since June 25. Among other things, it is too dangerous, not only because the conquest of Formosa by the Chinese communists might materialize at a time which would be highly embarrassing to us, both militarily and politically, but also because our inadequate preparations might well encourage an attack which would bring us into an undesired war with communist China at a moment chosen by the enemy. An equally important consideration to my mind is that for the longer term Course No. 1 is defeatist, in that a continuation of communist expansion in Asia is, by implication, accepted as inevitable.

. . . If No. 2 were chosen, then I believe that perforce we must resolve to treat the Chinese government as a sovereign power, shunning unilateral action and agreements involving China but without its participation or knowledge, such as we have shared in since Yalta, as well as avoiding public statements which the Chinese may regard as studied insults, whether or not we intend them to be. Obviously, there would be much more than that to Course No. 2, but our evident adoption of the tactics mentioned would seem prerequisite to other steps. . . .

. . . If our government should decide against both of the . . . two numbered courses, there would remain among other things the possibility of concerted action under the UN, perhaps by a regional association of nations having interests in the Pacific, as foreseen in the UN Charter, to assume joint responsibility for Formosa. No doubt this point is receiving careful study in the Department at the present time. I assume, therefore, that the necessity for the most painstaking advance preparation has been recognized. Unless an understanding were reached in advance with the Chinese government, for example, international action in Formosa might well encounter armed resistance by the

Chinese forces; even with prior general agreement, certain military units might make trouble. Moreover, we must not imagine that the Formosans themselves can take over the defense of the island or provide individuals capable of assuming full responsibilities of government for a long time to come. These would remain largely international, or American, responsibilities. It might easily require the use of more UN ground forces than are now in Korea to assure internal order and defend Formosa against communist aggression.

... However serious the defects of the present Chinese government, it is well to remind ourselves that today it compares favorably in efficiency and honesty with any other independent government in Asia, while its Armed Forces also are of high quality, judged by Asiatic standards. Certainly the civilian and military officials on this island include a large number of highly capable and patriotic individuals, many of whom are Western-trained and pro-American. Such qualifications are not so plentiful in Asia that they may be lightly cast aside.

MacArthur described convincingly the military considerations surrounding the Formosan question in his unfortunately timed message to the Veterans of Foreign Wars. . . . We want no territory or bases on this island, but we have definite obligations to see that it remains in hands which are friendly to the free world, particularly since this represents the undoubted desire of its inhabitants. The psychological effect upon other threatened nations in Asia and elsewhere is perhaps the most important consideration of all. I feel sure that we will not fail them.

The project of a United Nations commission to investigate American "aggression" in Taiwan was under active discussion in New York and elsewhere. After a talk with the Chinese Foreign Minister, I telegraphed to Washington on September 12, expressing the hope that such an investigation would not materialize. There was nothing to investigate, of course, but opportunities would be offered for a flood of propaganda calculated to undermine the position of the Chinese government on Taiwan. Nevertheless, I thought that a United Nations commission should be permitted to carry out inquiries on the island if one of appropriate composition were established. I shared the Chinese view that no country should be represented that had recognized the Peiping regime. Australia, Belgium, Brazil, and the Philippines were mentioned as probably not unacceptable to the Chinese, although they consistently opposed the whole project in principle. Fortunately it never materialized.

V

Our little house on Grass Mountain was becoming more comfortable. The plumbing remained as primitive as ever, but odd bits of furniture had been collected and repaired or painted, and we were able to begin some modest entertaining. Our bedroom was separated from the dining room only by Japanese paper doors. These were removed when we had guests, and our beds were stowed elsewhere to provide more dining space. Two years were to go by before this situation could be improved. The worst leaks in the roof were repaired, however, and Pauline was able to see the possibilities of making yet another attractive home for us.

The thirty-ninth anniversary of the revolution that overthrew the Manchu dynasty was celebrated on October 10, 1950, just two months after my arrival in Taiwan. The tenth day of the tenth month, or "Double Ten" as the Chinese call it, was observed in Taipei with speeches, a military review, and other events. The review was a brave and impressive effort. Since 1948 the remnants of some 130 army divisions had made their way to Taiwan from the China mainland; most of their equipment necessarily had been left behind. They had since been reorganized and retrained with what arms were available on the island. Good discipline and organization were evident in the review. A lack of adequate equipment was scarcely less obvious and, as we knew, the ammunition shortage was even more critical.

With the help of David L. Osborn, a young Foreign Service officer, I prepared an article for one of the principal Chinese daily newspapers on Taiwan for the celebration of the Double Tenth. It was unusually well received and was published in full by most of the Chinese dailies on the island, and in abbreviated form by papers in Hong Kong and elsewhere. In fact, press use of the article exceeded the usage rate of any previous item released by the United States

Information Service in Taiwan, attaining a distribution of 96 per cent of domestic press circulation. My own contribution was limited to a minimum of editing and the use of my name. Under the title "Revolution for Freedom," the article was intended to give encouragement in a dark hour.

I was fortunate in the American staff provided for the Embassy in Taipei. Alfred Jenkins had come over with me from Hong Kong as political officer and was continuing to apply his exceptional linguistic and other talents to the Chinese scene. Our military attachés were an extraordinarily able group. In addition to Admiral Jarrett, we had Colonel David "Dog" Barrett from the Army. He had spent a quarter of a century in China, and periodically threatened to write his memoirs with the title "From Assistant Military Attaché to Assistant Military Attaché in Twenty-five Years." His knowledge of the Chinese people and their language was remarkable. We missed him greatly when he reached retirement age a couple of years later, and typical Barrettisms were often recalled. One of these, when he saw some particularly wild country, was to describe it as a place where "the hand of man has never set foot."

The Air Force was ably represented by Colonel Leroy G. Heston, who had served with General Chennault in China and had trained many of the Chinese pilots who later came to Taiwan. Heston had played football at Michigan many years after his illustrious namesake, but not long enough to escape the same nickname of "Willy." Other officers in our little group, both civilian and military, were of similarly high quality, including the economic mission under Moyer's able direction.

VI

One of my first formal despatches from Taipei dealt with a subject that has given Americans and Chinese continuing trouble, ever since the national government was set up in Taiwan. The text is given here:

October 17, 1950

To the Department of State:

When Americans on Formosa hear Chinese speak of a "return

to the mainland" their first thought is of World War III, with the prospect of the United States again becoming involved in hostilities in China. At the same time an American is likely to experience a feeling of extreme vexation toward any individual or group of individuals who might cause or hasten such developments. All of this is a perfectly natural and healthy American reaction up to a certain point, but it may blind us to the wider implications of a "return to the mainland." We may forget that this basic urge has had its counterparts throughout history, that today it is encountered, with variations, all around the Iron Curtain and in other parts of the world as well. We should consider how this urge may be used to the advantage of the free world.

The American reaction just described is a sound policy guide in that the United States obviously should not provide encouragement, material or moral, for military adventures. American influence evidently should be exerted in every possible way to discourage courses of action which threaten to bring about hostilities. On the other hand, it seems no less obvious that in an effort to preserve peace important anti-communist forces should not deliberately be kept too weak to resist aggression, or that the millions of refugees among them should be denied the dream of an eventual return to their homes. Once that dream is lost, their value to the free world will be lost as well. In fact, many if not most of them would see no alternative to going over to the enemy camp.

It should be recognized, therefore, that a slogan which seems to mean war and bloodshed to Americans may mean everything that is good and desirable to a Chinese whom communist conquest has made a refugee from his home, his relatives, his friends. There can be no question but that the great majority of the millions of Chinese who have fled before the communists to various points abroad would prefer to return without fighting. Such a happy occurrence, of course, would be predicated upon a breakdown or other profound transformation of the Chinese communist regime. Many Chinese on Formosa firmly believe that such a breakdown will occur. . . . They refuse to accept the possibility of communist success in imposing definitively the Lenin-Stalin pattern of state and life upon the Chinese people. They foresee a partial collapse of the communists within the next few years, followed by chaotic conditions which would require the use of the armed forces now on Formosa to help restore order on the mainland. Whether the present Nationalist government would preside on that occasion, or some successor, may well prove to be a detail which will have solved itself by that time.

It is natural, also, that the purely military view should be widely encountered on Formosa under present conditions. The 600,000 men in the Chinese Armed Forces on the island are nearly all of mainland origin, and their officers include a large portion of China's best known military leaders. These men are professional soldiers with extensive combat experience in a country which has maintained a larger average force under arms during the past hundred years than any other nation in the world. It is not surprising that such leaders, in their thinking, should reduce the attainment of their great ambition to its most obvious (to them) terms: military reconquest of their country with such help from allies as may be necessary to success. Whether it is a real World War III involving Europe and other areas is, to them, incidental. The Chinese common soldier shares the overwhelming desire of his leaders to return home.

In addition to the undebatable preventive courses of action already mentioned, therefore, the United States is faced with a choice between (1) virtual abandonment of various anticommunist groups throughout the world, or (2) extending them sufficient moral and material support to preserve their morale and permit them to resist further communist aggression. In general, the United States has adopted the second course, and the question remains as to how such support can be given maximum effectiveness in various countries.

Maintaining morale quite evidently is related to the question of material support, but the two are by no means identical. The communists have demonstrated this conclusively on various occasions, where they won victories (as in China) or suffered defeats (as in Greece and Korea) with far less material support from their Soviet masters at critical moments than they might reasonably have expected. Assiduous attention by the Kremlin to the training of foreign political workers in the arts of revolution and propaganda, over a long period of years, and the influence which these workers have been able to exert over their fellow countrymen, have borne fruit for the communist cause which many billions in money and thousands of Russian troops could never have equaled. In its best sense, "Return to the Mainland" is the free world's answer to "Workers of the World Unite!" The importance of such slogans in the struggle between freedom and tyranny cannot be overestimated.

The extent to which opinion among Chinese refugees from communism veers from one course to another depends largely upon their evaluation of the success of the communists in consolidating their hold over China. When the prospects seem darkest for the forces opposed to communism, World War III appears to most refugee Chinese as their only possible salvation. The more enlightened may admit privately that it seems a counsel of despair, but they will quote many a prominent American to the effect that there are worse things than war. When the outlook seems brighter, as for example today with the success of United Nations' action in Korea, many Chinese will recognize the possibility of an alternative to a general war. Admittedly Korea is being liberated by force of arms, but open warfare between the great powers has so far been avoided. One may hope that the lesson will not be lost upon the Chinese people and their communist masters.

The two factors likely to exert the greatest influence during the coming months over Chinese opinion outside the Iron Curtain are the courses of action to be followed by the United States and by the Peiping regime. There is accumulating evidence that the Chinese communists are shifting emphasis from their announced aim of industrialization as a means of improving the lot of the people to one in which military considerations are paramount. There would appear to be no other explanation for the enormous number of men being kept under arms, or the extensive work being pushed on roads and airfields of primary military but negligible economic significance. Apparently authentic reports indicate similar expansion in the training of air and naval personnel, while there is no doubt of concentrated efforts by the Chinese communists in recent weeks to acquire materials and equipment of military significance from nearby sources.

Although present military and para-military activities of the Chinese communists could be related specifically to plans for early and large-scale aggression against Korea, Formosa, Indochina, or other areas, this is by no means certain. The coming months may establish that communist China is simply following the Soviet pattern of first building up a huge and permanent military machine, ostensibly for defense but actually for the purposes of suppressing internal opposition, indoctrinating politically the most virile segment of its population and, as occasion arises, overawing and swallowing up its neighbors. In such a picture the timing, place, and nature of new aggressions would become less significant than their inevitability.

Meanwhile, refugee Chinese on Formosa and elsewhere, as well as Chinese behind the Curtain, will be watching the United Nations, and particularly the United States, for positive steps toward preserving peace which give promise of canceling out communist steps toward war. Only if that materializes will opinion continue to veer away from accepting World War III as unavoidable and even desirable. Such noncommunist elements among the Chinese and others may require firm handling to discourage them from military adventures; equally essential will be the exercise of tact and understanding on our part if these elements are to be retained on the side of the free world. And their retention is the only hope for peace in Asia. Communist conquest of further important areas in the Far East will simply hasten World War III, after transferring to the enemy very considerable military, economic, and moral forces which are still on our side.

There will be a return to the mainland in any event. The questions are simply: When, and whose mainland? . . .

VII

Meanwhile the utter rout of the North Koreans following the Inchon landings was attracting world-wide attention. Along with the general rejoicing in Taiwan, were expressions of concern over a possible Chinese communist attack on our now greatly extended front in northern Korea. Intelligence reports of troop movements from Central and South China to Manchuria were sufficiently convincing to warrant serious attention. Some of these reports even antedated the North Korean attack on June 25. All available information had been sent on to Washington through military channels, but I telegraphed in the following sense:

November 6, 1950

To the Department of State:

Chinese military intelligence forwarded to Washington by the Embassy's service attachés during the past few days lends strong support to the assumption that the Chinese communists plan to throw the book at the United Nations forces in Korea and in addition to step up their pressure in Indochina. Allowance evidently should be made for wishful thinking among the Chinese military, most of whom regard a general conflict as the only means of liberating China from the communists. In the present instance, however, such a caveat still leaves an imposing array of apparently established facts, as well as evidence of sincerity among the best informed Chinese, such as to render quite possible the correctness of their consensus of opinion that all-out action in Korea by the Chinese communists should be expected.

The reasons why the Chinese communists have so far delayed their entry into Korea in force, quite aside from any speculation on influences exerted by Moscow, may include:

1. The Chinese communists had assumed that the North Koreans would win; hence they had not prepared to intervene earlier.

2. Postponing any major effort on their part until the fighting reached the region of the Korean-Manchurian frontier served to shorten their lines of communication—a particularly important point in view of the fact that United Nations forces control sea and air—and also gave them the maximum time for preparation. In addition to bringing up forces from other parts

65

of China, it was necessary to replenish stocks of equipment and supplies in Manchuria which had been seriously depleted in extending aid to the North Koreans.

3. In the above-mentioned frontier area full advantage can be taken of the degree to which world opinion has been conditioned to acts of aggression and now looks upon a few regiments being identified on the wrong side of a border as indicating rather less than overt action. Meantime the United Nations forces can be weakened and the exposure to bombing of Chinese communist lines of communications and bases can be postponed. Evidence of an all-out effort, including the expenditure of the Chinese communist Air Force, probably will be delayed as long as possible for the reasons mentioned in paragraph 2.

4. The support of public opinion in communist China for major military operations can be whipped up much more easily if it can be represented that an immediate threat to the Manchurian border exists; this notwithstanding the general assumption that Chinese communist leaders are aware United Nations forces do not intend to cross the frontier and would not attempt an invasion of Manchuria with a force of only ten divisions in any case.

5. United Nations successes to date can be most effectively countered by a crushing Chinese communist victory in North Korea, thereby enhancing Asian and communist prestige in relation to Western imperialism and eliminating as a fighting force an important part of the U.S. Army.

The above points necessarily are matters of opinion to a considerable degree, but the Chinese military on Formosa have access to more China mainland sources of information and have had more experience in this field of estimating Chinese communist intentions than others outside the Curtain; their opinions therefore warrant the most careful attention at this time.

The foregoing telegram was drafted before General MacArthur's communique reached Taipei.

MacArthur's communique announced the large-scale intervention of Chinese communist forces in Korea. My telegram was late, but was intended only to draw the Department's attention to information already available at the Pentagon. At least it might serve to emphasize the importance of the intelligence available in Taipei and Hong Kong.

VIII

At this point I recommended the removal of the somewhat informal restrictions that had been imposed on travel to Taiwan by American citizens in general and by the families of our official personnel in particular. The American colony on Taiwan was small at that time —less than three hundred, including military and civilian officials, missionaries, businessmen, and members of their families—and there was no early prospect of any substantial increase. However, I predicated my recommendation upon the assumption that the mission of the Seventh Fleet to protect Taiwan would continue. Replying to an inquiry from the Department, I pointed out that if Taiwan were to be written off at some critical juncture it might be impossible to evacuate any considerable number of persons on short notice. My telegram concluded:

November 9, 1950

To the Department of State:
The Department's telegram states that all possible steps would be taken to provide for the safety of Americans here in case of hostilities. In explaining to individuals the risks involved, however, it should be remembered that under certain conditions it might be possible to give very little assistance. For example, heavy air raids on Taipei and the nearby airfields and ports might well prevent the implementation of virtually all features of the evacuation plans now in existence. The only course would be to improvise in accordance with conditions as they might develop and in the light of Navy and Air Force capabilities for extending assistance at that time. It is believed that such air attacks are unlikely, but the possibility should not be excluded.

It is apparent from the foregoing that I was trying yet another way to obtain information on current policy development in Washington and to stimulate thinking in the State Department by posing practical problems. The restrictions on travel lapsed, which was encouraging, but I could not be sure that this was the result of any major policy decisions, or that the matter had been coordinated with all concerned. On the same day I sent another telegram, which may be paraphrased as follows:

November 9, 1950

To the Department of State:

The critical situation resulting from Chinese communist aggression in Korea makes it more urgent than ever that we be kept currently and fully informed of our government's policies and specific intentions as to military aid for the Chinese national forces on Formosa. I have raised these questions several times (for example, on August 18, October 9, October 19, and October 20), but so far our information is limited to one telegram from the Department about a shipment of ammunition and a Navy report regarding radar.

Our senior military attaché is responsible for liaison with the Seventh Fleet and for Mutual Defense Assistance operations at this end. To function effectively it is essential that he be given immediately the details of General MacArthur's "request of August 16," to which we had seen only a reference, and that he have copies of all recent reports by the military survey group from MacArthur's headquarters. Our attaché must be in a position to make recommendations in the light of a rapidly evolving situation, as well as to keep our Chinese friends informed to the extent necessary.

I assume that the Departments of State and Defense appreciate that Formosa holds the largest anti-communist military forces in the Far East, and that in total effectiveness they are second only to the United Nations forces in Korea. . . . there would be no excuse if lack of interagency coordination in Washington should result in failure to provide the Chinese national forces with their urgent and relatively modest requirements prior to a new crisis in which those forces might be needed here or elsewhere.

Another potential military asset for our side existed in Indochina, where some 25,000 Chinese troops had been interned after their withdrawal from China in the face of greatly superior communist forces. I reported as follows (in paraphrase):

November 10, 1950

To the Department of State:

The Chinese Foreign Minister told me yesterday that he considers the situation in Indochina to be hopeless unless the United States rushes additional aid and forces to the French to speed up the creation of a sizable and effective native army. Unless these steps are taken he sees no reason for sacrificing the Chinese troops now interned in Indochina, but if the French actually adopt a suitable program the Foreign Minister thinks that these Chinese troops could serve a useful purpose in bridging the present gap.

I have no direct information regarding the troops in question. Undoubtedly the Chinese are good soldiers when well fed, equipped, and led; I believe that the possibility of using these experienced troops on the spot should be looked into most carefully.

At this time we learned that President Chiang was considering the possibility of raids on the China coast opposite Taiwan, and that he probably would seek American logistic support. I telegraphed to the Department on November 20 that it seemed impracticable to achieve an early lodgment on the mainland, but that raids offered some attractions. Among these were the possibility of relieving pressure on Indochina, interrupting enemy communications with that theater, and perhaps even bringing about the diversion of some Chinese communist units from Korea. I said that a successful raid could raise morale everywhere in the noncommunist Far East. It will be recalled that things were going badly for us in Korea at that moment.

On November 16, 1950, we received our first important visit of Washington officials since my arrival in Taipei three months earlier.

☆ China Assignment ☆

Mr. William C. Foster, administrator of the Economic Cooperation Administration, was accompanied by Mrs. Foster and several officers of his organization. Realizing the importance of this opportunity to get across our thinking to Washington, political, economic, and military officers stationed in Taipei prepared carefully for the visit. First, we wanted to convince Mr. Foster of the soundness of our views on policy, about which all of us in Taiwan were in substantial agreement. Second, we hoped for an increase in ECA (economic aid) funds for the island. In the calendar year only twenty million dollars had been available, although Taiwan's deficit in international payments approached ninety million dollars. An increase of twenty million had been approved for the coming months, but we wanted at least sixty million for the fiscal year ending June 30, 1951.

Our first session was at the Embassy, where I read a general statement on the problems of Taiwan. Parts of the text are given here:

Unfortunately, the problems surrounding Formosa have generated so much heat as to leave many Americans bewildered if not actually singed. I was not at Wake Island and have seen no reports on the meeting of the President and General MacArthur other than those which appeared in the press. Nevertheless, I shall venture to give a brief summary of the positive aspects of American policy toward this island as I understand them. . . .

Long-term American policy toward the "question of Formosa" is that in fulfillment of the Cairo Declaration all appropriate steps should be taken toward its eventual incorporation into a friendly and peaceful China, under conditions acceptable to a majority of the island's inhabitants. I believe that to be a sound policy and one which we should always keep in mind. Unhappily, it is based upon hopes which present day realities have made remote to say the least.

As a guide for present action, therefore, we have a short- to medium-range policy. Reduced to its simplest terms, this policy is that the United States should exert all practicable efforts to keep Formosa outside the Curtain and, to the extent consistent with such primary policy, to prevent the outbreak of hostilities in this area. I believe such efforts to be in accord-

ance with the political, economic, and strategic interests of the
United States in particular, and of the free world in general,
besides being for the benefit and in conformity with the wishes
of a majority of the eight million people on this island. Moreover, the psychological influence of the fate of Formosa and
other threatened countries of East Asia is a matter of outstanding importance.

We cannot divorce the question of Formosa entirely from
the larger question of China. Obvious practical considerations,
as well as the long-term policy outlined above, make it necessary
that in dealing with this island the United States should have a
clear-cut position toward the two related but not identical questions of Chinese membership in the United Nations and American
recognition of one or the other existing Chinese regime. American policy is that there is no justification for changing the
status quo in this regard, at least as long as the Chinese government on Formosa makes a reasonably honest effort to sustain
the purposes and principles of the United Nations, while the
Peiping regime openly flouts them. Either the Chinese communists are so completely dominated by Moscow as to be unable to conduct themselves as a self-respecting sovereign state,
or their leaders have voluntarily dedicated themselves to undermining the world order created by the Charter of the United
Nations. In either case, the United States is justified in continuing to recognize the Chinese government on Formosa and to
oppose admission of the Peiping regime into the United Nations. . . .

We should not deceive ourselves, however, by assuming that
the United States can shift to others any considerable part of
the burdens of influencing United Nations opinion or of supplying the tangible outside support required to keep Formosa
in the orbit of the free world. The United Kingdom might have
helped and may yet do so if circumstances should force the
British government to acknowledge its mistake in recognizing
communist China last January. Meantime, while seeking all
possible moral support from friendly countries, the United
States must not expect to share with others besides the government and people of this island the practical responsibilities

involved. The vital questions arise, therefore, whether we can afford the necessary effort, in the light of American commitments elsewhere and whether we can obtain the essential degree of cooperation from the Chinese government in implementing our policy. . . .

During the past year the Chinese government has been forced to draw heavily on its holdings of gold and foreign exchange, besides virtually exhausting the $125 million grant extended by the United States in 1948. Internally, the currency situation has been kept from getting entirely out of hand only with the assistance which ECA was in a position to extend, and by various drastic measures which it may be impracticable to continue much longer. When it is noted that approximately 70 per cent of total government income is being devoted to military purposes, we need not look further for the first point of attack.

In absolute terms, expenditures for maintaining the defense establishment on Formosa are very low. . . . During and since the war [military "hardware"] equipment has been supplied to China very largely by the United States. At the present time [military aid] funds are being used to a limited extent for the extension of so-called selected military assistance to Formosa. The determination of such assistance is understood to be in the hands of the Joint Chiefs of Staff and, presumably, is based upon purely military considerations. No one here in Formosa has been given any idea of the extent, or more than a few details of the nature, of the military aid in prospect.

From the economic point of view, it obviously is desirable to coordinate military assistance with the ECA program. The supply of American shoes to the troops, for example, would not only increase their combat efficiency but could reduce or eliminate present local currency outlays of the Chinese government for inferior footwear of domestic manufacture. The soldier today is getting all the rice he can eat, but his health is impaired by lack of a balanced diet. The supply of supplementary foods from the United States would correct this condition and might release additional rice for export from the island. Consideration also could be given to increased imports of consumer goods, paid for by the United States, the sale of which on the Formosan market would provide local currency expressly to meet military requirements. All such expenditures evidently should be chargeable to military aid, but to date "selected" assistance to Formosa has not taken into account the economic implications of military expenditures other than as part of the direct dollar cost.

In a larger sense, of course, it may not matter in many cases whether the assistance given is labeled economic or military. The crucial point is that substantial increases in both categories are urgently needed. . . . Only by close coordination of military and economic assistance, however, can we hope to obtain optimum results. Such results, at comparatively moderate expense, should give promise of achieving our policy of keeping Formosa outside the Curtain, by making it self-supporting economically within a very few years and, with a minimum of military assistance, discouraging or preventing aggression against the island. In those terms, aid to Formosa seems very much worth-while in the light of our world-wide commitments. We cannot afford to lose further ground in the Far East if it can possibly be avoided.

So we come to the last and most delicate question—that of United States relations with the Chinese government. Many Americans have wondered during the past few years why, in view of all that has been said and done, we continue to recognize and to aid this government. Actually, the reasons pro and con may be less significant than the fact that we are still in here pitching. With due allowance for the force of circumstances, there is evidently something fundamental in the active American preference for Free China as opposed to communist China. There is at least a tacit recognition of the fact that in dealing with communist imperialism we cannot be neutral. To say, "A plague on both your houses," is no good; carried to its logical conclusion this means packing up, going home, and reverting to isolationism. . . .

The first consideration in our practical relations with the Chinese government, therefore, is whether we can obtain a satisfactory degree of cooperation in implementing American policy here. Our ECA Mission can tell you of past and present experience in this regard. My own experience during the three months I have been here is that the cooperation we receive compares not unfavorably in spirit and effectiveness with that in other countries where we are extending economic and military aid. With a fully coordinated program covering both fields it should be possible to obtain still better cooperation and thus improve the prospects of success in carrying out our policies.

Finally, I shall not evade the question whether the Chinese government is deserving of our help. Certainly it has many defects from the standpoints of efficiency . . . [but in Asia] this government is one of the more effective and maintains a satisfactory degree of law and order while preserving a considerable measure of personal freedom. Equally important, there seems to have been some improvement in these respects during the past year. There are signs of evolution into something more like what we call democracy, not into a communist strait jacket. This is all very important, and the United States should do everything in its power to encourage and even enforce further improvement. But we should not lose sight of the fact that reform is of immediate consequence to us only in so far as it contributes to the fulfillment of our primary policy. Reform, however desirable, must not be allowed to prevent effective cooperation between governments in attaining our more tangible and urgent objectives.

To achieve a maximum of success in Formosa, it seems evident that American support and cooperation must be wholehearted. This does not mean "all-out." The United States has many other obligations, to its own people, to the United Nations, and to friendly countries throughout the world. Nor does whole-hearted support imply our assumption of direct responsibility for keeping any particular government in power. We should be ready to work with any government which shows a sincere desire to cooperate, and our efforts should be directed toward making the most effective possible use of our relations with that government in obtaining practical results. Within the limits of such considerations, and of American commitments elsewhere, our attitude toward the government on Formosa should be frank, firm, friendly, and whole-hearted if we are to contribute our share to obtaining a maximum of cooperation on this island.

Chinese officials noted that Mr. Foster was the first high official of the United States government to visit Taiwan in many months. All of us in Taipei, Chinese and Americans alike, were pleased with the visit. Mr. Foster and his associates displayed a most intelligent and sympathetic interest in our problems. His subsequent article on Taiwan in the *Reader's Digest* was most helpful.

X

Before Mr. Foster's departure, other important visitors, Senator and Mrs. William F. Knowland, arrived. In retrospect, this visit also went off gratifyingly, but with some complications as the following despatch will indicate:

November 27, 1950

To the Department of State:

During a visit of one week (November 17-24, 1950) to Formosa, Senator and Mrs. William F. Knowland were the official guests of the Chinese government. A very full schedule was arranged for them by an official of the Foreign Office, who on request supplied the details of their activities shown on an enclosure to the present despatch. (American participation is indicated at various points on the schedule.) The Knowlands were met at the airport by a large crowd, despite the hour of 6:40 A.M., and were escorted to the government Guest House where they resided during their stay.

When news of the California Senator's prospective visit first reached Taipei, I expressed privately to Foreign Minister Yeh the hope that the Chinese would not "stand on their heads" to welcome him. I understood that they appreciated his sincere and indefatigable support, and that they naturally would wish to show this appreciation. However, I pointed out that Knowland's position on China was popularly considered to have a strong partisan bias. Under the circumstances, the Chinese government would do well, in its own interest, not to lend further credence to the already general impression that it was following

75

a partisan course in its attitude toward the two principal American political parties. The Foreign Minister expressed full agreement and said that he would do what he could along this line. However, he doubted that he would be able to influence matters appreciably. He remarked that he had long been aware of the "China Lobby" problem in Washington and expressed the hope and belief that the Chinese Embassy had been kept clear of it.

Telegrams from Seoul and Tokyo announcing the Knowlands' arrival in Taipei reached the Embassy, in encrypted form via Washington, during the night of November 16-17. With only one code clerk available, since the recent emergency transfer of its second code clerk to Seoul, it is not surprising that these telegrams were decoded too late to permit the Embassy to have an officer meet the plane before seven o'clock the next morning. (Note for Congressional relations: Such urgent telegrams should be sent in clear text, whenever possible, and by the most direct routes.)

In view of several previous discussions between the Foreign Office and the Embassy, I pointed out to Foreign Minister Yeh and Governor Wu that they should have shared with me their information on the hour of the Knowlands' arrival. I said that I knew Knowland, and was satisfied he did not mind that no one from the Embassy met him; nor did I mind personally. But from the Chinese viewpoint there would be only disadvantage to them in giving any further impression to the press and to the public that they were playing up to Republican senators (or SCAP) in the hope of putting pressure on the Administration or the Department of State.

Both the Foreign Minister and the Governor were profuse, and seemingly genuine, in their apologies for the oversight in not keeping the Embassy informed. The Foreign Minister made an immediate personal check of the press coverage of the Knowlands' arrival. The absence of Embassy representatives at the airport had been duly noted by various correspondents, but the Americans had accepted without question the factual explanation given them by the Embassy staff. Some speculation was

President Chiang Kai-shek and Ambassador Rankin, Taipei, 1962

Madame Chiang Kai-shek and Mrs. Rankin, Taipei, 1962

American Consul General's Residence on The Peak, Hong Kong

Ambassador Rankin's Residence at Tsao Shan (Grass Mountain) 1100 feet above Taipei

started in the Chinese press, but the Foreign Minister apparently succeeded in heading it off.

With due allowance for the somewhat unpropitious background described in the foregoing paragraphs, all of which is significant only because of the extreme delicacy of the Chinese question in general and that of Formosa in particular, the Knowlands' visit appears to have gone over quite satisfactorily. Their visit to Kinmen (or Chinmen) Island, near Amoy, and the resulting report that they had gone to the "Chinese Mainland," plus the fact that the communists dropped a few shells on that island the same day, added some color to an otherwise unspectacular if active itinerary.

In a two-hour conference with members of the Embassy staff on Thanksgiving Day, Senator Knowland gave a most helpful and reasonable review of recent developments in the United States as they might affect Far Eastern policy. He displayed none of the animus toward the Department with which he is often credited. In his approach to the practical and positive aspects of the "problem of Formosa," during this rather lengthy and frank discussion, no significant differences between the views of the Senator and of the Embassy staff were revealed. Those present included the chargé d'affaires, Counselor Dawson, Second Secretary Jenkins, Colonel Barrett (Army attaché), Colonel Heston (Air attaché), Commander Kilmartin (assistant Naval attaché, representing Admiral Jarrett who was out of town) and USIS Director Sheeks. The Senator had spent some time at the ECA Mission the day before, which explains why no one from that office was present.

Later on the same day, Senator and Mrs. Knowland had Thanksgiving dinner with members of the Embassy staff, which they seemed to enjoy thoroughly.

Press coverage of the Knowland visit was unusually extensive, but has either appeared in the United States or has been dealt with adequately in the Embassy's daily press telegrams and in the current "Weeka" [weekly review].

Senator and Mrs. Knowland had planned to depart for Hong Kong by a Philippine Airlines plane at 8 A.M. on November 24.

After circling the airport for two hours, the aircraft was unable to land, due to the low ceiling, and returned to Okinawa. I therefore arranged for them to proceed by the Naval attaché's plane at 9:30 A.M. Others among the numerous crowd at the airport to bid them good-bye included the Prime Minister, the Governor, and the chief of the ECA Mission, Dr. Moyer. Any lingering suspicion of coolness between the Knowlands and official Americans in Taipei should have been dispelled when they took off in a plane bearing a large American flag and conspicuously marked "United States Naval Attaché China." The Senator and his wife had been most cordial at all times.

This despatch is reproduced *in extenso*, partly because of the experience gained from the visit by the Chinese and the Embassy in preparing for the innumerable Congressional visitations that followed, and also because it is the last such despatch I ever wrote. Apparently Senator Knowland asked the Department to let him see whatever had been reported from Taipei about his visit. I had classified the despatch "confidential," and instead of refusing his request for that reason, as a matter of principle, the Department asked me whether I had any objection to passing it on to him. Had I said "no," presumably the Senator would have been so informed and left to suspect the worst. So of course I consented, but pointed out the unfortunate precedent being created. At the same time I told the Department that hereafter my despatches on Congressional visits would be unclassified and limited to a simple account of the schedules followed. According to press reports my despatch eventually was made available to a Senate Committee inquiring into the MacArthur episode. I might add that Knowland and I remained good friends.

XI

On December 5 I wrote as follows to an officer of the Department of State:

At the present moment we are all holding our breaths for the result of the Truman-Attlee meeting, which could be almost anything. One unpleasant possibility, in the event of another Munich, would be to have the 300-odd Americans now in Formosa given the Chinese equivalent of tar-and-feather treatment. Little as I should enjoy such a suit of winter clothing, I honestly couldn't blame them too much. However, I really don't expect anything of the kind.

Rightly or wrongly I have the impression that we have been developing a fairly positive Formosa policy since June 27, but it may have been rather late. We probably shall know very shortly whether events have overtaken us or overwhelmed us. Frankly, I do not see how we can give in on anything important; our position in Asia has already been reduced to a minimum. Any more losses on our side will put us out of the Far East entirely and permit the communists to concentrate on Europe. The Near and Middle East would go by default. Meanwhile, there is the grave military situation in Korea to consider, and I have no clear picture of just how that stands.

I suppose it must be evident to everyone by now that the United States should have maintained large and effective striking forces in Germany and Japan until such time as those two countries could be rearmed. . . . With them on our side we can balance the situation, and it seems to me that top priority should go to rearming them now. Any further delay may well be fatal.

All of the above sounds pretty pessimistic, and we shall hope that the Truman-Attlee talks will produce something constructive. But with those 800,000 agrarian reformers sweeping down through Korea, I cannot help remembering our modest efforts to promote a greater "sense of urgency" at Bangkok nearly a year ago.

The meeting of President Truman and Prime Minister Attlee ended reassuringly. Definitely, we were not to have another Munich. The following is a paraphrase of my telegram:

December 13, 1950

To the Department of State:

Local reaction is reserved but generally favorable to the final communique on the Truman-Attlee meeting, as already indicated in recent press review telegrams. It was widely expected here that Britain would favor giving Formosa to the Chinese communists in the vague hope of buying time or favor. The United States was expected to take a firm stand, and the fact that the British were won over to the American position except on the questions of recognition and UN membership is looked upon as a definite advance. However, in view of the situation in Korea and elsewhere, Chinese government circles and the local public will reserve judgment until a clearer picture becomes available of the course of action intended by the United States.

Opinion here cannot see how further consideration by the UN of questions affecting Formosa can contribute to a peaceful settlement and to the maintenance of security in the Pacific unless reinforced by continuing and effective steps to counter communist aggression. In the absence of such steps and in the face of the unyielding position taken by the communists and their avowed intention to take Formosa by force, further discussion in the UN could produce no substantial result at best; at worst it might bring forth an appeasing compromise which would open the way for communist control of the island.

Chinese government circles in general appreciate the soundness of American policy in continuing to make the greatest possible use of UN channels, in welcoming the discussion of any subject, and in avoiding in every possible way the use of the veto. At the same time no one expects the UN as such to establish and implement an effective program of safeguarding the "interests of the people of Formosa and the maintenance of peace and security in the Pacific" except in so far as such a program is proposed and supported by the U.S. Premier Chen Cheng remarked to me a few days ago, "The existence of the free world depends upon unity among the free nations, which in turn depends upon American leadership. All of us (i.e., all free nations) are looking for that leadership and are ready to follow it."

As a matter of fact, the United States already is embarked upon a positive course of action as regards Formosa, and I believe that the Truman-Attlee agreement furnishes a basis on which to carry such action through to its logical conclusion. This could be done without fanfare and without compromising our UN and other commitments. We need only to step up and to clarify action which is already under way:

1. While we should welcome UN or other international discussion of the "future of Formosa," I believe that we should overlook no suitable opportunity to repeat and to make clear our position that, under any circumstances, we shall resist the use of force to change the status of this island, and that its legal position can be settled only in a treaty with Japan. . . .

2. The ECA program for Formosa, calling for larger aid and the assignment of a modest number of United States technical experts, should be speeded up in every possible way to produce maximum results within the shortest space of time. This is already under way and is the most satisfactory and logical aspect of the American effort on this island.

3. Our present Armed Services attaché staff, numbering fifty Americans, should be enlarged to permit the detail of qualified officers and enlisted men to various units of the Chinese Army, Navy, and Air Force, where they would advise on training and the use of equipment in addition to keeping the United States government informed regarding Chinese military effectiveness, their equipment, and other requirements and on the end-use of American aid. This would be in effect simply an expansion of what we are doing already and would not need to be heralded as the "despatch of an American military mission." The additional personnel could be assigned as required to fill specific needs reported by the senior military attaché and would be under his orders; the total probably would never exceed two hundred. This plan is much to be preferred to the establishment of a formal "mission" along with the unwanted overhead and political implications, here and in the United States, which such action would inevitably involve.

Having taken the foregoing political, economic, and military steps we should be well on the way toward making Formosa capable of resisting aggression, self-supporting economically, and, in case hostilities should spread, a military asset. Training and equipping forces here should be for defense; this leaves enough to be done while avoiding the encouragement of any independent adventures. . . . When trained and equipped for the defense of this island, however, Nationalist forces could readily be fitted into possible combined offensive operations in case of a general conflict. On this point we should look ahead as far as the Chinese communists, who evidently expected a speedy North Korean victory last summer but nevertheless made plans long in advance to use their own troops if necessary.

XII

As 1950 drew to a close I reported the following conversation with an American citizen in a telegram (paraphrased):

December 26, 1950

To the Department of State:

Additional support for the opinion that the Chinese communists are committed to an all-out effort in Korea came today from a well-informed American who left Shanghai as recently as last month. He reported that the Chinese fully anticipated that the United States would bomb Manchuria and other points in China when Chinese communist intervention in Korea could no longer be hidden. He stated that this was an important reason why their open participation (in Korea) was delayed as long as possible; the communists feared bombings which would cut their lines of communication from North China to Korea before adequate amounts of military supplies could be moved (see also my telegram of November 6). This American added that our failure to bomb military objectives in China, when the Chinese communist aggression became apparent to everyone, was generally looked upon in Shanghai as evidence of American political and military weakness and was disappointing to the anti-communist majority of the population. Presumably the failure of the United States to undertake stronger military action with the crossing of the 38th parallel by the Chinese communists would confirm the opinion in communist China that the United States had accepted defeat.

☆☆☆

4: Consolidation

THE YEAR 1951 opened with the Chinese communist advance in Korea approaching high tide. Seoul was reoccupied by the enemy and it was widely accepted that he had the capability of pushing our forces entirely out of Korea. Two reports reaching Taiwan both puzzled and encouraged us. One was that the Reds were unable, apparently because of supply difficulties, to sustain an attack for more than four or five days. The second was that enemy aircraft rarely appeared over territory held by our forces. If the Chinese communists could not improve their supply effort, and if the Soviets were unwilling to risk their aircraft over our positions—whatever the reason or the nationality of the pilots—it was evident that we would enjoy two major advantages. Nevertheless, our armies were still retreating, and the question remained as to how Taiwan could be defended if we were defeated in Korea. Not only would large enemy forces be released for redeployment against the island, but the psychological impact of a major communist victory would compound our difficulties.

I was not satisfied with the preparations to defend Taiwan. All eyes naturally were on Korea, and there was no general agreement or understanding on how the Seventh Fleet was to carry out its mission in the Formosa Strait. That shallow, stormy hundred miles of water was being referred to complacently by press and public as the locus of formidable American naval forces. The habit, developed at that time, of referring to the Seventh Fleet as being "in the Strait," or its possible "withdrawal," persisted for years afterward. Informed persons recognized the significance of such expressions, but I fear that a far greater number imagined a long line of battleships down the Formosa Strait through which no enemy could pass. In fact, of course, the Strait is suitable only for the deployment of relatively small, light naval forces. Not infrequently during the Korean War no American naval vessel was seen within several hundred miles of Taiwan.

From the military standpoint we were not alarmed over ship movements that kept the Navy well beyond the horizon. Sea power is exerted over great distances, and in case of need a strong force presumably could have been moved in quickly. But we had to consider the effect on local Chinese morale if our ships remained out of sight for long. Moreover, we had to envisage the possibility of the Seventh Fleet being heavily engaged elsewhere in a crisis, with little help to spare for Taiwan. We could not overlook the possibility of a communist landing in strength on the island, whatever their losses en route, to be confronted by inadequately equipped national Chinese ground forces. Most frustrating of all from the standpoint of American officials on Taiwan, both civilian and military, was our lack of authoritative information as to what was being discussed and decided in Washington and Tokyo about military aid for Taiwan. On January 24, 1951, I wrote to an officer of the Department of State:

I agree with you that a strange situation exists in respect to military aid for Formosa. You may imagine how the Chinese here interpret a case in which numerous persons in Washington and Tokyo (even Radio Moscow has a figure of $200 millions) are informed on this subject, while Admiral Jarrett and I . . . have yet to see the Fox Report of last August. In one of my first telegrams to the Department after arriving here last summer I urged that in our relations with American military and economic officials the principle of full and free exchange of information should be established. I have been through all of this before, and I am convinced that our foreign relations cannot otherwise be conducted effectively. Frankly, however, I was not prepared for a situation in which, after five months, the Embassy and its Armed Services attachés are still studiously excluded from military plans for keeping Formosa outside the Iron Curtain. . . .

First, we have the very practical problem of making the Seventh Fleet's mission effective. It has been recognized all along and by all concerned that this island could not be defended successfully against a massive communist attack simply with the available strength of the Seventh Fleet, the Thirteenth Air Force, and the Chinese Nationalist forces as the latter existed on June 27, 1950. Our avowed intention, therefore, was to increase the effectiveness of the forces on Formosa by "selected military aid." During the past seven months, such aid has been limited to one shipload of ammunition. Important as this shipment was and is, the net effect is to leave the island even less well prepared to resist aggression than it was last June. Equipment has suffered wear and tear in the meantime, and not inconsiderable amounts of ammunition and other supplies have been used up in normal processes of training and maintenance.

We shall be much interested in seeing a copy of the Fox Report, which you say will be sent to us as soon as it is available (it has been available to persons in Tokyo for the past five months). Inevitably the report is already out of date, which need not have been the case had it been in the hands of our attachés in the meantime; and with the best will in the world it could not have been complete in the first place. We learn, for example, that no provision was made for supplying aviation and motor gasoline and fuel oil, to say nothing of the large incidental expenditures involved in handling, storing, maintaining, and utilizing an important amount of military equipment. The Chinese government is close to the end of its financial tether, and has no funds for such purposes. Moreover, our latest information is to the effect that the entire project is being held up while Tokyo pares down the Fox lists to meet new limits fixed by the Joint Chiefs of Staff (reportedly fifty million dollars for the Chinese Army, five million dollars for the Navy, and sixteen million dollars for the Air Force).

The exact amount to be allotted for military aid to Formosa is far less important, however, than the filling of urgent needs immediately in preparation for a possible attack in March or April. . . . One of the most urgent needs at the present moment is for anything up to 250 propeller-driven fighter aircraft, with the necessary spare parts and fuel. Whether or not these aircraft are here and operational at the time of a communist attack may well determine the fate of Formosa. If they are not here, and this island is lost, someone will have to do a lot of explaining which will transcend such questions at to whether aid to Formosa should amount to $212.2 million or only $71 million, or who should not have been allowed to see the Fox Report. Presumably funds have been available all along which could have covered really urgent needs, and I understand that the fighter aircraft required are available in our mothball reserve.

Second in importance to filling urgent military requirements without further delay is the determination of the form of organization the United States should employ on Formosa to assure the effective use of our aid. Indications are that an "Advisory Group" may be established. I have suggested a somewhat different approach, as you may have noted, which would involve starting from where we are rather than from where we left off in 1948 with something less than glory. At the present time I believe that the United States government has a good team in Formosa. The Embassy proper, the ECA mission, and our Armed Services attachés are operating harmoniously and in the closest liaison. We have joint weekly meetings, and files of current telegrams, etc., of each group are made available to key personnel in the other groups. Moreover, we are all in general agreement as to what should be done and how we should go about it.

I am sure that I need not argue a case with you in favor of retaining the coordinating authority and responsibility for the conduct of our foreign relations in the hands of the Department and the Foreign Service. But all past experience points to the probability of the military taking over if and when they are given huge sums to spend, along with the authority to decide when to withhold information and otherwise act independently of American civilian officials. Failure of the Department to take a stand on this issue in advance will be equivalent to abdicating primary responsibility for the conduct of our relations with

China. If it is necessary to do this, then let us proceed with our eyes open and have the record straight at the outset.

The foregoing opinions should not be construed as indicating any lack of appreciation on my part of the enormous difficulties to be overcome in carrying out a new military aid program for China. It will require the best efforts of all of us, civilian and military. Actually, our work might be simplified by letting the Army assume major responsibility, while we sat back to enjoy such commissary, PX, APO, club, transportation, USO, and other facilities as they might provide. But I do believe that broad political decisions should govern rather than military. Sound political decisions take account of military and economic factors. Military decisions often are based on purely military factors of relatively short-range character. It seems to me the clear duty of the Department and the Foreign Service to play the central, coordinating role in developing and implementing our foreign policy in all of its phases.

I may add that I have the very highest respect and admiration for General MacArthur, and that I recognize the desirability of his having authority over any military operations which may involve Formosa, the Philippines, and various other areas in the Far East. But the fact remains that MacArthur is not on Formosa, and that we have here a sovereign state which our government recognizes. I would have no secrets from General MacArthur, but he is an extremely busy man; I would avoid any bottleneck, in the form of subordinates in Tokyo or elsewhere, between Taipei and Washington, where all major and many minor decisions will have to be made in any case. This would apply to political and economic affairs under any circumstances, as well as to administrative and other military matters not involving actual operations.

I justify this incursion into the military field primarily on political grounds, but I also have in mind an episode of 1942. Operations in Egypt were not receiving a high priority in the allocation of American tanks and planes; our minister in Cairo, Alexander Kirk, kept hammering at Washington on the urgent need for both if Egypt and the Suez Canal were to be held. Members of his staff were later convinced that but for his efforts Alamein would have been Rommel's victory. Montgomery got the credit, deservedly enough, but who can say what would have happened to the Allied cause in the Middle East had Kirk kept strictly out of the military field?

II

At this time our small Embassy staff was strengthened by the assignment of Robert W. Rinden as chief of the political section. One of our Chinese language officers, he had been with me briefly in Canton, en route to Tihwa in western China. The same events that kept me from Shanghai prevented Rinden from reaching his post, and he had been sent to Indonesia instead. Now, I was delighted to have him in Taipei. Excerpts from his first monthly political report are given here:

During January 1951 the thinking of military and political leaders in Formosa was dominated by a deepening conviction that the hardening of the United States attitude toward the Peiping regime presaged large-scale American military assistance to Nationalist China and, as a corollary, abandonment of the military neutralization of Formosa and accelerated moves for the mainland's reconquest.

Ambassador Gross's statement that the United States would participate in no conference involving Chinese Nationalist interests at which they were not present, and that American military security considerations would enter into the United States viewpoint on the "Formosa problem," was officially and editorially acclaimed as evidence of a reversal of American policy toward Formosa and Nationalist China. Subsequent official explanations in Washington that there was no change in China policy did little to modify the original reaction to the Ambassador's remarks.

United States unwillingness to parley further on the basis of the limited cease-fire counter-proposal [in Korea], American efforts to have the United Nations condemn the Chinese communists as aggressors, and the Senate and House resolutions denouncing Red China were interpreted to mean that the United States had passed the point of no return in its negotiations with the regime of Mao Tse-tung.

Besides the apparent logic of the situation, Senator McCarran's proposal to give Free China one billion dollars of war material, press reports that from forty to sixty million dollars of military aid would soon be granted Formosa, and well-publicized discussion in the United States Congress and press of the folly of not arming Nationalist troops for a counter-attack on communist China, all created the impression that military assistance in large amounts and lifting the ban on a counter-offensive were near at hand. Heartened by the prospect of substantial American support, Nationalist China's leaders talked and planned more than ever for a return to the mainland.

Although during January the mood of Nationalist China was predominantly one of rising optimism and morale there were a few bad moments—notably when the United States accepted the final United Nations cease-fire proposal. Its provision for a conference on Formosa and other Far Eastern problems, to be participated in by the Chinese communists (but presumably not by the Chinese Nationalists) aroused no little alarm and protest in Taipei. The Foreign Minister declared: "The proposal for the participation of Chinese communist representatives in the General Assembly's attempt to settle Far Eastern problems would be to sell out not only Free China and Korea but also the United Nations itself."

After the Chinese communists' rejection of the last cease-fire proposal, local officials and editors warned the United States against further hope of making peace with the Chinese communists and castigated Nehru, the British, and the Arab-Asian group for delaying action in the United Nations on the United States resolution to brand the Peiping group as aggressors. Not only members of the United Nations were excoriated, but the organization itself was found a source of disenchantment. In this connection the Nationalist Government Spokesman recently stated that the Formosa question should be settled at the Japanese peace treaty conference—not by the United Nations.

☆ China Assignment ☆

With March not far off—when the heavy monsoon seas in the Formosa Strait subside—thought was given to the possibility of a communist attack on Formosa as well as to plans for a Nationalist invasion of the mainland. Reports of increased military activity in East China—reinforcement of coastal garrisons and construction of airfields and highways—Soviet transfers of former Japanese naval vessels to the Chinese communists, aircraft over Shanghai and Canton, and the arrival in Canton of a number of Soviet advisers were disquieting. At the same time, however, there was evidence of Chinese communist withdrawals from coastal areas and other preparations on their part more indicative of defensive than offensive intentions toward Free China. Massing of Red Chinese troops near the Indochina border, further such troop movements in that direction from Central China, Soviet-communist China-Vietminh military conferences at Nanning, construction of a Soviet submarine base on Hainan Island, and the presence of Russian submarines in the South China Sea were reported; all suggested that Indochina, rather than Formosa, might be the next object of a major communist aggression.

III

By coincidence, our military position in Korea began to improve on the same day that my January 24 letter was written. It was too soon to say that the communist tide was ebbing and that the immediate danger in Korea and Taiwan was past. But evidently we were to have time to prepare for the next round. I recommended that the Department order me to Washington for consultation. This was done.

Before leaving Taipei I called on Premier Chen Cheng, for whom I had already gained a high regard. He seemed a quiet man, but his distinguished military record, which had carried him up to the position of chief of staff on the China mainland, was evidence of iron in his soul. Moreover, as governor of Taiwan and later premier, he had shown an appreciation of social and economic problems not often found among professional soldiers in Asia or elsewhere. In this conversation General Chen stated that although the national forces were not yet prepared for a landing on the mainland, with our help they could be ready in three to six months. I asked where he thought the landing should be made. The Premier replied that the stronger his forces, the farther north he would attack.

General Sun Li-jen, Commander-in-Chief of the Chinese Army, called on me to discuss the same project of a landing on the South China coast, which was still regarded as an early possibility in conjunction with military operations in Korea. The General thought that a sufficient number of the troops under his command could be made ready in four months. He noted that United States naval and air cover would be necessary, however, in addition to logistic support.

On the day before my departure, President Chiang Kai-shek invited me for tea. Madame Chiang was present, as were Foreign Minister Yeh and the President's able English secretary, Shen Chang-huan. President Chiang emphasized the urgent need of fighter planes for the Chinese Air Force to meet the ever-present threat of communist air raids on Taiwan and mentioned other needed items of military equipment. Madame Chiang interjected, "He expects you to bring home the bacon." I remarked that he was expecting me to accomplish what General MacArthur had so far not succeeded in doing. President Chiang replied with a chuckle that the General had not left his wife behind as a hostage when he departed. There was, of course, no particular reason for Pauline to go with me to the United States on so hurried a trip in midwinter.

In the course of our conversation, the President observed that in past relations between his government and United States military missions there had been difficulties only with General Stilwell. This had been owing to communist intrigues and to lack of understanding of Chinese personnel problems as a result of Red infiltration. The same question was to arise again and again in subsequent years, and in my own opinion there was much to be said for President Chiang's viewpoint. Americans usually evaluate a Chinese on the basis of his apparent professional competence and, not infrequently, his knowledge of English. These qualifications are important, but of limited value unless supported by proven loyalty. In all of our experience with subversion in the United States, only an infinitesimal number of Americans have committed treasonable acts within living memory. We have taken this extraordinary advantage for granted. Most other countries have not been so fortunate, and in China the situation was enormously complicated by massive communist aggression and subversion, combined with the countless divided loyalties inevitable in a civil war.

IV

On February 14 I left Taipei by Northwest Airlines, headed for the Great Circle route, and two hours later arrived in Okinawa. Here I spent two days while the airport at Tokyo, our next stop, was being cleared after an exceptionally heavy snowfall. In the sunshine of Okinawa it seemed incredible that winter could be so few hours away. I used our wait to see something of the island and to call on Major General Stearley, commanding the Twentieth Air Force, which was giving heavy bomber support to our forces in Korea.

Sebald met me at the Tokyo airport. We exchanged recent experiences while my plane was refueling. The next stop was at Shemya Island, in the Aleutians, where we arrived in a snowstorm about 3 A.M. I let the pilot do the worrying, but his job of finding this tiny and remote island reminded me of the little jingle we heard while crossing the South Atlantic during the war: "If I miss Ascension, my wife gets a pension." Next day, approaching Anchorage, we had magnificent views of the Aleutians and of the great Alaska Range to the north. Awakening interest in Taiwan was evidenced by correspondents who questioned me when the plane stopped at Edmonton, again at 3 A.M., and by others who interviewed me on arrival at Minneapolis.

On my first day in the Department I had talks with Dean Rusk, Assistant Secretary of State for Far Eastern Affairs, whom I met for the first time, and several other officers dealing with Chinese affairs. I expressed myself frankly and repeatedly on China, advocating a policy of action for the United States. My impression of Rusk was particularly favorable, and nearly everyone was helpful and sympathetic. In continuing my calls around the Department, I sensed occasionally some latent antagonism to the Chinese government on Taiwan, but could find no one who would come out and fight. Our difficulties in obtaining information and decisions apparently were caused largely by a degree of mutual suspicion among various government agencies and individual officials, with resultant foot-dragging at various points along the line.

92

☆ *Consolidation* ☆

A common story at the time was that communists in the Department of State were sabotaging policies toward the Western Pacific that were favored by many members of Congress and by the Navy and General MacArthur, while the rest of the Army, interested solely in Europe, was much annoyed over its unforeseen involvement in Korea. I was not satisfied with this explanation. In long years of experience I had never known an identifiable communist in the Department, although doubtless there have been and will be a few such scattered individuals throughout the United States government. But I had met a considerable number of well-meaning officials who, without realizing it, had never advanced their thinking on world affairs beyond the isolationism of pre-1917. When things went badly for the United States in a given area abroad, they naturally blamed the benighted foreigners concerned; and if the answer was not war, then it must be disengagement. And so back to isolation.

v

Senator and Mrs. H. Alexander Smith of New Jersey, who had stayed with us in Hong Kong, invited me to dinner at their apartment in the Wardman Park. I had a most enjoyable evening and confirmed my earlier impression of the Senator and his delightful wife as kindred spirits. He had been executive secretary of Princeton University when I was a student there, but of more immediate consequence was our virtual identity of views on Far Eastern problems. Senator Smith said that he intended to arrange a luncheon at the Capitol where I would speak to about a dozen Senators. My chief assignment would be to "convert Bob Taft."

The Chinese ambassador, Wellington Koo, gave a stag luncheon for me on February 20, attended by several members of his staff and officers of the Department. I had met the Ambassador once before, and was again impressed by his abilities. Other diplomats seemed inexperienced and unsure of themselves in comparison to this accomplished Chinese gentleman, who had first served abroad as minister plenipotentiary thirty-six years earlier, not to mention prior experience in his government at home, and later service as finance minister, foreign minister, and premier of China.

My rounds in the Department continued, with numerous discussions on military and economic aid. No decision had been reached on sending a military mission to Taiwan, but substantial shipments of arms and other equipment were in prospect. I urged that they be speeded up, particularly in the case of fighter aircraft. These were to be World War II Thunderbolts, with which the Chinese Air Force was thoroughly familiar. I gave a talk on Taiwan at the Under Secretary's weekly conference, and spent an hour on the same topic with the Department's Policy Planning Group. A similar session was held at the Central Intelligence Agency, and later I addressed a "gold plate" briefing group of perhaps seventy-five officers, including several generals, at the Pentagon. In some cases surprise was expressed in private conversation afterward that I spoke so frankly in advocating a policy of action in favor of Taiwan and the Chinese government, but no one suggested that I tone down my remarks.

I called on Dr. John Leighton Stuart, who continued to hold the position of ambassador to China although he had been incapacitated by illness since his return to the United States in 1949. I found him a charming elderly man with a vast store of wisdom about China, where he had spent half a century as an educator.

The luncheon at the Capitol, as arranged by Senator Smith, was a particularly interesting experience. The guests included Senators Cain, Ferguson, Flanders, Hickenlooper, Knowland, Martin, Saltonstall, Taft, Thye, Tobey, and Wiley. Both Senator Knowland and Senator Smith made kind remarks about me, after which I talked. Everyone seemed most interested and friendly, although I could not assume anyone was actually converted from whatever previous views he held on Taiwan. Further calls and discussions took place with Senator Margaret Chase Smith, Senator Brewster, Senator Green, and Senator Ellender.

Between appointments in Washington I found time to spend a week in Maine, visiting my father and Pauline's sister and her husband. On the way back, I called at the headquarters of the Voice of America in New York to see two old friends, Foy D. Kohler and Edwin Kretzmann. Here, as I had in Washington, I urged that we try to help the Chinese government with technical assistance and equipment to improve their broadcasting facilities.

While in Washington I had talks with the Secretary of State, Dean Acheson, and, later, with the man who was to succeed him,

94

☆ Consolidation ☆

John Foster Dulles. Acheson had just returned from a Congressional hearing where, he remarked with a broad smile, he had been "insulted" for two hours. The Secretary asked me what I thought our policy should be toward the regime on Taiwan in case either a stalemate should develop in Korea or the communists should undertake further aggression elsewhere in Asia. I replied, in effect, that in either event the only practicable course was to support the government on Taiwan as an asset to our side.

Dulles had been serving as consultant to the Secretary of State and, as personal representative of the President with the rank of ambassador, was undertaking the negotiation of a peace treaty with Japan. He was keenly aware of the importance of strengthening our legal position toward Taiwan in connection with the Japanese treaty. I mentioned the project of landing troops from Taiwan on the China mainland to support our operations in Korea and, if possible, to detach South China, at least, from the Soviet orbit. I was glad to find that he favored a policy of action.

VI

After a luncheon at the Capitol with Congressmen Robert Hale and Walter H. Judd, the latter arranged an informal gathering of members of the Far Eastern Subcommittee of the House Foreign Affairs Committee to discuss Taiwan. Some twenty persons were present, including Congressmen Mansfield, Kee, Judd, Vorys, Reece, and Roosevelt. They questioned me for two hours in a friendly atmosphere. The memorandum that I left with the Department describing my activities on Capitol Hill closed with the following paragraph:

I shall not undertake to detail what was said on the occasions mentioned above. However, I might make a few observations for whatever they may be worth. First, everyone seemed most friendly and interested, irrespective of party affiliations and individual views. Second, in so far as they expressed opinions in my hearing, all of these Senators and Congressmen appeared to favor a policy toward Formosa substantially in line with that now being developed by the Department in conjunction with JCS, Defense, and ECA. Third, there seemed to be a rather general feeling that they were not being consulted sufficiently and otherwise kept informed of such policy developments and implementation. This was no less true of the Democrats than of the Republicans.

During my peregrinations in Washington and New York I made many inquiries about the "China Lobby." What was this strange organization which reportedly interfered in American domestic politics and otherwise misbehaved? Other countries spent far more money in hiring public relations counsel, distributing propaganda material, and entertaining American Congressmen and other officials. Yet no one ever heard of a British Lobby, or a French Lobby, or an Indian Lobby; the derogatory term "lobby" was not even applied to the Soviet propaganda apparatus. I asked who headed this China Lobby? The answers included such names as those of Senator Knowland, Alfred Kohlberg, Rabbi Benjamin Schultz, and Congressman Judd. Yet as far as anyone knew, these gentlemen were simply good Americans who believed that support for a free China was in the best interest of the United States. Certainly, no one was better informed or more selflessly devoted to furthering our interests in the Far East than Walter H. Judd, whose subsequent visits to Taiwan were always an inspiration. I could only conclude that the term "China Lobby," however casually it might have originated, had been propagated by elements hostile to the Chinese government as part of a smear campaign. Perhaps my current activities in Washington qualified me as an agent of the Lobby pro tempore!

Before I left Washington, May Craig and Doris Fleeson, those terrors of successive Presidents, invited me to dine at the F Street Club. Pauline and I had done some small favors for them in Hong Kong, which they later returned several times over. Other guests were Senator and Mrs. Douglas, Senator and Mrs. Sparkman, Senator and Mrs. McMahon, Senator and Mrs. Knowland, and Navy Under Secretary Dan Kimball. Doris made a nice little speech to which I replied, thanking her "on behalf of the poor old State Department."

After two and a half busy weeks I started back to Taiwan. Edmund Clubb, Director of the Office of Chinese Affairs in the Department, who had been most kind and helpful, saw me off at the airport.

Next day I was in Honolulu again, and made a point this time of stopping at the Moana Hotel, where my grandmother had stayed in 1901.

Driving out to Pearl Harbor for the first time since November, 1941, I called on Admiral Arthur W. Radford, who was currently Commander-in-Chief Pacific and Commander-in-Chief Pacific Fleet. Technically, Taiwan was still in MacArthur's territory rather than Radford's, but it was the Navy's mission to defend the island. The Admiral made a highly favorable impression on me, both because of his personality and his enthusiasm for a policy of action. We were to meet frequently thereafter and to become close friends. I believe that a large share of the credit for maintaining our position in the Western Pacific, both during and after the Korean War, belongs to Arthur Radford.

The next stop was Manila, where I was met by an old friend of Prague days, Counselor Vinton Chapin. Ambassador Myron Cowan kindly offered me an air-conditioned bedroom at his residence, and I had just time to look up four old friends, two Filipinos and two Americans, from the days of our internment by the Japanese. Pauline met me in Hong Kong, where I called on the Governor and on General Sir Robert Mansergh. One more short flight and I was back in Taipei, after a rather exciting stretch up the Tamsui River at an altitude of a hundred feet or so because of the low ceiling. The trip had been useful to me personally and, I hoped, to our China effort. If I had not brought back the "bacon," perhaps I had helped a bit. The bacon—more than we had dared to hope for—came along in subsequent months and years.

VII

Just before my return, the Fox Report finally had been made available to Admiral Jarrett by the Far East Command in Tokyo. His comments had been forwarded, emphasizing the financial inability of the Chinese government to find the local currency necessary to make effective as large a program of military aid as we now envisaged. Chinese resources already were strained to the limit simply to feed, clothe, pay, and provide a minimum of shelter and training for their armed forces. The monthly gasoline allowance was three gallons per vehicle. As supplies and equipment arrived from the United States, far more gasoline would be needed, warehouses and pipe lines would have to be built, bridges would have to be strengthened and widened to carry heavy vehicles and equipment, radar sites would have to be developed. It was urged that priority in delivery be given to items most urgently needed and, other things being equal, to those involving the least expense to the Chinese. Finally a limited number of American officers from all three services were needed to help in supervising the program.

On April 17 Moyer and I sent a lengthy telegram to the Department and the Economic Cooperation Administration on the economic aspects of the military assistance proposed for Taiwan. We suggested a figure of eighty-five million dollars in economic aid for the coming fiscal year, simply to close the existing gap in international payments. In addition, we suggested that this figure be increased by perhaps 30 per cent of the value of military "hardware" to be supplied in order to cover the additional cost of caring for and operating the new equipment. We were alarmed over the size of the figure being proposed in the Department of Defense for military hardware ($237 million for the fiscal year 1952, which was later cut substantially), because of the seeming impossibility of absorbing such a quantity of material in a short time on Taiwan. A few days later we telegraphed again, urging that consideration of huge military deliveries in the future should not be permitted to delay the shipment of equipment needed immediately for Taiwan's defense.

VIII

During February our forces in Korea began to advance once more, and by the end of March had fought their way north to a line approximating the 38th parallel. But the fact remained that the Soviets were not extending all of the assistance within their power to the Chinese communists and the North Koreans. This applied particularly to air support, and the possibility of Soviet ground forces appearing on the Korean front could not be excluded. Perhaps atomic bombs on a few strategic points in Manchuria would have brought decisive victory, but there was no serious thought of using them. High explosive bombing of enemy communications north and west of the Yalu might have forced a decision, but the United States preferred to avoid the attendant risks.

With our self-imposed limitations in effect, and with no certainty as to the corresponding limitations which Moscow might see fit to impose on communist military action, it was necessary to assume that total enemy capabilities in Northeast Asia were superior to those of the United Nations in the same area. Even a drive northward to take the North Korean capital and shorten our line was looked upon in many quarters as unwise in the face of objections by our allies. Moreover, the superiority of the United Nations forces in the vicinity of the 38th parallel had not yet been established clearly enough to convince all concerned of our ability to make another substantial advance. There remained the possibility of offensive action in other areas where the risk of open Soviet intervention would be much less. I touched upon such considerations in a telegram to the Department on April 12.

During 1951 special units of the Chinese national forces mounted a number of raids against the communist-held mainland, some with and some without our prior knowledge. These were of value for morale and intelligence purposes, besides having some diversionary benefit for our forces in Korea. General Claire L. Chennault, a great fighter and commander, believed that a vital opportunity was being lost. With American logistic support he believed that a Chinese force from Taiwan could have established a beachhead in South China in 1951. The result, he was convinced, would have been the hasty withdrawal of Chinese communist armies from Korea and the liberation of all of that country, plus the possible collapse of the communist regime in Peiping. Certainly the Red Chinese armies put forth in Korea the maximum military effort of which they were capable in 1951. Any substantial diversion in South China could not have been without effect in the north. Moreover, it was generally accepted in the Far East that the Soviets would not intervene directly in fighting south of the Yangtze River, and probably not south of the Yellow River.

We shall never know whether Chennault was right. I had a high regard for his judgment, and in this case I believe that his instinct was sound. In addition to other pros and cons, however, there were two practical objections that seemed insurmountable at the time, and these also appear to have been the decisive factors in preventing the use of Chinese national troops in Korea. First, certain of our major partners in the United Nations effort in Korea would not have gone along with us. Second, we apparently lacked sufficient arms and equipment to give the Chinese national forces what they needed at that time without depriving the United Nations forces or the Republic of Korea of desired equipment. Chennault would have said to put first things first and win the war.

I first met Claire Chennault in Athens in 1945, when he was returning from China to the United States accompanied by several of his officers from the 14th Air Force. Pauline and I took them to dinner at a seaside restaurant, where we were joined by our ambassador, Lincoln MacVeagh. My most lasting recollection of that night was the obvious devotion of his officers to their leader. I also gained a fuller understanding of what Churchill is reported to have said after meeting Chennault and noting his jutting jaw, "I am glad he is on our side!" In Hong Kong and later in Taipei I saw Chennault frequentlly, and we went on hunting trips together. He was a quiet, kindly man in my experience, and I admired him greatly. Early in 1958 I called at Walter Reed Hospital and saw him for the last time. He seemed almost his old cheerful self, despite the knowledge that he had only a short time to live. Chennault died of lung cancer a few months later, after a deathbed promotion to lieutenant general, which should have been his fourteen years earlier.

IX

I was talking with Foreign Minister Yeh in his office when his telephone rang. He listened a moment, put the receiver down and said to me in a level voice, "Truman has sacked MacArthur." We looked at each other in silence. It is difficult for anyone who had not lived in the Far East during the preceding decade to appreciate the impact of this announcement. General MacArthur was not only the architect of military victory but the proconsul who, to a large extent, had made policy in Japan and elsewhere in the Far East. As I have suggested, he was almost a prophet. What could his departure mean in terms of American policy toward the Far East in general

100

and toward China in particular? The Chinese had regarded Mac-Arthur as one of their strongest friends and supporters.

In military terms, the transfer of General Matthew B. Ridgway to head the Far East Command and the appointment of Lieutenant General James A. Van Fleet to command the United Nations Forces were both reassuring. I telegraphed to Van Fleet on April 16: "Warmest congratulations on your momentous assignment. They could not have made a better selection. Best wishes for your success."

Van Fleet acknowledged my message cordially. He had come to Greece as head of our military mission at the beginning of 1948, when I was chargé d'affaires, and I knew him well. In addition to being an eminent and offensive-oriented field commander, he was a natural leader. He had quickly gained the confidence, admiration, and cooperation of the Greeks. I was certain that he would do the same in Korea. The Eighth Army was in good hands.

x

With a stalemate in prospect for Korea and a large program of military aid to Taiwan decided on, the time seemed appropriate for further efforts to explain our China policy to the public. Later, more specific statements on Taiwan would be in order, but these evidently should derive from broad United States policy toward China. In September, 1950, the Department had issued a pamphlet, "Our Foreign Policy," which devoted about three pages to China. The conception of the pamphlet was good, but I was not satisfied with everything that was said about China. Moreover, there were significant omissions. Assisted by Robert Rinden, therefore, I drafted a statement which we hoped would be of some use. Particular care was given to avoiding controversy, while retaining a positive approach. The text was forwarded to the Department on April 23, 1951:

For nearly twenty years the Nationalist Government of China had fought against Japanese penetration and open aggression. In 1945, with the help of its Western allies and despite more opposition than assistance from the U.S.S.R., China had won that desperate struggle. In this process the government had brought about the abolition of extraterritorial rights with which China had been burdened, as well as foreign control of its taxes and customs. At last it seemed to many that the Chinese could concentrate on internal reconstruction and reforms without fear of being absorbed or torn apart by foreign enemies. But as Japan in the 1930's feared growing Chinese nationalism, so in 1945 the Kremlin was unwilling to see China become a strong independent nation which could not readily be transformed into a Soviet satellite. Moscow decided that the time had come to amalgamate China into what Stalin has called the "single state union"—Soviet communism's pattern for world rule.

In August 1945 the Soviet Union drove several hard bargains with the Nationalist Government of China, taking advantage of the latter's weakness after years of war and enemy occupation. These agreements went far beyond what the United States had envisaged at Yalta. The Soviet Union got full authority over key ports and railroads in what was universally recognized to be Chinese territory. In effect, the U.S.S.R. obtained control of Manchuria, whose rich natural resources, large industries and strategic location were of such significance that the Nationalist Government considered its retention essential to China's continued existence as a sovereign power. Forced to compromise with the Soviets, the Chinese Nationalists steadfastly refused to abandon Manchuria altogether until forced to do so by communist armies in 1948.

In the thirty-year Treaty of Friendship and Alliance signed in 1945, the Soviet Union agreed to "render to China moral support and aid in military supplies and other material resources," and to give such support and aid only to the Nationalist Government of China. Once the Kremlin had obtained a legal foothold in Manchuria, however, the undertaking to support only the Nationalist Government was conveniently forgotten. The Soviet Union not only transferred its material and moral support entirely to the Chinese communists, but in less than five years (February, 1950) had concluded a Treaty of Friendship and Alliance and Mutual Assistance with these open enemies of the Nationalist Government.

Even if militant Soviet-supported communism had never

existed in China, the country could scarcely have avoided a postwar period of unrest and confusion. The Nationalist Government had been driven by the Japanese from the chief centers of population and production to the remote wartime capital of Chungking. It was ill prepared in 1945 for the gigantic task of resuming the administration of the most populous and one of the largest in area of the world's countries. A ruinous inflation was in progress, communications were disrupted and resistance or guerrilla movements of various political complexions were not ready for an orderly and peaceful existence. Moreover, despite gratifying progress recorded in the early 1930's, China had never in modern times enjoyed peace and prosperity over a sufficient period to permit the development of a system of civil administration adequate to the needs of a modern state. The essential fact remains, however, that with active Soviet support and a ruthless Russian-trained cadre developed over a quarter of a century, and with all of the advantages of being a "new broom" in a country where nearly everyone had reason to be dissatisfied with things as they were, the communists were not only the positive but also the decisive factor in bringing China behind the Curtain. In the absence of militant communism, the Chinese Nationalist Government probably would have been able to surmount postwar difficulties, despite its freely admitted defects and many other handicaps, and to take a leading position in the family of free nations.

There can be no definitive answer to the question whether communist conquest of China could have been avoided by various steps which the Nationalist Government and the United States, among others, might have taken. The Soviet Union consistently displayed its readiness to flout solemn international agreements. In direct violation of such an agreement, it deliberately offset American aid to the Nationalists in restoring order, by arming the communist rebels with captured Japanese weapons. This action, and many others, suggests that the Soviets were prepared to go to any lengths to gain control of China under the unique opportunity afforded by chaotic postwar conditions. To inquire regarding the extent to which the communists were able to win the allegiance of the Chinese people away from the Nationalists must also remain in large part rhetorical. However, it is important to note that China's crowding millions, at least 75 per cent of whom are still illiterate and politically inert, have been for centuries preoccupied with averting starvation for their families and themselves. They are not interested in political dogma, but from time to time in history they have accepted new rulers who were strong in battle and free with promises. Rarely have these promises been fulfilled, and under communism today the disillusionment of China's masses may well be greater than ever before. Among the literate 25 per cent or less, there is also a growing realization that initial evidences of discipline and personal integrity among the communists have not kept them from yielding the sovereignty of their country to Moscow and supporting their internal position by political persecution on an almost unprecedented scale.

Time and again the Chinese people have shown a capacity to liberate themselves by outlasting and absorbing their conquerors. Will they be able, in time, to free themselves from Soviet domination? Among those who know and understand China there is a strong belief that the traditional pride and independent spirit of the Chinese people will, in the long run, triumph over every foreign attempt to dominate them—including the present attempt. Whether or not this judgment turns out to be right will depend on many factors, both in and outside China. It will depend on the toughness of other Asian peoples in standing up for their independence against communist pressure. It will depend on the strength we can add to theirs, and on American example.

The policy of the United States is to use every effective method of further enlightening the Chinese people on the true nature of Soviet aims as opposed to those of the free world, while actively extending all practicable assistance to them in regaining their independence, as well as their administrative and territorial integrity. Meantime, the United States will continue to oppose by every feasible means any and all acts of aggression against China's neighbors to which the communist regime lends itself in brutal disregard of China's peaceful tradition.

XI

On May 1, Major General William C. Chase arrived in Taipei with a small number of officers to set up a Military Assistance Advisory Group (MAAG). The decision finally had been reached in Washington to reverse our earlier position that no further missions of this kind would be sent to China. I had thought that we might do well enough on an informal basis, by enlarging our staff of military attachés. But it probably was better to face the matter squarely, and General Chase made an outstanding contribution during his four years in Taiwan. He carried out his professional responsibilities in guiding the equipment, training, and organization of the Chinese armed forces in a most creditable fashion. Equally important from my standpoint, Chase always worked closely with the Embassy and recognized our primary responsibility in the field of policy. On June 15, 1951, I sent the following telegram (paraphrased) to the Department:

My concurrence in Gen. Chase's recommendation of a total staff of 777 Americans for MAAG was contingent upon his assurance that only slightly more than 100 of these would be located in Taipei, while the others would be stationed in various parts of Formosa with Chinese military units.

The number of American officials stationed in Taipei is nearing a level where the law of diminishing returns will begin to be felt. Administrative problems, including housing, will then increase in geometric ratio with the numbers involved. No less important is that the political effect of giving Taipei the appearance of an "occupied" town should be avoided. At the same time, qualified United States military personnel in any reasonable number could be scattered about the island on training and advisory assignments with actual Chinese units and yet avoid unwanted effects.

The present totals of United States government employees serving in Taipei, excluding MAAG, are as follows: Embassy (regular program) 16, Marine guards 5, USIS 6, ECA and affiliated agencies 42, service attachés 50, total 119. Some increases will be necessary, especially in view of the expanded ECA and USIS programs, but I sincerely hope that the total number of official Americans located in Taipei, including MAAG, will be limited to about 250. If these are properly selected, I believe that a good job can be done—actually better than with a larger number of Americans of equal quality, and much better than if the average quality is lowered as the numbers increase, which is most likely to happen.

The question of increasing the American staff of our economic mission also came up at this time, and I followed up my June 15 telegram with a letter to an officer of the Department of State on the same day. The following is an excerpt.

One thing I am sure of, however, is that our problem will not be solved simply by increasing the size of our ECA staff. Some further increase doubtless will be necessary, but I am already alarmed by evidences of our old American custom of shooting the works once we get started. Hence my telegram of June 15.

You know far better than I about our recent experiences and mistakes in China, but I suspect that not the least of the latter was the huge staffs of Americans we had hanging around Shanghai and Nanking, not to mention the new "imperialism" evident in our acquisition of over ten million dollars worth of elaborate office and residential quarters. Well, the communists are enjoying them now!

XII

Meanwhile, in Korea, the Eighth Army had brought yet another enemy offensive to a standstill. The front line was again south of the 38th parallel, but Seoul remained in our hands and heavy losses had been inflicted on the "human sea" which the Chinese communists threw against us. After May 20, General Van Fleet resumed the offensive and within a month not only regained the territory lost in the preceding weeks but pushed on close to what was to become the Armistice Demarcation Line over two years later. The American Joint Chiefs of Staff had prescribed that the Eighth Army should not advance appreciably north of the 38th parallel. In Taiwan we did not know whether the enemy was aware of these instructions when, on June 23, the Soviet delegate to the United Nations proposed cease-fire discussions between the opposing forces in Korea. It was evident that the Chinese communist armies of some 700,000 men had been decisively defeated and sought a cease-fire only when our forces were in a position to drive them far to the north, if not to the Yalu, then at least to the "waist" of Korea, above the 39th parallel.

☆☆☆

5: *Progress*

I

For two years events in East Asia evolved under the shadow of the truce negotiations in Korea. During this period, fighting occurred on a considerable scale. In fact, the statement frequently was heard that our forces could have driven to the Yalu with no more casualties than were suffered in maintaining a position only slightly above the 38th parallel until the Armistice was signed on July 27, 1953. Perhaps this was not literally true, but it reflected the frustration felt among military leaders. Meanwhile the enemy steadily built up strength from his precarious situation of mid-1951, when the Soviets proposed truce talks. We were certain that their primary purpose was to gain time. But was this in preparation for a new offensive against the United Nations forces in Korea or elsewhere? Would the Chinese troops on Taiwan yet be needed to help retrieve the situation? We did not have answers to these questions until the latter part of 1953, when it became apparent that the next target for communist aggression was Southeast Asia.

The actual and potential aggressors enjoyed the advantage of knowing what they intended to do and being able to plan accordingly. In retrospect it is not difficult to see that they had reached a major decision by the middle of 1951. Communist forces, both North Korean and Chinese, had been defeated in their effort to overrun all of Korea. Indochina, to which the Chinese communists doubtless had given a high priority all along, was to be the next point of attack. Time was needed to replace trained men and materiel, to construct a

Calligraphy by President Chiang Kai-shek presented to Ambassador Rankin on his departure from Taiwan. Inscription reads, "Same boat, mutual aid." Left to right: Mme. Chiang, Mrs. Rankin, Mr. Rankin, President Chiang

Left to right (front row): Admiral Robert B. Carney, Chief of Naval Operations; Foreign Minister George K. C. Yeh; Secretary of State John Foster Dulles; Premier O. K. Yui; Ambassador Rankin; Defense Minister Yu Ta-wei; Assistant Secretary of State Walter S. Robertson; Admiral Felix B. Stump, Commander-in-Chief Pacific; General Peng Meng-chi, Chief, Supreme General Staff. Taipei, March, 1955

Ambassador Phillip C. Jessup with Major General and Mrs. C. L. Chennault at American Consul General's Residence, Hong Kong, January, 1950

Exchange of ratifications for the Mutual Defense Treaty. Left to right: Foreign Minister Yeh, Assistant Secretary of State Robertson, Douglas Mac-Arthur II, Ambassador Rankin, Secretary of State Dulles. Taipei, March 3, 1955

heavily fortified line against another possible offensive from South Korea, to strengthen their defenses on the coast opposite Taiwan, and to prepare for the conquest of Tonkin. For an indefinite future period their effort north of the 38th parallel would be a holding operation, until some new opportunity could be found to absorb the Republic of Korea. Meanwhile, by engaging in truce negotiations, the communists could be reasonably certain that their opponents in Korea would neither undertake major offensive operations against them nor help the Chinese on Taiwan to do so. When ready on all fronts, in 1953, they signed an armistice and turned their attention to Southeast Asia.

Our problems on Taiwan during the period of truce negotiations were complicated by the necessity of planning both for a relatively long period of stalemate and the possibility of hostilities on short notice. In mid-1951 the Korean War was a year old, and my first year in Free China, as we called it more and more frequently, was drawing to a close. Whatever the outcome of the truce negotiations in Korea, our program of support for the government of the Republic of China was well under way. Sufficient funds had been authorized to close the gap in Taiwan's international payments. On the military side, if large-scale fighting in Korea were to cease, it seemed probable that materiel would be readily available to supply Free China with almost everything that might be needed.

II

At this time, press and other reports indicated that the United States and the United Kingdom had reached a compromise agreement by which neither the Taipei government nor the Peiping regime would sign the proposed multilateral peace treaty with Japan. At first glance this seemed an almost inevitable compromise under the circumstances. Since the Soviet Union would not be among the signatories, which included most of the countries at war with Japan, it was evident that neither would Peiping sign. On the other hand, the government of the Republic of China would have been quite ready to do so. Of particular importance to that government, and indirectly to the United States, was the fact that the international legal position of Taiwan was involved.

A draft of the multilateral treaty had been completed on June 14.

☆ *China Assignment* ☆

The Chinese asked us to postpone its circulation among the interested parties until agreement could be reached on a bilateral Chinese-Japanese treaty. They wished, if possible, to avoid public discussion of the draft until their own position had been assured. As a matter of fact, they assumed that the British had shown the text to the Peiping regime, and that either it would leak out or be made public officially any day. The Chinese on Taiwan were vitally interested, not simply because of their legal position on the island, but because of their prestige, both at home and abroad. Moreover, they considered that a treaty between themselves and Japan would serve as an effective barrier to any possible rapprochement between Tokyo and Peiping.

The text of the proposed treaty with Japan was made public on July 2, 1951, and public reaction on Taiwan was no less unfavorable than we had anticipated. Queried by the press, I issued the following statement on July 25:

The Chinese Nationalist Government on Formosa and many elements friendly to that Government, both of Chinese and other nationality, are deeply hurt by the omission of China from the list of countries invited to sign the multilateral Japanese peace treaty. Their chagrin parallels that of the Philippines and Korea, although for reasons differing in detail. It should not be difficult to understand these bitter feelings on the part of countries so intimately involved in the late war with Japan. This is particularly true of Free China, which lost all but a small fraction of its huge territory and population as an indirect result of that war. Moreover, the Chinese Nationalists say and believe that the influences which exclude them from the Treaty are the same which favor extinguishing what remains of China's independence by turning over Formosa to the tender mercies of the communists. No less important in their minds is the necessity of continuing their mission on Formosa: to provide a rallying point which some day will play a vital part in liberating their homeland from the communist yoke.

On the other hand, we may expect a growing realization among the Chinese outside the Curtain that the draft Japanese Peace Treaty, as published on July 12, 1951, protects Chinese interests as well as any such document could be expected to do, with or without the signature of the Nationalist Government. Careful study of the draft also will reveal to them few if any political features to which China could object, other than its omission from the list of signatories. It may also be expected that Free China in general will come to accept, as many of its leading citizens already do, the paramount importance to the free world of a magnanimous peace treaty with Japan, including as many important countries as possible and to be signed at the earliest possible date.

There will remain the delicate but essential task of restoring normal relations between Japan and Free China as soon as possible, along lines similar to those of the draft treaty. Despite all that has happened in the past, the good will and common sense existing on both sides make success both possible and probable. Any necessary support from friends abroad should not be withheld.

III

Nearly five months had passed since my latest visit to Washington, and on August 13 I wrote a long letter to Assistant Secretary of State Dean Rusk. I reviewed recent developments and current problems of military and economic aid. I felt a modest optimism over the short- to medium-term outlook. For the more distant future I had misgivings. I concluded as follows:

In the process of looking ahead it is also important to keep our thinking clear on the fundamental problem of overpopulation in so much of the Far East. The communists have promised higher living standards without caring whether these promises could be kept. Americans have tended to outbid them in this regard, with the best of intentions but without realizing the full implications of such promises. During the current fiscal year we are by way of assuming at least a degree of responsibility for the economic welfare of nearly 700 million people in Asia and its nearby islands. For this program we propose to spend an average of about 54 cents a head. A great deal of good can be done with this money, but no one can pretend that it will produce any discernible rise in general living standards. As a matter of fact, we shall be doing very well indeed if we can prevent present standards from declining in the face of fears and dislocations caused by the communist menace.

Of course we can and should push on with our programs of technical assistance and of direct economic aid to meet emergency conditions. But we know that improvements in the fields of agriculture and public health will be offset by a net increase in population as regards any general effect on living standards in most of Asia, including Formosa. Only when such efforts are complemented by wide-scale industrialization and birth control will the economic lot of the common man in Asia begin to improve. This is not only a very long-term conception, transcending any aid program we have ever envisaged, but it also involves fundamental questions of economic security. Elimination of colonialism also did away very largely with sound currencies, reasonable credit facilities, and a conception of property rights essential to private enterprise. However much the colonial powers may have profited in the past, a very large number of Asiatics benefited economically from colonial rule. Now all of them are being thrown back upon the oldest of all forms of economic security: breeding the largest possible number of children. The communists could not have ordered matters better toward the attainment of their ends.

We are feeling all of this here in Formosa. The population is increasing rapidly from an excess of births over deaths. Due to this fact, and to the much more rigorous collection of taxes from the largely agricultural population, some of our best American experts have become convinced that the average inhabitant of this island is worse off economically than he was a year or two ago. Yet during this period there have been very real improvements in agricultural production and in marketing methods, largely as a result of the assistance of ECA and its affiliated JCRR. Now we are complicating this problem enormously, although quite properly, by a large-scale program of military aid. It is none too soon to undertake a careful study as to where all of this is leading us. . . .

In the midst of the excitement over the Japanese peace treaty we were visited in Taipei by Governor Thomas E. Dewey. His trip was unofficial, but scarcely could have been private. The Chinese had long looked upon him as a firm friend and supporter. They gave him a warm welcome. His experiences and impressions have been recorded in his book, *Journey to the Far Pacific* (Doubleday, 1952), which devotes a chapter to Formosa. I may add a few recollections.

As so often happens when important Americans visit a foreign capital, the Embassy had no advance information on Governor Dewey's plans and wishes, except in the most general terms. Some visitors arrive with the desire to be kept on the jump from early till late. Others prefer to be left to their own devices. Naturally, Chinese officialdom wanted to entertain the Governor on a considerable scale. Before his arrival, we had assembled a list of the organizations and individuals who wished to see and entertain him. Persuasion had been used to simplify the official agenda in order to allow some time for seeing the country and the plain people. Even so, when I showed the proposed schedule to the Governor, he blew up. I cannot say that I blamed him; the weather was very hot. But after the interests and sensitivities of those concerned had been explained to him, and two Chinese social functions combined into one, he went along with the program most agreeably.

I took Governor Dewey to call on President and Madame Chiang at their residence on Grass Mountain, next to ours. The conversation proceeded normally and pleasantly until someone mentioned the peace treaty with Japan. This time President Chiang blew up. The Governor recorded the rest of the conversation in his book as one of the most violent political discussions he had ever had. He described the President and Madame as the most furious people he had met in the Orient. Governor Dewey explained the American attitude very effectively, and I attempted to pour oil on the waters. Our hosts realized, of course, that we both appreciated China's difficult position and the call ended on a friendly note. But I was glad that a prominent American visitor had been faced so bluntly with the problem that I had been trying to explain to the Department. The accounts he gave orally and, later, in his book were most helpful.

Before Governor Dewey's departure from Taipei we enjoyed a

good old-fashioned bull session until a late hour at General Chase's quarters. Perhaps twenty Americans were present, including all of the senior civil and military officers on duty in China. The Governor was in good form and posed many penetrating questions. It was one of the most stimulating evenings in my memory.

v

The completion of my first year in Taiwan encouraged me to write an article, which I called "Free China's Rallying Point." I had no confidence that it could be published. But writing with a view to possible public use is a better exercise than drafting confidential telegrams or despatches to the Department. These are read by a few people and then filed away and forgotten. If the author is guilty of mistakes in his facts or opinions, the chances are that he will never hear of it unless he is very far off the beam indeed; and a confidential classification supposedly prevents any harm being done. Diplomats are much more careful in preparing for publication. They must make a particular effort to be sure of their facts and to avoid unnecessary controversy or offense. With such considerations in mind, I completed an article of 5,000 words on August 30, 1951, and sent it to the Department.

My thesis was that the preservation and development of Taiwan as a rallying point for all freedom-loving Chinese could be a promising step toward eventually freeing all of China from communist domination. I went on to sketch the history of Taiwan. I suggested that the record of the Soviet Empire since 1917, under initial conditions basically like those of mainland China since 1949, provided no grounds for predicting the early downfall of the Red Chinese regime. We could only go on the assumption that it would remain in power for a long time. However, I pointed out that Formosa gave China an important advantage that freedom-loving Russians never enjoyed after communism had established itself in their country:

Within one hundred miles of the China coast lies Formosa, a highly productive, militarily defensible rallying point, containing an almost purely Chinese population who, whatever the political differences among them, are substantially united in opposition to communism. Is such a rallying point the hitherto missing ingredient in the struggle against communist conquest? At the very least it would seem that the free world's successes to date against that enemy are not so gratifying as to warrant overlooking what might prove to be the Achilles heel of communism in Asia. . . .

I described how our aid programs, economic and military, were making it possible for the island to develop as a strong and prosperous center, and traced its recent political and social progress. I concluded:

It remains to be seen whether sufficient good will, patience, and determination on the Chinese side will be matched by the necessary good will, patience, and understanding on the part of Americans to bring about success. If only from military necessity, the two nations will be going most of the way in any case. Why should they not continue on together until communism is forced to relinquish its hold upon Asia's greatest country?

The response to this article from Assistant Secretary Rusk was that it made a "great deal of good sense" and contained little which would be questioned from a policy point of view. However, it was believed that the article could not be published without the authorship becoming known. The ensuing year (1952) would be one of active political controversy over issues such as those that I had discussed. I was not a politically controversial figure in the United States and it seemed better to leave it that way. I accepted this decision.

VI

Meanwhile the armistice negotiations in Korea and preparations for the signature of the multilateral peace treaty with Japan had been proceeding. One of our major preoccupations was the maintenance of Chinese morale during this period of uncertainty. It is not easy for an American to imagine himself in the position of an official in a country whose fate is being decided by others. Decisions affecting either Korea or Japan could redirect the whole course of events in East Asia. Yet the government of the Republic of China was

115

allowed to have no part in these negotiations. There were practical reasons for this, but they did not satisfy or reassure the Chinese.

Ambassador Dulles was making every effort to keep the Chinese Embassy in Washington informed of developments affecting the Japanese treaty. We supplemented this effort as best we could in Taipei. No less than forty-eight countries were to sign the treaty; several others were vitally interested. The task of keeping all of them informed currently but not prematurely was one of the first magnitude. Changes in the treaty draft eventually required the consent of all the prospective signatories. Dulles succeeded in obtaining acceptance of certain Chinese suggestions which largely removed their practical objections to the treaty before it finally was signed on September 8, 1951.

To Richard T. Ewing, a most capable China language officer who had joined the Embassy's Political Section, I assigned the job of writing up our activities in connection with the Japanese Peace Treaty. It turned out to be an imposing document. One of our principal efforts had been to explain the continuing and mounting Chinese reaction to the Department. The Legislative Yuan, or parliament, was particularly exercised over the details of a preliminary draft of the treaty, which had leaked to the press in Washington or elsewhere. With the first official information that the British government had refused to sign a treaty which bore the signature of the government of the Republic of China, I had discussed with Foreign Minister Yeh the possibility of a parallel bilateral treaty between China and Japan. The conversation was reported to Ambassador Dulles in London, who replied that he was thinking along the same lines. This was in June, 1951.

It was not easy to persuade President Chiang and the Legislative Yuan of the acceptability of a separate treaty. However, there were certain provisions of special interest to China and Japan which could not easily have been included in the multilateral agreement. This provided a face-saving device for China as well as possible practical advantages. The major difficulty remained that Japan, the ex-enemy, might be placed in a position of choosing which Chinese regime should be dealt with, Taipei or Peiping. The Chinese on Taiwan held that it was the moral responsibility of the United States to see that matters should not come to such a pass. On the other hand, the Department did not feel that the United States could do much more until a formula had been found by the Chinese and Japanese for the effective power of the government of the Republic of China on Taiwan to bind all of China. A stream of telegrams went back and forth between Taipei and Washington over a period of five months, with explanations, proposals, and counterproposals. No substantial progress had been made when the multilateral treaty was signed at San Francisco in September.

The next effort was to accomplish a Chinese-Japanese treaty by the date on which the multilateral treaty took effect. The problem had come to the attention of certain members of the Foreign Relations Committee of the United States Senate, who understood and sympathized with the Chinese position. Senator H. Alexander Smith visited Taipei at this time and subsequently did effective work in high Japanese circles in Tokyo. More discussions took place in Washington and Taipei, and more telegrams were exchanged. Active negotiations were begun between the Chinese and Japanese. A formula was found which made the treaty applicable, in the case of China, to "all the territories which are now or which may hereafter be" under the control of the government of the Republic of China. The bilateral treaty was based specifically on the one signed at San Francisco, in which Japan renounced all claims to Taiwan and the Penghu, Spratly, and Paracel Islands. China waived all further claims for reparations, partly by implication, and Japan similarly assumed all claims by its subjects as a result of the Chinese seizure of enemy property on Taiwan.

The Treaty of Peace between the Republic of China and Japan was signed in Taipei on April 28, 1952, the same day on which the multilateral San Francisco treaty came into force by proclamation of President Truman. A major step had been accomplished in establishing the position of the Chinese government on Taiwan and in creating further important ties between the new Japan and the free world. Foreign Minister Yeh sent me an informal note on May 2:

I would like to present you with one of the Chinese writing brushes with which the Sino-Japanese Peace Treaty was signed on April 28, 1952.

I should be glad if you would accept this memento as a mark

of my appreciation for the personal interest you have taken in the negotiations and the valuable support you have given me in bringing about the successful conclusion of the Treaty.

VII

At the turn of the year 1951-52 Francis Cardinal Spellman visited Taipei after spending Christmas with our forces in Korea. I had never met him before and was immediately charmed with his personality. A combination of modesty and assurance such as his is rare indeed. He was to visit us several times over the years. I recall one occasion, which to me was most revealing. The entire diplomatic corps had been invited to attend a Mass at which the Cardinal would officiate. It was conducted in the large hall where the Legislative Yuan held its sessions. The stage was trimmed attractively with pine boughs, and I thought at once of the danger of fire from the candles close to the branches. During the Mass one of the boughs broke into a feeble flame. The Cardinal was on his knees at a solemn moment. Before anyone else on the platform reacted, he rose, and, with great dignity, walked over to the incipient fire and put it out with his hands. Then, with no break in the ritual, he returned to his place and knelt again. The Cardinal's visits were of great value to all of us, Chinese and Americans alike, whatever our religious affiliations.

VIII

In early 1952 the number of official Americans in Taiwan passed the five hundred mark, not including dependents. A majority of these belonged to the Armed Services, but our economic mission, now known as MSA China, was expanding too. I was asked to talk to the economic staff, which included a large proportion of new arrivals, about American policy. Passages from my remarks on April 1, 1952, are included here:

Popular mythology represents the United States either as having no foreign policy whatever or as being guided in its foreign relations by highly secret and often sinister influences which can be only partially unmasked by continuous investiga-

tions on the part of Congress and the press. In actual fact
American foreign policy not only has a very real existence but
is largely an open book. Secret understandings with foreign powers have been rare, and seldom have remained secret for long.
The most decisive single factor in shaping policy is American
public opinion, which is influenced by overt far more than by
covert means, by the press and radio rather than by clandes-
tine propaganda. As long as the American press and radio are
substantially free, we need worry only to the extent that such
media of information permit themselves to be misled. And there
are too many of them for a majority to be wrong most of the
time.

How then have these myths about our foreign policy gained
such wide acceptance? I shall try to explain certain reasons for
this and to illustrate them by examples from our own experience
in Formosa.

In the first place we must remember that foreign policy is
largely determined by domestic policy—by domestic "politics,"
if you wish. This is particularly true in a democracy which is at
the same time a great power and therefore capable of exerting
a decisive influence on the course of world events. (A minor
country has its foreign policy determined largely by external
influences.) To those of us who believe in democracy—government by the people—all of this is as it should be. In fact, I may
go so far as to say that the basic tenets of American foreign
policy are a reality only to the extent that they are understood,
accepted, and supported by the American people.

Yet our public has only in recent years come to realize the
power and responsibilities of the United States in world affairs.
The tradition of isolationism—not inappropriate to our country in the nineteenth century and even in the early part of the
twentieth—remains strong. It still inclines the American public
to some suspicion of foreigners and foreign entanglements.
This, in turn, leads our responsible officials in their public statements to avoid the appearance of being so far in advance of
public opinion as to produce an undesired and negative reaction. Sometimes they lean over backward in this respect, and

thus encourage the myth that "we have no foreign policy." What this really means, of course, is that official policy may appear negative rather than positive. In either case a policy exists.

Turning now to Formosa, a number of interesting official policy documents labeled "secret" and "top secret" have dealt with this island during the past several years. The usual reasons why they have been so labeled were either that opinions were set forth which represented simply the views of an individual or group, rather than the accepted position of our government, or that they were so far in advance of public opinion at home and abroad as to make it unwise to risk unfavorable reaction by making them public. In the second case consideration always must be given to how much it is desirable for our enemies to know, and in which instances it is wise to announce in advance an intended course of action contingent upon circumstances which may never arise.

Yet the broad lines of American policy toward Formosa are not secret. Before, during, and since World War II this island has always been recognized as of unquestionable importance, strategically and otherwise. The differences of opinion were as to the degree of its importance and what we should do about it.

In the months prior to the communist aggression in Korea our positive program was limited to the extension of a modest amount of economic aid to Formosa as the only Chinese territory where such a program could still be carried on. Before June 25, 1950, it was widely hoped and believed—I personally shared the hope but not the belief—that the Far Eastern situation would work itself out in due course without further large-scale hostilities. The events of mid-1950 belied that hope and the importance of keeping Formosa out of communist hands, by the use of American sea and air power if necessary, was accepted immediately by our government and public as a matter of policy. Perhaps this policy had existed all along, unavowed. However that may be, the deployment of American forces to defend Formosa would have aroused serious opposition at home prior to the outbreak of war in Korea; after that event it was accepted almost as a matter of course. Such are the workings of a democracy in the conduct of its foreign relations.

In retrospect we may note with some satisfaction that our government was by no means entirely unprepared for the new responsibilities which it assumed toward Formosa on June 27, 1950. We were already represented here by a Foreign Service establishment, with Armed Services attachés, able to make the necessary political and military arrangements with the Chinese government in a matter of hours. Our small but effective ECA mission was ready to take over the expanded duties implicit in the new responsibilities which we had assumed. The Seventh Fleet was prepared to start its patrols without delay. Perhaps it was in part simply good luck that we found ourselves in a position to undertake these responsibilities so quickly. But there had been thinking and planning too, of the kind which before the event is appropriately labeled "top secret." Discreet advance preparations for such an eventuality furnish a good example of what government officials in various categories can contribute toward making American policies succeed once they are officially implemented.

It was quite clear, however, that sea and air patrols, plus a small-scale economic program, were by no means adequate to the situation which faced us on Formosa in mid-1950. They were at best stopgap measures, and it was becoming increasingly apparent that only a comprehensive medium- to long-term program offered hope of accomplishing what had become an essential feature of American foreign policy: to build up countries which were threatened by communist aggression, both to preserve them as a part of the free world and to discourage the spread of open hostilities. This broad policy, which had found formal acknowledgment in the Truman Doctrine in 1947, was now to be implemented in the Far East.

At this point I should like to explode another myth: that American officials serving abroad are mere messengers, engaged chiefly in transmitting to the local authorities the texts of communications emanating from Washington. Even so well-informed a publication as *Time* recently repeated this legend as a fact, with the further intimation that the practical value of our officials abroad depended largely upon their ability to obtain local popularity by back-slapping and related methods. I am sure that I do not need to persuade any of you here today of the falseness of this myth. As a matter of fact, the foreign representatives of a democratic government such as ours have incomparably greater opportunities to influence policy than the minions of a dictatorship. We may never be responsible for the determination of basic policy, but in its implementation abroad, in our day-to-day relations with Washington and with the local authorities, our attitudes and approaches often have the greatest significance.

Suppose, for example, the Embassy and the ECA mission had adopted a negative, defeatist attitude toward the problems of Formosa after mid-1950. Suppose we had persuaded ourselves that this was simply another "Operation Rat Hole." Is it not quite likely that we should have inclined our government as a whole toward the same conclusion? As a matter of fact we took a positive approach. . . .

Our present policy toward Formosa is the result of political decisions influenced by military and, to a lesser extent, by economic considerations. This fact becomes clear when we consider what our program probably would be if it were based on purely military factors related to the Korean conflict. Under such circumstances we would have supplied the Chinese government with its most immediate military needs, notably in ammunition and POL, to cope with the relatively moderate sized communist forces which might be able to survive our naval and air attacks and effect landings on the island. Such aid would have been supplemented by sufficient economic support to prevent an increase in disease and unrest. The sum total would have been a minimum program on a short-term basis until the "future of Formosa" could be decided by international agreement.

It is obvious to all, however, that our actual program for Formosa is now on a comprehensive, medium- to long-term basis which foresees making the island economically self-supporting except for such assistance as may be required to maintain a larger-than-normal military establishment until peace and security are re-established in the Far East. It is true that funds are voted by Congress only on a fiscal year basis, but the amounts made available during the calendar year 1951, and the programs on which these amounts were based, are the best evidence that the United States in fact has accepted the longer term and more comprehensive view, even though this may not yet have appeared with finality in public policy statements.

Here, then, is another point to watch for in the development of American foreign policy: action not infrequently precedes words. The policy in question may have been in existence all along, but for various reasons was never made the subject of an open commitment by our government. After June 27, 1950, the most significant events in the development of our policy toward Formosa were (1) the allocation of approximately fifty million dollars in equipment and supplies for the Chinese Army on February 16, 1951; (2) the communication to the Chinese government on April 20, 1951, that a MAAG would be established on Formosa; (3) the allocation on June 21, 1951, of nearly forty-two million dollars in additional economic aid to be obligated in the last days of fiscal year 1951; (4) the passage of the Mutual Security appropriations in October, 1951, which included totals based on estimates of some three hundred million dollars in aid for Formosa in the fiscal year 1952.

Such are the tangible factors to note in the development of American foreign policy no less than the public statements of high officials. . . . If such policy development seems at times halting or illogical, we should remember our own duty as government officials to give our best thoughts to what can and should be done in connection with our particular jobs, and to make recommendations through proper channels when we have something constructive to offer. When final decisions are made, of course, it is our simple duty to carry them out to the best of our ability.

IX

Late in 1951 the Department assigned Howard P. Jones as first secretary and, on my recommendation and prior to his arrival early in 1952, raised his designation to that of counselor. The appointment was a particularly fortunate one. Jones was about my age and had spent many years in public life. It was his first assignment in the Far East, but in a short time he gained a full appreciation of the sensitive problems confronting us. Pauline and I had not enjoyed a real vacation in nearly three years. We were looking forward to home leave, and I was happy that so mature and competent an officer as Howard Jones was there to assume charge.

Having had so many threads in my fingers during the recent past I prepared a lengthy memorandum for Jones on April 16, 1952, before my departure for the United States. Excerpts are given here:

When I arrived in Formosa on August 10, 1950, I found our Foreign Service establishment here in the last stages of decay. It had never been designated as an embassy, but was simply a consular office in which the principal officer was also chargé d'affaires, a.i. The staff had been reduced even below what is usually considered a "skeleton," much of the best office and household equipment had been shipped out to save it from the expected communist invasion, while the buildings and the remaining equipment were in a sad state of repair. Files had been largely destroyed and operations were virtually limited to keeping evacuation plans up-to-date and exchanging current information with the Department to the limited extent permitted by the tiny staff and other sketchy facilities.

Under the circumstances just described it is scarcely surprising that American government operations in Formosa were not being closely coordinated. Personal relations were cordial enough among the various agencies, but they were functioning in several almost water-tight compartments. In addition to the skeletonized "regular program" Foreign Service staff, there was a USIS operation with two Americans. The Armed Services attachés had been expanded in number after June 27, 1950, but certain of their most important responsibilities toward the Embassy, the Seventh Fleet and the Chinese government were by no means clear. A group of some forty officers and men from the Far East Command in Tokyo had arrived on Formosa but had been forbidden to maintain official relations with the Embassy or its military attachés. Finally, the small ECA mission and its two affiliates were carrying on, independently, a modest but constructive economic program.

With no position other than that previously occupied by several officers considerably junior to me, with almost no staff or other facilities, and in the face of a tradition of suspicion and dislike between the Department and the Chinese government, I set about to see what could be done. First, members of the Far East Command and of the ECA mission were invited for the first time to attend our weekly staff meetings. These have continued regularly and are now attended by an average of about twenty persons, usually including the chiefs and other representatives of the MSA (economic) mission and of MAAG (military). A free exchange of views takes place on these occasions, covering the entire field of American interests, each person present being individually invited to say something. On my recommendation the Department agreed to call our establishment an embassy, even if it could not be headed by a resident ambassador. Modest recommendations were made to improve and expand our staff, as well as office and housing facilities. But most of all I concentrated upon familiarizing myself with the larger aspects of the "problems of Formosa" and seeking ways of coordinating our American efforts on this island.

In view of the unfortunate background of distrust which existed between representatives of the Department of State and the Far East Command at the time of my arrival in Taipei, I was particularly anxious that relationships between the Embassy and MAAG should get off to a good start when the latter was established here on May 1, 1951. The Department's directive on this point was satisfactory, and the chief of MAAG has been most cooperative. As in the case of MSA, important matters touching upon policy have been referred to me before they were taken up with Washington or with the Chinese authorities. With occasional agreed exceptions, all contacts between MAAG and the Chinese President, Prime Minister, and other high civilian officals have been maintained through the Embassy. The chief of MAAG has continued to discuss with me not only policy but also major personnel questions and other subjects of importance to our joint effort here.

Visits of prominent American officials and others to Formosa have been utilized not only to acquaint the visitors themselves of what we are doing on Formosa but also to emphasize the close coordination of our efforts here. This emphasis is intended to impress the Chinese government and the numerous Americans in our government agencies on this island, who already number over five hundred, fully as much as the visitors from abroad. By taking the lead in preparing itineraries and programs, by arranging joint briefings in which members of the Embassy staff take an important part, by accompanying visitors during official calls and on itineraries, in addition to arranging social events, I have endeavored not only to inform them of our activities but to establish the position of the Embassy as the coordinating American authority here, both in Chinese and in American eyes. . . .

Such visits almost always include a briefing at the Embassy, calls on the President, the Prime Minister and other high Chinese officials, visits to points of interest such as military installations, a reception or other function given by the Embassy and a dinner invitation from President Chiang. The President almost invariably invites not only myself but also the heads of MSA and MAAG on such occasions, thereby giving our visitors from the United States further evidence of close cooperation. Important officials of our government who have been so treated include Senators Sparkman, Magnuson, Brewster, H. Alexander Smith, and Knowland; also Representatives Armstrong, Mack, Martin, and Hall, as well as Navy Secretary Kimball and Ambassador William D. Pawley.

American military visitors to Formosa have been numerous; it is sufficient to mention General J. Lawton Collins, Vice Admirals A. D. Struble and Harold M. Martin, the Commanding Generals of the Ryukyus and the Twentieth and Thirteenth Air Forces, and the Army Chief of Information and the Army G-3 from the Pentagon. In such cases I have made particular efforts to support the desires of General Chase, as for example in stressing the need for clarifying channels of command and speeding up the arrival of materiel. In all of this the gap which existed between the Embassy's Armed Services attachés and the

Far East Command has been replaced by a close working relationship among all of our military representatives. The attachés, in addition to their other duties, perform intelligence functions for General Chase and his staff. MAAG, in turn, keeps the attachés informed on matters of mutual interest and invites them to attend military exercises, briefings, etc.

Other notable visitors of the past year were Governor Thomas E. Dewey and Francis Cardinal Spellman. The press has been well represented by Hanson W. Baldwin, Gardner Cowles, Paul C. Smith, H. V. Kaltenborn, Edgar Ansel Mowrer, and many others. These names and others mentioned in earlier paragraphs by no means constitute a complete list. My purpose in mentioning them is to emphasize that in the case of all of the most prominent visitors, as well as many others, the Embassy took the lead in steering them around despite our woeful lack of representational facilities and shortage of staff. The desired effect has been noted in virtually every instance, several of the visitors having been kind enough to remark that the coordination among the various agencies of the United States government seemed unusually good in Taipei. In a letter subsequent to his Formosa visit Governor Dewey said that he had never seen a "more united and sympathetic group representing the United States in any country." I should like to think that this reflects not only appearances but also a large degree of reality.

With minor exceptions our more prominent guests have been persons who favored aid to the Chinese government on a substantial scale; those holding a contrary view usually omit Formosa from their itineraries. Again, with some exceptions, our visitors arrived with a critical attitude toward the State Department, suspecting that no opportunities were being overlooked to slow down the aid program for Formosa. I believe that we have been able to disabuse them of such notions to an important degree. Probably the most effective single factor in accomplishing this has been the evidence of cooperation among the American agencies here and between all of them and the Chinese government. It has been a surprise to many visitors to find such close agreement among our American diplomatic, economic, and military missions on the island as to what should be done in Formosa. It has also been gratifying to be able to tell them that our Formosa programs have received excellent support from Washington, particularly since the early part of 1951.

I hope and believe, therefore, that a pattern of coordination under the Embassy is well established. But this is no more than half of the battle at best. In the earlier stages we at the Embassy have been able to help the other American missions in many ways, due to our past experience, to our contacts among the highest Chinese officials, and to such meager facilities as we possessed. . . .

While without various advantages which could have contributed to the Embassy's prestige and authority, as mentioned above, plus the continuing handicap that we have no announced long-term policy toward Formosa, I have endeavored to reestablish the mutual confidence and respect in our dealings with the Chinese government which are essential to the prosecution of our program here. The "White Paper" atmosphere was still very much in evidence when I arrived in Taipei. The Chinese government considers that the United States let them down badly in publishing that document. With minor exceptions they would not quarrel over the facts presented, and they derived some inner satisfaction in forbearing to issue a detailed reply. But they hold that the White Paper does not tell the whole story, and that additional documents which they possess would, if published, have a devastating impact upon the White Paper's thesis. In Chinese eyes, however, the most serious aspect was that the United States had displayed not only animus but bad manners. In refusing repayment in the same coin, the Chinese not only obtained merit in their own eyes but, like the realists they are, left the door open for a change of heart on the part of the United States.

In establishing satisfactory working relationships with the Chinese against the background just described, I have combined telling them the plain truth with observing all diplomatic niceties. The latter are important to the Chinese in any case, and particularly since they have fallen so far from their former high estate. Free China shares with most of the other countries we are aiding a "pawn complex" which we must always keep in mind. Especially to be avoided is public criticism, however frank we may need to be in talking with local officials privately. The Embassy staff should set the tone in this regard, but it is scarcely less important to keep officials of other United States government agencies on the same track. "Running down the natives" is one of the oldest sports among Americans living abroad; it is a direct product of ignorance and isolationism. For an official American to indulge in such pastimes is ample evidence that he is not in sympathy with our Mutual Security program; he should be allowed to have no connection with it. I believe that present official relations between Chinese and Americans here are such as to indicate substantial progress in the right direction since mid-1950. That correct relations have done no harm is borne out by frequent statements from persons of experience that practical working cooperation between Americans and Chinese were never better than they are today.

Along with other activities, I have written a series of letters to the Department dealing with matters bearing on policy. Obviously we in the Embassy must not outrun policy as developed in Washington when we deal with the Chinese government. However, I consider it our duty to look ahead as far as possible in policy matters and to make recommendations to the Department in this connection. During the past year practical accomplishments and commitments in Formosa have tended to outrun avowed policy. To maintain the Embassy's position and influence in giving political support to our economic and military programs, it is our duty to suggest to the Department how the balance can be redressed. My letters illustrate such efforts.

Good luck to you!

x

In general I avoided public speaking in Taiwan, except for a few complimentary remarks on official occasions. I had little time to prepare speeches, and there was always the possibility of misinterpretation in the press or otherwise, due both to language problems and to the highly sensitive character of various facets of our Far

Eastern policy. On occasion, however, I responded to an invitation to speak when I thought it might help Chinese morale or give them greater confidence in the American officials stationed on Taiwan.

On May 1, 1952, a few days before departing for home leave, I responded to a request from the Taipei Rotary Club with an autobiographical talk. It was still a common opinion in China that officials of the Department of State were soft on communism. It seemed appropriate, therefore, to sketch some of my own experiences in the past under the topic of "Contacts with Communism." I started with my arrival in Batum for a tour of duty of two and a half years as construction superintendent for one of the large American relief operations then in progress in Soviet Russia. Excerpts follow:

In 1922 one could still be impressed by the handsome cities, which compared favorably with those of Western Europe despite the neglect and stagnation which had occurred toward the end of the war and during the subsequent years of communist rule. One could see that the Russian railroad system had been among the finest in the world. Yet when I arrived in Russia it was unable to transport sufficient food from surplus areas to prevent starvation a few hundred miles away. But worst of all was the evident terror under which the people lived. Every community had its "Cheka," or special police, which knew no rules but its own. Private trading was still permitted at that time, and a frequent sight was a merchant being marched down the street to prison for "profiteering," escorted by police with rifles and fixed bayonets. Whether he was guilty of anything—even of improper thoughts—no one outside the Cheka would ever know. In every city truckloads of victims were taken periodically to the outskirts, forced to dig their own graves, shot and pushed in. Most of them undoubtedly had done nothing worse than express an indiscreet opinion or display a degree of conscientiousness in their daily jobs which had embarrassed some good communist.

In our work as a foreign organization we were accorded certain privileges not extended to others. There was much speculation as to why we were there. A common idea, of course, was that we were simply spies. Another was that the American capitalists had large surpluses of agricultural and other products which they wanted to dispose of, and that we were accomplishing this by sending these surpluses to Russia while the American "workers" footed the bill. There was, of course, a distorted element of truth in this latter explanation. In actual fact, the "workers" were either American taxpayers, who fully understood and supported the idea of relieving famine in Russia, or citizens who made voluntary contributions, largely through religious organizations in those days. No American "workers" were being fleeced by "capitalists" in the process, but all of this was simply beyond the comprehension of more than a handful of people in Russia. And this handful included few if any communists.

However, anyone could see that we were bringing in millions of dollars worth of food and other necessities, without which many more millions would have died of privation. So the communist officials as a rule did not interfere too seriously with our operations.

Private business firms had a very different experience. Although the remaining assets of most of those established before the war had since been seized by the communist regime, new victims were enticed into bringing in capital for new projects. Once these were started, they became targets for all kinds of persecution. Modern labor legislation, copied largely from Germany, had been put on the books but never enforced, least of all in enterprises operated by the communist government. But a newly established foreign firm was called upon to do the impossible, with no consideration of cost factors. In due course all of them were driven out, but not before they had contributed in money and technical assistance to the communist regime.

Although most of my time in the Soviet Union was spent in the south, I visited both Moscow and St. Petersburg. Everywhere the picture was the same. The communist process is one of leveling down rather than grading up. The Soviet Union was and is the world's greatest poorhouse.

It was with a sense of great relief, therefore, that I sailed out of Batum on a little French ship in February, 1925. Not that I had ever been particularly worried about my personal safety. Like nearly everyone else, I had been shot at several times, but in an impersonal fashion. And I had been arrested only once. It was the atmosphere of terror that I was escaping. Of course I would continue to wonder what had happened to many of my good friends, Russian and others, who could not leave the Red paradise. I would grieve when I heard bad news about them. But in a perhaps selfish way I could not help being thankful that I would no longer hear the shot in the night, the police making an arrest at the customary hour of 3 A.M., or the fusillade at dawn.

My next contact with communism came two years later, in 1927, when I was assigned to the American Legation at Prague. Czechoslovakia, as you know, was at that time about as close to a genuine democracy as could be found in Central or Eastern Europe. It had defects, of course, but a large degree of freedom, justice, and prosperity prevailed. Even at that time, however, the Communist party was the second largest in Czechoslovakia; it was exceeded in membership and in parliamentary representation only by the Agrarian party. Most people were not then particularly disturbed by such evidence of communist strength. There were many political parties in Czechoslovakia and the communists, as I recall, controlled only 10 or 12 per cent of the popular vote.

With my recent experiences in Russia, however, I was not happy about what I saw in Prague. The communists were obviously well organized; they were a rough and ruthless lot. I recall discussing the question at that time with a foreign diplomat who now holds a high place in the service of his country. He thought that communism in Europe was attracting not only certain so-called intellectuals, who provided a "front," but also much larger numbers of persons who, if they had been in the United States, would have been gangsters. This diplomat had served in Washington, and his opinion was not intended as a criticism of America. He was simply making the point that our large degree of individual liberty, and our comparative laxity in law enforcement, provided opportunities for crime of which a counterpart in Czechoslovakia and other liberal European countries could be found only in political gangsterism. I believe that he had something there.

In any case, despite its strong democratic and liberal traditions, Czechoslovakia later proved ripe for the plucking when orders came from the Kremlin after World War II. Czech communists had done their work well.

During the 1930's I spent several years in Greece, where communism was generally regarded as a negligible factor. But the Reds were by no means idle. Cadres were being developed. Carefully selected individuals went to Moscow for intensive training in the arts of revolution and treason. Greece at that time had two large political parties of almost equal parliamentary strength, the Liberals and the Populists; but the small communist fraction and a few fellow-travelers held the balance of power on certain issues where the two major parties opposed each other. This encouraged one of the latter to seek communist support at a rather critical moment in 1935, which in turn encouraged the conservative Acting Prime Minister to obtain the King's approval for the dissolution of Parliament. For eleven years thereafter Greece was without a parliamentary government, thanks to the threat of communism.

In the spring of 1939 I left Greece, and for the next five years my chief troubles were with the Nazis in Belgium and Yugoslavia, and later with the Japanese in the Philippines. In attacking the Soviet Union, and in declaring war on the United States, Hitler made us the temporary allies of the Kremlin. But even with our common struggle against Nazi Germany still far from won, the communists played their own games at our expense. For example, they took over important elements among resistance groups in various countries in preparation for attempts to assume power when the Nazis were defeated. This had occurred in Greece, and when I returned to the Near East early in 1944, Greek army and navy elements in Egypt were suffering from internal dissension, stimulated by communist activities, in which the British had to intervene with force.

These troubles in Egypt seemed to have been patched up, however, and in October, 1944, we embarked on what might have been called "operation Shoestring." Greece was to be liberated by a handful of British troops supported by a few Greek units. Members of our Embassy staff accompanied this expedition. It had been correctly assumed that the main German forces in Greece would withdraw to Yugoslavia without offering resistance, while isolated units on Crete and other islands would be immobilized by Allied control of the sea and air. But no adequate preparations had been made to cope with communism.

It would be interesting to speculate as to what might have happened in various other European countries, where the communists had substantial forces in the form of armed resistance groups, had the liberating Allied armies arrived with only a corporal's guard to maintain internal order. Fortunately, this seems to have been tried only in Greece. At the outset many people were hopeful of the new Greek government, which embraced all elements including the extreme Left. The test came quickly, however, when the Prime Minister and the British Commanding General called upon the communist-controlled resistance forces to submit to their military orders. No satisfactory reply was forthcoming, and early in December, 1944, street fighting broke out in connection with communist demonstrations. I watched a part of this from a window in our Embassy. The crowd was made up largely of sixteen to twenty-year-olds, of both sexes, directed by older men with red armbands. They were being urged to charge a group of police, stationed at the street corner, who shot over their heads and caused no casualties or damage except for some broken windows in our building. In other parts of the city, however, numbers were killed on both sides. This was the prelude to revolt.

During succeeding weeks, until nearly the middle of January, 1945, the communists controlled virtually all of Greece except at points such as the center of Athens, where a few British or loyal Greek troops were able to hold out—hundreds against thousands. Remember, we were still fighting Germany, and there were still many more German troops in Greece than British. The latter had to be diverted from their main job to deal with a communist revolt ordered by our allies in the Kremlin! Moreover, it was obvious that if the situation was to be brought under control, substantial reinforcements would have to be withdrawn from the Italian front and brought to Greece. It was a bad moment, and Greece owes her rescue largely to one man: Winston Churchill. . . .

British reinforcements began arriving in Athens, brought from Italy by American transport planes. Others followed by sea with tanks and artillery. When sufficient strength had been built up to deal with the estimated 25,000 armed communists surrounding the city, an offensive was ordered. Some of the British said later that it was the worst fighting they had seen during the war. They fought from house to house, down narrow streets where the communists had created road blocks by dynamiting buildings, and finally out into the open country in pursuit of the fleeing enemy. Small operations in other parts of Greece completed the collapse of the communist effort. But it was bitter while it lasted, as the large and well kept British military cemetery near Athens reminds the visitor of today. Here was a sacrifice of Allied forces who should have been fighting the Germans but had to be diverted to establish the authority of the Greek government which the communists had agreed to support and then almost immediately attempted to overthrow by force. That it was all ordered by Moscow cannot be doubted.

While British losses in this unnecessary fighting were serious enough, Greek casualties on both sides were far greater. Battle deaths were only a small part of the total. The communists took thousands of hostages from the environs of Athens, including many prominent individuals, men, women, and children. They were marched away into the hills in the dead of winter. Many died of exposure; others were slaughtered. Meanwhile the communists were killing thousands throughout Greece because of their political beliefs or because they had remained loyal to their military or police duties. Many were subjected to indescribable tortures, of which the perpetrators included members of a communist youth organization called the "Opla," who had been trained in terror and were armed with peculiar curved knives carried inside their shirts.

All of these developments were new to the Greeks. True, they had enjoyed their periodic revolutions in the past, but these ordinarily had involved little bloodshed. Rarely had anyone been executed for his political beliefs. Something had been imported—from Moscow.

With British help, order was re-established throughout Greece. General elections were held early in 1946, from which the parties of the Left abstained but which demonstrated convincingly that the entire "Left" accounted for no more than 15 per cent of the population, and most of these were only fellow-travelers. The hard communist core was scarcely 5 per cent. The elections were conducted peacefully and fairly; Greece seemed to be embarking on a new era of democracy and prosperity.

I was in charge of our Embassy in Athens during the 1946 elections and for several months thereafter. Then I was transferred to Vienna to experience new contacts with the Russians. It was the same, old, sad communist story, and I shall not prolong my remarks with details of that year in Austria. But having said so much about Greece, I should like to round off my story of communism in that tormented country. Late in 1947 I was told that I would shortly be ordered to Shanghai as consul general. Imagine my surprise, therefore, to receive a subsequent message telling me to return to Athens immediately. Our ambassador there had gone to the United States for medical treatment and I was to relieve him. After a few months of tranquillity in 1945-46, new orders had come from the Kremlin and another Greek communist revolt was in full swing. Things were not going well for the Greek government or ourselves, and Washington seemed to want an old hand on the job.

For seven months, beginning in December, 1947, I was again in charge of the Embassy in Athens. The communists once more controlled a large part of the Greek countryside, while units of the Greek army and police were tied down to defensive duties in the towns. Communist guerrillas raided villages within a few miles of Athens, and more than half a million refugees left their homes in the country and crowded into the cities for safety. The communists finally captured a town in northern Greece and announced the setting up of a government in this temporary capital. Their forces were well armed with automatic weapons, mortars, land mines and some artillery. The leaders had received intensive training in nearby communist countries, and when any of their units were hard pressed by the Greek Army they would simply retire into one of the sanctuaries to the north.

Our military advisory group, which was headed by General James A. Van Fleet, assisted the Greeks in a number of ways which eventually produced good results. The striking power of the Greek Air Force was increased, particularly in fighter-bombers which proved particularly effective against guerrilla units and fortifications in the mountains. Carefully selected farmers were armed and thereby enabled to defend their villages against all but major attacks; troops and police were thus released for offensive action. The mobility of the army was improved, and two or more divisions were used at a time to surround an area where communist forces were active. Advancing in several concentric circles, as a precaution against infiltration, such areas were cleared consecutively. Refugees were then encouraged to return to their villages and assistance given them in repairing their houses and other property. Wherever possible stone houses were built, which gave them new confidence, for a stone house can also serve as a fort against lightly armed attackers.

It was a long struggle this time. . . . In any event, the corner was turned in 1948 and by mid-1949 the campaign was brought to a successful conclusion. Refugees, who had exceeded 10 per cent of the country's total population, returned to their homes, and the reconstruction of Greece could be resumed.

I concluded by observing that it was superfluous for me to draw parallels between the events I had just described and those my listeners had experienced in China. But I mentioned a few considerations from which we might take hope for the future. First, I was convinced that a regime which could exist only by terror and the denial of human rights was essentially not only inefficient but weak. Second, we had learned that aggression could be stopped by collective action. Third, I reminded them that in contrast to most countries which had fallen prey to communist aggression, Free China had been able to retain a substantial and secure rallying point of its own, on Taiwan, where hope could be kept alive.

☆ *China Assignment* ☆

Taiwan is almost half way around the world from Washington, and Pauline and I started for home on May 11, 1952. We flew to Hong Kong, Saigon, Angkor Wat, Bangkok, Rangoon, and New Delhi. At Saigon we stayed with old friends, Ambassador and Mrs. Donald R. Heath. In the Indian capital, Counselor Everett F. Drumright, who was to succeed me in Taipei six years later, kindly offered us his car for a trip to Agra. The heat was terrible but the Taj Mahal was more than worth it. I called on Ambassador Chester Bowles and found him charming and enthusiastic about India. In Beirut we were met at the airport by more old friends, Ambassador and Mrs. Harold B. Minor, with whom we had served in Athens. Consul General and Mrs. Elbert G. Matthews received us most hospitably in Istanbul. Athens, where we had served three times for a total of ten years provided opportunity to see many more friends during a short stay.

The next stop was Rome, where the Chinese Ambassador James Yu entertained us with the American Ambassador and Mrs. Ellsworth Bunker, and Counselor and Mrs. Llewellen E. Thompson. In Paris as in Rome, our Embassy was closed for four days over the Memorial Day weekend. During this extensive trip I found that Taipei was a minority of one on Saturday closing, irrespective of local customs around the world. I made a mental note that in Taipei we would have to start closing on Saturdays, which we had not done because Chinese government offices worked a full six-day week. But I wondered whether all of our communist adversaries were also permitting themselves the luxury of a forty-hour week.

In Paris I saw Ambassador James C. Dunn and many other friends and acquaintances. One evening, at dinner, I fear that Cyrus L. Sulzberger of the *New York Times* and I succeeded in boring our new Assistant Secretary of State for Near Eastern Affairs, Henry A. Byroade, with our long reminiscences about various countries in his area. We flew on to New York and Washington arriving on June 8, 1952.

During my 1952 trip to the United States I spent a total of five weeks on consultation in Washington, with seven weeks of leave in between. Pauline stayed in Washington with me for only a few days. She and I both needed a real break after so considerable a period of tense activity abroad. And my time in Washington was anything but restful. Father was eighty-four at that time, and it was to be our last long vacation with him. Pauline and I thoroughly enjoyed the Maine scene and its people.

In Washington my rounds followed the familiar pattern. There were scores of calls and conferences about China and about our administrative problems in Taipei. John M. Allison had become Assistant Secretary of State for Far Eastern Affairs and I saw him frequently. We did not always agree on Chinese issues, but no one could have been more meticulous than he in carrying out official policy. We got along well and have remained good friends, as have our wives. During one conference in his office, Robert Scott, Assistant Under Secretary of State and Allison's opposite number in the British Foreign Office, was present. I tried to disabuse him of the idea that we were planning with Chiang Kai-shek for an early attack on the China mainland. We were simply preparing to resist new aggression and to support offensive action from Taiwan only in response to such aggression.

Other meetings took me to the Pentagon, the Central Intelligence Agency, the Department of Commerce, the Mutual Security Administration, the Psychological Strategy Board, the Capitol, and various units within the Department such as the Policy Planning Staff.

At the Pentagon I saw William C. Foster, who had become Deputy Secretary of Defense, as well as Secretary of the Army Frank Pace, and Secretary of the Navy Dan A. Kimball. All were well informed and well disposed to what we were doing in Taiwan. I gave them a current report on China. Admiral Radford was at the Pentagon and had been urging that the delivery of military equipment for Taiwan be expedited. Major General George H. Olmsted, then in charge of military aid programs, invited me to a luncheon at the Pentagon where I added further urging. The "gold plate" briefing of my previous visit was repeated. Several general and flag officers were among the sizable group present. I talked for half an hour and answered questions for thirty minutes more.

Pauline and I dined with former Ambassador William C. Bullitt, the guests including Mrs. Alice Roosevelt Longworth, Mrs. A. Mitchell Palmer, Senator and Mrs. Andrew F. Schoeppel, Ambassador Donald R. Heath, and the new counselor of the embassy for Manila, William S. B. Lacey, with his wife. After dinner we were joined by Senator Knowland, Admiral and Mrs. Radford, and Mr. and Mrs. Arthur Krock. It was an animated evening. Our host was in good form; few could equal him as a conversationalist and raconteur. But the guests were not silent.

XII

Secretary Acheson was charming and reasonable as always when I called on him. I reviewed the situation in Taiwan briefly, mentioning the good progress being made with the help of our military and economic aid programs. I believed that Taiwan and our present policy toward that island were amply justified in terms of the "situation of strength" being created there. I did not pretend that we had found a solution for the larger problem of China, but what we were doing could contribute toward a solution. We were receiving excellent cooperation from the Chinese government.

At the same time I took up with the Secretary the question of my personal prospects. I was nearly fifty-four, and no less than three of my juniors and subordinates in Athens had been appointed ambassadors or ministers plenipotentiary after I left Greece for the Far East in 1949. Acheson promised to discuss my status with Assistant Secretary Allison—he did so, helpfully, a few days later—and then told a story on himself. He was sixty, and had been doing some work on his place with the assistance of a Negro of the same age. It was hot and the Secretary was soon winded, remarking to his helper, "You're a better man than I." The reply was to the point, "Ah has to be!"

I had spent more time in Washington than I had intended. During most of this period Congress was not in session, but I saw Senator H. Alexander Smith and Senator Margaret Chase Smith, for whom we had come to have a high regard both as a person and as our Senator from Maine, where we had maintained legal residence for many years. Another opportunity to meet members of Congress was provided when Secretary of the Navy Kimball invited Pauline and me to dine on the U.S.S. *Sequoia*. Among the guests were Senator and Mrs. Homer Ferguson, Senator and Mrs. J. William Fulbright, Senator Knowland, and Ambassador and Mrs. Wellington Koo. On another occasion May Craig and Doris Fleeson again gave a most pleasant dinner at the F Street Club, where we saw Senator and Mrs. H. Alexander Smith and Congressman Mike Mansfield, among others. On still another pleasant evening May Craig invited us to dine at her house with Mrs. Eleanor Roosevelt.

Shortly before leaving Washington I called on President Truman at the White House. He stood up from his desk as I came in and shook my hand cordially. In response to his question, I repeated what I had said to Secretary Acheson about progress on Taiwan and the cooperativeness of the Chinese government. He remarked that my review was rather more optimistic than he had heard from others. The President asked me about the Chinese military establishment on Taiwan, and whether the defects demonstrated on the China mainland had been corrected. I admitted these defects, but pointed out that in 1945 China was in a state of disorganization on a vast scale. This explained much of what had happened. Now, I said, there was marked improvement all around. As our talk ended, President Truman said that he believed our country's position to be much stronger than when he took office; otherwise he would not have refused to run again. My call lasted about twenty minutes, during which I talked rather more than half the time. Later I was told that it usually was the other way around.

XIII

The Washington atmosphere was distinctly more favorable toward Free China than for several years past. I had encountered a residue of the classic criticisms which had been directed at the government of the Republic of China in previous years, but our policy of active support for that government was rarely questioned. The one point that seemed to warrant particular attention was an incipient revival of demands for "reform" in the Chinese government, but without clear or practical notions of what this might entail. I prepared a memorandum on June 23, for circulation in the Department, from which the following passages may be quoted:

> The need for "reform" in the Chinese Nationalist government often is mentioned without specifying the character of reform desired. When one attempts to analyze the approaches to this problem which have been favored by Americans over the past

few years, it becomes apparent that they have at different times proposed courses of action ranging from one of unqualified support of the Nationalist regime to one of permitting or even aiding the communists to take over China. It seems important, therefore, to clarify our thinking on this subject before deciding upon any new course of action. As a first step, therefore, I suggest that we should determine to support the government of the Republic of China, as currently established on Formosa and within the framework of the Constitution of 1946, to the extent feasible in the light of our own resources and of that government's actual and potential effectiveness in contributing to the furtherance of American foreign policy. As a corollary, we should refrain from actions which would undermine the National Government's effectiveness, such as giving support to subversive minorities or publicly castigating that government in a manner liable to lessen its prestige without at the same time accomplishing more than equivalent gains in enhancing its effectiveness.

If we accept the basis set forth in the preceding paragraph, it may be that we would do better to substitute the word "improvement" for "reform," since the latter has at times been taken to imply fundamental changes in form of government as well as in the details of administration. Having thus delimited our field, it may be convenient to divide our possible courses of action into four general groups:

1. Improvement of the effectiveness of Chinese government operations, in the military and economic fields, which have a direct bearing on the success of our aid programs.

2. Improvement of the Chinese governmental administration in preparation for its eventual resumption of authority over part or all of mainland China.

3. Improvement of the political posture of the Chinese government, within the framework of the 1946 Constitution and without ourselves engaging in intrigue or subversion, such as to gain greater popular support for that government both in Formosa and on the Chinese mainland.

4. Improvement of techniques to persuade the free world that the Chinese government has evolved into one worthy of general sympathy and support.

☆ *Progress* ☆

The first numbered course of action mentioned above is one which is followed rather consistently in all areas where American aid programs are in progress, including Formosa. It represents a direct approach which is justified by our duty to obtain maximum results from the aid made available by our government. It also has the advantage of dealing with practical questions with which our aid missions are familiar and on which their opinions therefore are most valuable. This approach, if properly used, not only contributes directly to the success of our programs but also indirectly exercises a wholesome political influence. For example, our efforts to introduce better budgetary control through the Economic Stabilization Board in Formosa not only have encouraged economy and probity but have raised public confidence in the Chinese government. Similarly our insistence upon maintaining a single chain of command in the defense establishment, in the interest of military effectiveness, is ameliorating various undesirable features of the Political Department of the Ministry of National Defense. Yet such steps need involve no objectionable assumption of direct American responsibility for the detailed handling of Chinese finance or for combatting subversion in the Chinese Armed Forces.

Before considering a possible extension of such efforts as those mentioned in the preceding paragraph, however, it is important to weigh them in relation to our current practices in other countries where we are conducting aid programs. Specifically, there would be no grounds for exerting greater pressure on the Chinese government in this connection than we do elsewhere, except in so far as that government might be less effective and less cooperative than others. Otherwise, our actions in Formosa would be in conflict with our general policy of supporting, in a spirit of cooperation, the sovereignty and administrative integrity of free states. In actual fact, the present effectiveness, probity, and cooperativeness of the Chinese government compare very favorably with other governments now receiving American aid. In comparison to other Asian governments, that on Formosa stands close to the top of the list in these respects, while on a world-wide basis it undoubtedly would rate better-than-average. While efforts in this field are producing results, therefore, and should continue to do so, there would appear to exist no justifiable or promising opportunity at present for a general approach to the Chinese on the subject of "reform" within the immediate framework of our aid programs.

Passing on to the second numbered type of improvement which the Joint Chiefs of Staff may have had in mind when they referred (December 17, 1951) to enhancing "the Chinese Nationalists' capability of contributing to the containment of communism in Asia, and thus to lead to the possible eventual liberation of Communist China by the Chinese people under Chinese Nationalist leadership supported by other free nations of the world," we enter a broader field which has no counterpart in other countries where we are conducting aid programs. Certainly, this proposal is deserving of the most careful consideration by all concerned. . . . While the initial step might be taken on a broad basis of principle, it seems to me that at the outset we should have clearly in mind just what we intend to seek in the way of reforms or improvements, and just how they are intended to support our struggle with communism. . . .

If after due consideration of all factors involved, we should decide to ask the Generalissimo and his government to yield what might be regarded as a certain amount of sovereignty in return for our support in re-establishing themselves on the mainland, their reply very likely would be in the affirmative. In the absence of any significant commitment on our part, however, and depending somewhat upon the details of our proposal, a negative reply could be anticipated.

The third numbered form of improvement mentioned above— "political"—offers a promising field, within the limitations mentioned, and does not necessarily involve any general approach to the Chinese government on the subject of "reform." In public administration, for example, the Chinese would welcome expert advice as to improvements in their civil service system, in fiscal procedures, etc. These are not only important in terms of direct governmental effectiveness but also in raising standards of probity and in gaining popular support for the government. Until adequate scales of pay and retirement are introduced into the civil and military services, for example, it is futile to expect the complete elimination of "squeeze" in Formosa or elsewhere. In this connection, equitable systems for promotion and "selection out" could be developed with our assistance. The MSA mission has plans for activity in these fields, and it is regrettable that the American military fiscal officers requested last year have not yet arrived. With military expenditures absorbing half of Formosa's public revenues, and in view of the traditional laxity of Chinese military finances, it is particularly important that this opportunity for improvement should not be lost.

In considering the need for political improvement on Formosa it is important also to recognize the considerable progress which has been recorded in the past two or three years, largely on Chinese initiative. Popular elections, the inclusion of a majority of Formosans in the civil service, improvements in court procedures, and the attainment of a degree of law and order probably unequaled elsewhere in Asia yet without significant restrictions of freedom of movement, all give evidence that the Chinese government is evolving into something better. Certainly this is very different from the straitjacket of communism.

The fourth category of improvement listed above is largely in the field of public relations. The Chinese government today is in fact very much better in every way than its reputation abroad. Overshadowing its admitted faults in the past, and the ample room for improvement still remaining, the Chinese government's greatest moral handicap is the fact of its colossal failure in losing the China mainland to the communists. However the blame for this catastrophe may be apportioned, the Chinese Nationalists were incomparably the most obvious losers. World opinion, further influenced by unwarrantedly virulent adverse propaganda from many sources . . . is not basing itself on facts as they are today. Here, then, is a most fertile field for cooperative effort on the part of the American and Chinese governments. Something has already been done in this regard; much more can be done in the future. . . .

A glance at . . . aspects of American policy toward Formosa is sufficient to suggest the profound changes in our programs which would be necessary if the Chinese Nationalists were to become involved in open conflict as a result of initiative taken by either side during the next two to five years. Planning for either eventuality should be pursued actively here in Washington, and the Chinese government should be consulted to the fullest extent possible as these plans are developed. The improvement or "reform" of the Nationalist Government would be an important aspect in this development, not as an end in itself but as one of various means to a far greater end. As suggested in the preceding paragraphs, such improvement can be stimulated by various types of effort on our part, all coordinated as to form and timing with the development of our total policy toward Formosa, China, and the Far East as a whole.

XIV

On September 11, 1952, I said good-bye at the Department. Ambassador Koo, who had again entertained us most agreeably at the Chinese Embassy, saw us off at the Washington airport. We arrived in Los Angeles that evening. Ray Moyer, formerly in charge of our economic mission on Taiwan, had joined the Ford Foundation in Pasadena. He took me to call on Chester C. Davis, associate director of the Foundation, whom I tried to interest in Taiwan. Specifically, I thought it would be preferable for a private organization to undertake a study of public administration on the island, rather than extend our official American activities into this field. We had a great deal to work with in the way of capable personnel in the Chinese government, but often there were many employees doing the same job. Recommendations, after appropriate study, from an organization such as the Ford Foundation could result in the shifting of many public employees into industry, which was expanding rapidly with the help of our economic program. Davis and John B. Howard, whom I had known in Greece, seemed interested, but nothing came of my effort.

We spent two days at Yosemite, en route to San Francisco, and found it deserving of all the double stars awarded by our 1909 edition of Baedecker's *United States*. Madame Chiang was in a San Francisco hospital receiving treatment for her recurrent skin difficulty. Pauline and I called on her. She was feeling better, but impatient to return to Taiwan. The same afternoon we called on former Ambassador and Mrs. Henry F. Grady, with whom we had served in Greece. Whenever asked who were my favorite chiefs in the Foreign Service, I have cited Henry Grady and Lincoln Mac-Veagh. This was the last time I was to see Henry.

On the night of September 18 we flew by Pan American to Honolulu. Commander James G. Hedrick, Admiral Radford's aide, met us the next morning at the airport. We were to be the Radford's guest in the house where Fleet Admiral Nimitz and other famous officers had lived. Admiral and Mrs. Radford were most considerate hosts, and we enjoyed our visit thoroughly. At his headquarters, a short distance away, I had talks with Radford's two chiefs of staff and other officers of all the services who were interested in Taiwan. This was my first opportunity to discuss our problems in detail at Pearl Harbor, and I was delighted to find comprehensive knowledge and keen appreciation of our situation on all sides. This gratifying experience was repeated every time I passed through Honolulu thereafter. I only regretted that so great a distance separated Taiwan from Headquarters, Commander in Chief Pacific.

The Radfords included us in a luncheon party at the Royal Hawaiian for military representatives from Australia and New Zealand, who were in Honolulu for an ANZUS conference. Our visitors from down under impressed me most favorably. This was followed by a buffet supper at Admiral Radford's quarters, after which we took off again by Pan American. A typhoon had damaged facilities at Wake Island and our fuel stop was at Midway instead. It was not yet daylight, but I got off the aircraft in the hope of seeing the famous gooney birds. Apparently they were still in bed when we took off once more for the Far East.

☆☆☆

6: *Armistice*

I

OUR PLANE landed in Tokyo on September 23, 1952; we were met by Counselor and Mrs. William T. Turner of the Embassy. They kindly helped us to get installed at the new Nikkatsu Hotel. We were quite comfortable, but missed the Frank Lloyd Wright atmosphere of the old Imperial.

Next morning I called on Ambassador Robert D. Murphy. We had a good talk, and I was glad to find ourselves in full agreement on how to deal with the Chinese communists, particularly as to the commonly exaggerated fear of "provoking" them. I was reminded of a passage in Mao Tse-tung's writings. He posed the question of what to do when confronting a man-eating tiger in the forest. As Mao correctly put it, whether the tiger is provoked or not is beside the point. What matters is whether you kill him before he eats you.

We lunched with the Turners at the large and attractive house which had been purchased for the use of our second ranking diplomatic representative in Japan. Ambassador and Mrs. Murphy invited us for dinner. It was the first time Pauline and I had seen the official residence in Tokyo; since the war it had been occupied successively by Generals Douglas MacArthur and Matthew B. Ridgway. The buildings erected by the United States in the Japanese capital about 1930 formed an imposing group. Tokyo was one of the first capitals in which we built an embassy with attention to the prestige of our country. But the architecture puzzled me. There were a few Japanese details on some of the secondary buildings, but the Ambassador's residence appeared to my layman's eyes as Spanish rather than either American or Oriental. However, the general effect was both spacious and pleasing.

I called on General Mark W. Clark, with whom I had served for a short time at Vienna in 1946-47. He had followed MacArthur and Ridgway as Supreme Commander Allied Forces Pacific, and I was not surprised to have my understanding confirmed that Clark shared MacArthur's view: There is no substitute for victory. By arming additional Korean forces, already trained, and bringing in two Chinese divisions or so from Taiwan, he believed that decisive victory in Korea could be achieved. It should be recalled that at this time the truce negotiations were being dragged out unconscionably by the communists, with no indication that they wanted a just and peaceful settlement. General Clark remarked that he wanted to visit Taiwan, and I hoped very much that he would do so.

Coming out of SCAP headquarters I noticed a large sign across the street, evidently soliciting American trade for a Japanese fur store. A donkey and an elephant were saying in unison, "We like mink!"

I saw Ambassador Murphy again to give him the substance of my talk with General Clark. He also wanted to visit Taiwan, and I urged him to come. It was suggested that he and Clark come together, which I thought would be most desirable.

We arrived back in Taipei on October 1, after a stopover in Hong Kong. A considerable group met us at the airport. In addition to American officials, there was Finance Minister C. K. Yen, Chief of the General Staff Chou Chi-jou, Commander-in-Chief of the Air Force "Tiger" Wang Shu-ming, General J. L. Huang, the Chief of Protocol, and others. Howard Jones had done a most creditable job as chargé d'affaires in my absence. We were glad to be "back home."

Before I left for the United States we had completed arrangements to lease another small Japanese-style house next to ours on Grass Mountain. The two were then connected by a short passageway, and not long after our return from home leave Pauline and I were able to enjoy the luxury of two bedrooms and two simple but convenient bathrooms. No longer was it necessary for us to sleep in one end of our little dining room.

Corresponding improvements were made at the chancery. By

compensation payments, the Taiwan Provincial Government had persuaded our squatters to move. We were able to demolish the various ramshackle structures, haul away many tons of junk and rubbish, and complete a masonry wall around the entire area owned by the United States. In due course, a garage, parking lot, and lawn appeared on the land thus vacated. Our chancery might still be the shabbiest in the world, as an Associated Press correspondent once called it in a story, but the property as a whole was at least clean and tidy. Operations became more efficient at the same time.

II

The results of the 1952 elections in the United States were received by the Chinese on Taiwan with quiet gratification, but with no great expectation of a decisive change in foreign policy. The Korean trip of President-elect Eisenhower inevitably started rumors. One of these was that Eisenhower and Chiang Kai-shek were to meet on Wake Island. Another was that the President-elect looked with sympathy upon proposals of Generals Clark and Van Fleet for a major offensive in North Korea to replace stalemate with victory. The first story appeared to be a pure fabrication. As to the second, the 1952 elections had made it apparent that the American public shared with Western European opinion a determination to avoid aggressive action in Korea appreciably to the north of the 38th parallel. Only some new and particularly scandalous act by the communists would have changed this attitude.

One of the last communications received by the Embassy in Taipei from the Department of State before the new administration took office in January, 1953, was a draft paper on United States policy toward the Republic of China. We were asked to comment. It seemed an auspicious moment to raise a number of pointed questions and follow these with recommendations. Excerpts from my reply of February 3, 1953, are given here:

Although the U.S. military and economic aid program for Formosa in its present expanded form is less than two years old and has been carried out largely on an *ad hoc* basis, its size and scope imply a medium to long-term policy transcending the admitted objectives of defense and containment. In order to clarify the U.S. position and permit sound planning, therefore, it would be desirable to have answers to the following questions:

a. *For what purposes and on what date or dates does the U.S. wish to have Chinese Nationalist armed forces ready for possible combat other than in defense of Formosa and the Pescadores?* Until recently there has seemed to be no practicable alternative to accepting responsibility for equipping and training of the forces actually existing on Formosa and the Pescadores, within the limits of equipment and supplies available from the U.S. and within the capabilities of the Chinese officers and men at hand. Two years ago the combat efficiency of these forces was such that, despite the large number of men immediately involved (approximately 500,000), all of them were needed for defense. With the substantial improvement in their effectiveness since 1951, however, and in view of the evident necessity for continuing the assurance of American air and naval support in any case, the ground forces on Formosa may be stronger today than is necessary for purely defensive purposes and for maintaining internal order. The margin should be much greater a year hence. (Chinese Nationalist air and naval forces presumably should continue to be considered primarily as supporting elements for the ground forces and should be equipped accordingly.) The possible uses for this resulting strategic reserve, say within the next year or two, require early definition to provide a basis for both military and economic planning during the immediate future.

b. *Does the U.S. wish to assist the government of the Republic of China in expanding production on Formosa so that the island can become self-supporting within, say, four years, except for extraordinary defense expenditures?* This would represent the logical continuation and realization of the economic program actually followed more or less consistently since mid-1951. Economic aid is already so involved with the military program, however, that any significant change in the latter is liable to upset the stability which now obtains, and nullify efforts to increase economic production, unless adequate funds are made available for all necessary purposes.

c. *Does the U.S. wish to make formal commitments to the*

government of the Republic of China, either now or in the foreseeable future, involving the legal status and/or defense of Formosa, or envisaging support in its objective of liberating the China mainland from communism, or for other purposes? The Chinese Nationalists are keenly aware of the fact that while the United States has signed a security pact with the ex-enemy, Japan, no formal and continuing commitment has been made to Nationalist China, either as to the defense of Formosa or as to their legal position with reference to the island. . . . the Nationalists do not exclude the possibility that the U.S. may at some future date favor turning Formosa over to a "trustee" or even to a China mainland regime which had promised to behave. U.S. commitments on these points would help to consolidate the structure of mutual confidence between the U.S. and Nationalist China which has been laboriously re-erected since 1950. The Chinese would, of course, welcome any additional steps by the United States which might support their "return to the mainland."

a. If the answer to the first question above indicates that Chinese Nationalist forces should be made ready for possible combat outside of Formosa, within the foreseeable future, urgent consideration should be given to the following:

1. The delivery of military supplies and equipment, and the staffing of MAAG, should be accelerated and expanded in a manner to permit adequate and timely training and equipment of the units required without unduly weakening the forces which would remain on Formosa for its defense.

2. The responsibilities of MAAG for training and equipment of Chinese Nationalist forces should be extended to units now stationed on Kinmen, Matsu, and Tachen Islands (numbering about 75,000), paralleling present responsibilities for those on Formosa and the Pescadores (about 500,000).

3. In connection with (2), consideration should be given to transferring responsibility for various anti-communist guerrilla activities, as carried on at present from offshore islands, to the regular Chinese Nationalist armed forces and hence to the purview of MAAG. These activities would include blockade duties

and raids, but presumably would not extend to guerrilla operations inland.

4. Equipment, American advisers, and funds should be provided to step up the training of reserves and replacements.

5. It should be borne in mind that of the $102 million allocated for "economic aid" to Formosa during the fiscal year 1953, less than 23 per cent is for capital goods to expand production and for technical assistance, while nearly two-thirds of the total goes directly and indirectly for the support of the large military establishment required to defend the island. The remaining 10 to 11 per cent is for consumer goods to balance Formosa's international payments. Any increase in the military program, therefore, should be accompanied by adequate expansion of economic support for such increase, leaving intact the funds needed for balancing international payments and for such technical assistance and capital investment as may be considered desirable.

6. In arriving at totals for economic support of the military program, provision should be made for better pay and allowances, particularly in the case of officers and men who have families, as essential to maintaining morale.

If, on the other hand, the U.S. wishes the Chinese Nationalist armed forces to continue to play an almost purely defensive role, then the military aid program should be re-examined immediately in that light and urgent consideration should be given as to how the government of the Republic of China might be reconciled to such an objective.

b. The U.S. should determine whether it wishes to support something along the lines of the Chinese government's Four-Year Plan (1953-56, inclusive) to make Formosa economically self-supporting, which foresees the need for U.S. economic aid of approximately $250 million during that period. Actually, this figure includes a substantial amount (around $100 million) for imports of consumer goods which would serve the dual purpose of helping to balance international payments and at the same time provide local currency (counterpart funds) for direct support of the military program and for balancing the national budget deficit resulting from other outlays for defense. In any event, the continuation of the most modest military and economic aid program will require the balancing of international payments and of the national budget, as well as better compensation for civilian employees as well as military. Only on capital investment and technical assistance, totaling perhaps $75 million for the four years, would any saving be possible in the economic field.

c. Early consideration is recommended of U.S. desires as to bilateral or multilateral agreements affecting the government of the Republic of China and/or Formosa. The absence of any formal and continuing U.S. commitment makes all programs and policies of a tentative and possibly temporary nature. Political, military, and economic relations are influenced accordingly. The Chinese Nationalists feel that they must continue to plan for the eventuality, however remote it may seem at present, that the U.S. may again leave them on their own at a crucial moment. Under such conditions the mutual confidence necessary to full cooperation evidently is lacking, private investment is discouraged or prevented from assisting in economic recovery, and future planning often seems academic.

The basic decision to be made, of course, is whether U.S. policy toward Free China is to be static or dynamic, neutral or positive; whether Formosa is simply a strategically important island which should be denied to the communists or an important factor which can be helped to play a significant part in the eventual liberation of mainland China from communist rule. The Iron Curtain in Asia will either move forward or back. Dynamic communism will use every means to push it forward; only a dynamic free world can push it back. To what extent does the U.S. wish to encourage the use of the considerable potential of Formosa and the Chinese Nationalist government to that end?

III

Early in February I was instructed by the Department to inform President Chiang that the Seventh Fleet would no longer be used to shield communist China from attack by forces based on Taiwan.

This problem had plagued our relations with the Chinese ever since the "neutralization" order issued at the outbreak of the Korean War in connection with the Fleet's mission to protect Taiwan. It continued to plague us long after the Korean Armistice in 1953, and to produce thousands of bitter words, spoken and written, all over the world, most of them beside the point.

The facts in the case were quite simple, and the considerations primarily political rather than military. The armed forces of the Republic of China were in no position to conduct more than hit-and-run raids on the China mainland, whether in 1950 or in subsequent years, without American logistic and other support, including sea transport. In return for our willingness to assist in the defense of Taiwan—shortly afterward extended to include Penghu, or the Pescadores—the Chinese government was quite prepared to forego any and all offensive action against the communists for an indefinite period after the outbreak of hostilities in Korea. From a diplomatic standpoint it would have been desirable to seek mutual agreement before directing the Seventh Fleet to defend Taiwan. But events were moving rapidly in mid-1950, and information on enemy dispositions was scanty. In any case, the government on Taiwan had proffered its agreement immediately in a manner intended to give the appearance of bilateral rather than unilateral action.

The amendment to the Seventh Fleet's directive, issued about the first of February, 1953, ending any protection for the communist-held mainland, again was unilateral. It had been reported extensively and accurately in the press before instructions reached me to inform the Chinese. Our position in Formosa remained basically unchanged, owing to the tangible factors which continued to govern; but the Chinese, not unnaturally, interpreted our step as suggesting the possibility of American support for offensive action on their part. To minimize the danger of any misunderstanding, I therefore took the occasion of my call on President Chiang to ask that no such action be initiated by his armed forces, particularly if aircraft or armor were involved, without consulting the senior American military officer on Taiwan, General Chase. He readily agreed. To this extent was the Chinese government "unleashed"—unfortunate word—and a moment later, "neutralized" once more.

The Chinese on Taiwan followed with interest the "Captive Peoples" resolution in the United States Congress, which was to represent disavowal by the United States of commitments permitting the "enslavement" of other peoples. The Tehran, Yalta, and Potsdam conferences had been cited in this connection, and Yalta was a fighting word in China. An American policy envisaging the "liberation of captive peoples," even though "peaceful means" were specified, suggested new initiatives against Red-held China. Hence, the eventual shelving of the resolution was a disappointment to Free China.

IV

The next major problem in United States-Chinese relations involved the "Kuomintang troops in Burma." Again, a great deal was said and written which provoked ill feeling and distrust between Free China and its friends; and again, much of what attracted public attention was either grossly exaggerated or quite beside the point. A few essential facts may be given here.

While much larger numbers of Chinese national troops were retreating into Indochina before the advancing communists, some regular units, totaling perhaps two to three thousand men, withdrew into the Shan states of northeastern Burma. They formed part of a far larger refugee movement of Chinese into Burmese territory from 1949 to 1951; some estimates placed the total figure as high as 50,000. This efflux took place in one of the wildest and most remote parts of the world. No established authority existed in large areas on both sides of the frontier. In fact, the location of the border itself was in question. A Chinese commission sent to study the matter after World War II had simply disappeared. Certainly, the simple and illiterate people in the area were unaware of any need for passports and visas to cross a frontier of which they were barely conscious. Nor was there any awareness of an ethnographic line to the southwest of which people were "Burmese."

This refugee movement was simply another southward flow of people from China in response to pressure from the north, such as had occurred from time to time over many centuries. Coming into a sparsely settled region with little or no constituted authority, it was inevitable that considerable numbers of men should attach themselves in some way to the Chinese military units there, at the same time trying to make a living as best they could. The leaders of these

156

units began to boast of their military strength and to entertain hopes of renewing offensive action against their communist enemies to the northeast. They claimed to have organized several "divisions," and in 1951 at least one sizable incursion into Yunnan was undertaken. Defeat followed a pitched battle with communist forces and they retired into Burma once more. These "KMT troops" never totaled more than ten to twelve thousand, and only a small proportion of these men had sufficient arms and training to be considered soldiers.

After the abortive operation of 1951, the refugees in northwest Burma settled down to live by farming, trade, and, in some cases no doubt, by banditry. During my visit to Rangoon in 1952 no one even mentioned them to me. A few months later, however, the Peiping regime stirred up the question to the great alarm of the Burmese. The mere presence of foreign military units in the country without Rangoon's consent was a reflection on the Burmese government's strength and authority, but more immediately serious was the possibility that Peiping might use them as an excuse for aggression against Burma. In retrospect it does not appear that Red China took the matter seriously except as it provided opportunity to strain relations between Rangoon, Taipei, and Washington.

In any event, my first task after the new administration took office in the United States was to persuade President Chiang Kai-shek to evacuate the anti-communist Chinese forces from Burma. The President and his advisers were genuinely surprised. We had raised the question on several occasions during the previous year, suggesting that these troops be withdrawn, but now we were insistent. From the Chinese point of view, the units in Burma were significant as the only sizable anti-communist Chinese military force remaining on the mainland of Asia. We were fighting the Chinese Reds in Korea. We were talking about the liberation of captive peoples. It was far from certain that we would get a satisfactory peace or even a truce in Korea. New aggression against Southeast Asia was in prospect, and the forces in question might prove useful where they were. Why oblige the enemy with a propaganda victory and another military retreat?

The negotiations over this affair during the succeeding weeks were among the least pleasant of my China experiences. We at the Embassy were caught between a series of sharp exchanges which illustrated basic considerations in the conduct of foreign affairs. In the first place, it is important to remember that objectivity should not be looked for in relations between states. What may appear to be objective is more likely to reflect indifference toward a given issue as not touching important interests of the country in question. And on major questions it is too much to expect a government to reverse its position simply in response to a detailed presentation of information by a diplomat whose eyes are of the right color. Most governments today are well informed on matters of importance to them, and national interest, real or imagined, is not sacrificed simply to please a foreigner. Prestige or face are of major importance, and it is essential in persuading another country to change its position that a graceful way out be provided. As the Chinese say, one must have "steps to come down."

The Chinese and ourselves were both quite subjective on the Burmese affair. Their interest was more direct, but ours was based no less on what we considered our advantage. Perhaps the chief difference lay in our primary desire for peace, while the Chinese wanted above all to liberate their country from the communists. Recourse to cruder methods of negotiations, such as the carrot and the stick, remained, but one does not use such methods among friends if he expects to keep his friends. After reviewing the entire subject in great detail and on many occasions with President Chiang, with his able and understanding secretary-general, Wang Shih-chieh, and Foreign Minister Yeh, as well as with the commander of the troops in question, General Li Mi, I endeavored to reduce the whole problem to a balance of relative advantage. In the end I had no choice but to stress the desirability of acceding to this first request of our new administration as an auspicious beginning for continued cooperation. On March 27, 1953, the Chinese government authorized us to inform the government of Burma of its readiness to cooperate in the withdrawal to the best of its ability. In subsequent months nearly 7,000 persons, including a number of dependents, were airlifted to Taiwan. No one could be quite certain of the net advantage of this evacuation at the time, but in the light of subsequent developments on Korea it was all for the best.

Meanwhile, in February, 1953, I was appointed ambassador to China. My friends in the Department had been patient with me and I was properly grateful. Despite all of my fulminations about China policy, it seemed that I was still not a controversial figure. Certain others who reportedly had been considered were less fortunate in this respect, and in the absence of serious opposition I got the job. It was, of course, very gratifying, after nearly twenty-six years of foreign service for the United States. I presented my credentials to President Chiang on April 2. At a press conference the next day I made the following statement:

It is a particular pleasure to meet the press after presenting my credentials to President Chiang.

First, I should like to send to the Chinese people my warm and friendly greetings. I am delighted at the prospect of continuing my close association with them, which has been a most gratifying experience during the past two and a half years.

When I say "Chinese people" I am thinking both of the people of Free China and of their enslaved brothers on the mainland. As Secretary Dulles has said, Americans "never have acquiesced, never will acquiesce in the enslavement of other peoples. We do not accept or tolerate captivity as an irrevocable fact which can be finalized by force or by the lapse of time." The government of China has dedicated itself to the liberation of the mainland from communism. Americans share Chinese hopes for the success of this great enterprise.

At the present time it seems to me especially important that we should distinguish between taking the initiative and undertaking aggression. The first is an essential part of American policy; the second is communist policy. We are building strength —our own and that of our friends—to meet aggression if and where it comes. But taking the initiative need not and must not stop there. There is still much to do in building up the military strength of Free China. Meanwhile we must all exert our best efforts in developing moral strength to reinforce military power until the combined effect is overwhelming. This involves taking and retaining the initiative in the best sense.

Finally, let us bear in mind that among the countries suffering under communist tyranny only China is fortunate enough to have its Taiwan, a bastion and rallying point where hope is being kept alive and preparations made for a better future.

VI

Official American visitors to Taiwan were increasing steadily in numbers. We had a brief visit by Senator John Sparkman, who made an excellent impression, and by Senator Bourke B. Hickenlooper, whom the Chinese regarded as a stanch friend. General and Mrs. Mark W. Clark came in March, followed by Ambassador Robert D. Murphy, who was being transferred from Tokyo to the United States. In cooperation with the Chinese Foreign Ministry we developed a routine which was followed hundreds of times in succeeding months and years. We met visitors at the airport, where military honors were given when appropriate, and escorted them to their quarters. A schedule, prepared in advance, was produced for their approval. An informal briefing at the Embassy and a luncheon or dinner at our house were followed by calls on the President and other Chinese officials, and a social function offered by the Chinese. We tried to limit social affairs to one under Chinese auspices and one at the Embassy, but our hospitable Chinese friends often were difficult to restrain. Depending on the length of a visit, additional briefings and field trips were arranged. Separate programs were arranged as desired for the ladies of a party. President Chiang invariably was generous with his time. In most cases he gave a dinner for the visitors, inviting them to call an hour in advance for a talk before sitting down at the table. Pauline and I were included on all occasions; at times we became almost regular boarders.

Shortly before General Clark's party arrived, we learned that it included a British Major General who was on his staff. No senior British military officer had visited Taiwan since the United Kingdom recognized the communist regime in Peiping. However, the British Consul with a small staff had remained on the island, and we arranged for him to be on hand when Clark's plane arrived. If there were any signs of embarrassment, the Consul was to whisk his Major General away for the duration of the visit. Everything went smoothly on arrival, but the question remained whether the British officer should be included in any official functions. I drove General Clark and the Chinese Chief of Staff, General Chou Chi-jou, from the airport to town and raised the issue en route. Clark asked that Major General Stephen N. Shoosmith be invited to social affairs and General Chou agreed. This included dinner at the President's, where I was gratified to see President Chiang raise his glass in an informal toast to his British guest. More than once British officials had admitted to me ruefully that their actual relations with the government on Taiwan continued to be far better than with the regime in Peiping which they had recognized.

Other important visitors during the spring were Admiral Radford and Assistant Secretary Allison, who was soon to replace Murphy as ambassador to Japan. John Allison's next stop on this trip was Tokyo, and I told him that he should expect our military leaders to argue for a new offensive in North Korea. He recognized that the project was not without attractions. Meanwhile, in United States military terms, Taiwan had been shifted from the territory of the Far East Command in Tokyo to that of CINCPAC at Pearl Harbor. Admiral Radford therefore had new responsibilities which he discussed during his visit. In particular, he took up with President Chiang the question I had raised about letting us know of any plans for offensive military action. The Admiral was satisfied with the assurances he received.

Another welcome visitor, whom I had not seen since our commencement at Princeton thirty-one years before, was Adlai E. Stevenson. In addition to the usual round of calls and social affairs, we drove out in the country to the west of Taipei so that he might get some notion of the beauty and productivity of the island. This also provided opportunity for an informal review of world affairs. I was glad we were in substantial agreement. He was planning to write something on Taiwan for publication, and I agreed to send him a memorandum for possible use.

VII

At this time we had one more flurry over possible offensive action by the Chinese forces on Taiwan. I was instructed to obtain assurance on this score before we would deliver the first lot of jet fighter aircraft to the Chinese Air Force. It appeared that these instructions had been issued without reference to and perhaps without knowledge of the assurances which Admiral Radford and I already had been given and had reported. So we went through it again, arousing considerable irritation in the process, both on the part of the Chinese and at Pearl Harbor. The Navy seemed to suspect that the Department of State was deliberately making trouble. Actually, it turned out to be nothing more than lack of coordination at some level in Washington. My comment at the time to the Department was, "We simply must keep this gap bridged between State and Defense."

There had been many personnel and other changes in Washington during the early months of the new administration and it seemed essential to me to touch base once more. I suggested that I be called home for a brief period of consultation. This was done. A few days before my departure President Chiang invited us to luncheon. Only the President and Madame Chiang, and his secretary, Sampson Shen, were there in addition to Pauline and myself. President Chiang was in a good mood and enlarged on his favorite thesis that China was the key to the world problem. The Soviets were concentrating their aggressive schemes in Asia for the time being, and mainland China was being integrated into their scheme of five-year plans. If China could be liberated from communism, the threat to both Asia and Europe would be largely removed. Of course, he added with a smile, this was the viewpoint of a Chinese.

On May 22, 1953, I started out once more by Northwest Airlines, over the Great Circle route, and arrived in Minneapolis the next day, by the calendar. The short intervening day provided by the International Date Line made spectacularly rapid travel possible but failed to provide an equivalent amount of restful sleep. I was glad to be met by my cousins, Helen and Ellwood Newhart, at the Minneapolis airport and taken to their home for a pleasant evening and a comfortable night. At the airport I experienced my first television interview and saw myself on the screen later in the evening. It might have been worse.

I went on to Washington the next morning and started the familiar routine. One of my first calls was on the new Assistant Secretary of State for Far Eastern Affairs, Walter S. Robertson, the fourth incumbent of that key position since I went to China in 1949. I liked him at once and soon realized that we shared the same sympathies for China and the same desire for a strong and positive Far Eastern policy. He had served at our wartime embassy in Chungking and later on the Marshall Truce Commission. Robertson and I had numerous discussions during my stay in Washington. He was particularly helpful in obtaining funds for two of our most urgent projects: the repatriation of Chinese troops interned in Indochina, to which France had agreed at last, and the improvement of airstrips on Taiwan for both military and civilian use. I felt that our Far Eastern interests could not have been in better hands. Robertson was ably assisted by Walter P. McConaughy, formerly consul general in Hong Kong, who had taken over as director of the Office of Chinese affairs.

VIII

Appointments on Capitol Hill included breakfast with Senator Knowland, luncheons with Senator Margaret Chase Smith and Representatives Robert Hale, as well as calls on Senators Hickenlooper and Frederick G. Payne. At the Pentagon I saw Admiral Radford, whom I arranged to see again at Pearl Harbor on my way back. Also I attended a large briefing session under the chairmanship of the Army's G-2, Major General Richard C. Partridge. Here, as in the Department, I urged the need to define the "mission," as we saw it, of the armed forces of the Republic of China. The beginnings of our military aid program in 1950-52 scarcely went beyond covering minimum needs for defense. Where were we going now? This, of course, was an essential feature of our China policy as a whole.

I called on Under Secretary of State Walter Bedell Smith, whom I expected to scold me about some of my rather heated telegrams on the Chinese troops in Burma. The matter had been handled largely through his office, I was told, and the tone of messages in both directions at times had been barely polite. To my gratification he was most cordial, and passed lightly over the Burma affair. His final injunction as I left was, "Keep your tail up!"

The new Under Secretary of State for Administration was my Princeton classmate, Donald B. Lourie. We had two sessions on the organizational problems of the Department and the Foreign Service. On the first occasion he asked me to review two draft papers on the new set-up for the Foreign Operations Administration, which was to be responsible for our foreign economic aid programs, and the new United States Information Agency. I went over these carefully and gave him my opinion a few days later. The projects were well drawn, it seemed to me, but the conception was unsound. I believed that both agencies should be directly under the Secretary of State, each headed by an under secretary or assistant secretary. Only in this way could we insure that the Secretary of State was in control of foreign policy. Lourie seemed inclined to agree with me.

Secretary Dulles impressed me as a harried man when I called on him for the first time in his new capacity. He quite evidently continued to favor a strong policy in the Far East, but pressures from many quarters, domestic and foreign, were making his position extremely difficult. The old questions of recognizing Red China and allowing it to take a seat in the United Nations were coming to the fore again. I thought that either or both would be disastrous, and the Secretary did not disagree.

On May 31 I called on President Eisenhower at the White House. After a few minutes' wait, General Collins came out of the President's office. We shook hands, and I went in to see President Eisenhower for the first time, in the same room where I had called on President Truman the year before. He greeted me cordially; I conveyed President Chiang's compliments and his thesis that China's liberation was the key to the communist problem, as he had requested. President Eisenhower told me to assure him that he had China very much in mind. He went on to review the Far Eastern situation, and to say that we must not lose Korea, Japan, and Taiwan to the communists. I observed that the free world's position in Asia was such that we could not afford to lose anything more. The President agreed. I then gave him General Chase's greetings, adding that he was doing a fine job on Taiwan, and took my departure.

IX

I flew to Maine for a few days with my father. We drove to Boothbay Harbor for a day and a night; then to the Poland Spring House for a short stay and back to South Bridgton. I went on to Honolulu, stopping over briefly in Seattle en route. The China Club of Seattle invited me to make some extemporaneous remarks at a luncheon on

☆ *Armistice* ☆

June 18, 1953, which was given between sessions of a conference on China being held by the Far Eastern Institute at the University of Washington. I reduced my remarks to paper afterward:

While attending this morning's session of the China Institute I was reminded once more that to Americans the Far East is in fact the Far West. The large and interested audience was appropriately assembled in Seattle because your city looks west toward China.

The traditional European approach to the "Far East," by way of the Mediterranean and India, has exerted a profound influence on our thinking. Yet by air Seattle is closer to the principal centers of the Far East than is Bombay; by sea the advantage is even more in Seattle's favor. So it seems to me important to remember that we Americans do have a different set of problems and, legitimately, a different outlook when dealing with what is to us the Far West.

I am not for a moment suggesting that we are uninterested in the traditional approach as well. The responsibilities of the United States today are world-wide, and we have a very genuine interest in developments in the Near and Middle East, both in themselves and as they affect the Far East and other parts of the world. Certainly I am not in any way suggesting that we should try to "go it alone" in our Far Eastern policy. But in common with its American neighbors looking out over the great Pacific Ocean, the United States shares direct and vital interests in the Far East which need not and should not be complicated by all the myriad problems existing between the Straits of Gibralter and those of Malacca.

It is most encouraging to observe the very real interest being shown in this China Institute, and I want to compliment the organizers on their evident success. I am sure that all of you may be counted on to oppose any relaxation in our present efforts to make America strong, and to preserve a determined, positive, consistent, long-range policy toward the Far East—to us, the Far West.

Honolulu was the next stop. I saw Admiral Radford and members of his staff, and enjoyed another interesting and stimulating series of discussions. An engine went out just before we landed at Guam and I was able to see something of the island while repairs were being made. The American population, it seemed, had become more numerous than the Guamanians, who had largely given up their traditional pursuits of agriculture and fishing to operate shops and services for the Americans. These were largely Navy and Air Force personnel. Labor needed for construction and similar work had to be imported from the Philippines.

Ambassador Raymond A. Spruance, whose reputation as one of our greatest naval commanders had long interested me, was at the airport and took me to his home. Pauline was there, waiting to go back to Taiwan with me. We enjoyed knowing Admiral and Mrs. Spruance, who were perfect hosts. The Admiral and I had several long talks; these impressed me with his wisdom and experience, although we were not in full agreement on China policy. On June 26 Pauline and I flew to Taipei.

X

A serious misunderstanding had developed between Washington and Taipei while I was on my way back. The truce negotiations in Korea were at a critical stage; we were having difficulty in satisfying President Syngman Rhee. Someone in Washington apparently had been persuaded that President Chiang was encouraging the Korean President in his alleged intransigence. An unfortunate message had been drafted in Washington, seemingly without adequate coordination because of our overriding desire for a truce, and transmitted to the Chinese. President Chiang was offended, both because the report of his intervention with Rhee was untrue and because of what he regarded as an implied threat in the message. My first call on him after my return from the United States provided an opportunity to put the matter in a somewhat better light.

When I saw the President with the Foreign Minister on July 1, 1953, I explained that the Korean issue was at an extremely delicate stage and suggested that President Chiang consider the offending message quite simply as a recognition of what might come to pass. In the event that United Nations forces were withdrawn from Korea in the near future, many phases of American policy toward the Far

East would have to be reconsidered, including our policy toward Free China. One conceivable result might be a substantial increase in aid to Taiwan. As evidence of our continuing sympathy I cited two telegrams just received from the Department. One of these, of which I gave the President a paraphrase, was a circular to all of our diplomatic missions abroad, outlining the positive support we intended to give Free China's representation in United Nations bodies and instructing them to seek the views of each government concerned. The other telegram contained renewed assurance that no discussions affecting friendly countries would be taken at the forthcoming Bermuda conference without consulting them.

I went on to describe my conversations in Washington, including that with President Eisenhower. I said that prospects seemed good for accelerated deliveries of military equipment and that in addition to extra funds for airport construction we had obtained a substantial sum to help finance the repatriation of the Chinese troops interned in Indochina. (The Chinese Navy did an excellent job in handling this movement, involving about 24,000 soldiers and 5,000 dependents, but of course there were considerable expenses for fuel and many other items before, during, and after the evacuation.) I hope that I left the President in a better frame of mind.

Meanwhile a grave situation was in prospect on the so-called offshore islands. The Chinese communists had been building up their strength on the mainland opposite the coastal islands still held by Free China, particularly since the truce negotiations started in Korea. Avowed American responsibilities extended only to assistance in the defense of Taiwan and the group of small islands almost in the center of the Strait known as Penghu or the Pescadores. Our military assistance program had been limited to the same area. But the offshore islands were Free China's front line; we could not be indifferent to what was happening there. Only the largest island (variously called Kinmen, Chinmen, or Quemoy, pronounced "Jinmun" in Mandarin, and meaning Golden Gate) was rather strongly defended, partly in deference to its sizable civilian population of over 40,000. The other islands were lightly held by "guerrilla" units, which had been raiding the mainland from time to time and, in general, possessed no weapons besides small arms, grenades, and light mortars. They were in no position to resist large-scale attacks.

The most northerly group, known as the Tachen Islands, were particularly vulnerable, because of inadequate preparation in an otherwise rather strong natural defensive position.

Our military opinion was that if the Chinese really wanted to hold the offshore islands, they should improve their defenses so as to deter anything less than a major enemy assault. Deliveries and training under our military aid program had reached a point where, if the Chinese wished to do so, our Joint Chiefs of Staff had no objection to rotating a few of their regular American-equipped units to the islands. This had been mentioned informally, but no action had been taken and it seemed wise for me to try to bring matters to a head. I called on President Chiang again on July 6, having let him know in advance what I wished to discuss.

I began by referring to a report that had been prepared by MAAG officers after a recent visit to Tachen. The President said that he had read the report, and he led me to a map that had just been hung on a screen in his office. He pointed out the airline distances between Tachen and various communist air bases on the mainland, which ranged from thirty to one hundred miles, while the nearest bases from which air support could be given were on Taiwan and Okinawa, both more than two hundred miles distant. Under these circumstances, he observed, the defense of Tachen against air attack would be extremely difficult. I admitted this, but remarked that similarly exposed islands had held out for months, or even throughout World War II, despite almost overwhelming enemy air superiority. I cited Corregidor and Malta. I said that of course Tachen could not be made impregnable; the communists could take it if willing to pay the price. But, I added, there were very few points around the periphery of the Iron Curtain which were impregnable or could be made so; Taiwan was perhaps the strongest. In every case, however, the prospect of a determined defense could help to deter aggression.

President Chiang then asked me to transmit three requests to the Department. The first was that renewed consideration be given to the formal integration of the offshore islands in the combined defense system for Taiwan and Penghu, which would mean the assumption of direct responsibility by the United States to aid in their protection. Since a decision on this point might take some time, however, the President urged an immediate public expression of United

States interest in the offshore islands as a deterrent to the communists. Third, he asked for early and favorable action on a recent Chinese request for certain shallow draft naval craft for use in the offshore island area.

I told President Chiang that I would be glad to transmit his requests, but added that whatever action might be taken on them eventually, I thought it would be unwise to expect quick results. Important questions of policy were involved, which probably would have to await further clarification of the situation in Korea and might also require consideration by the newly-appointed members of our Joint Chiefs of Staff. Meanwhile, there might be an attack at any time and the Chinese should not look to us for assistance on short notice.

President Chiang made a remark to the effect that to deter an enemy from aggression he should be warned not to step over a given line. I questioned the applicability of this method in all circumstances, particularly in cases like that of Tachen. I asked pardon for suggesting that military men were inclined to be perfectionists. Before determining and announcing a line beyond which the enemy could not advance with impunity, it was right and proper that one's military experts should be consulted. However, they were prone to favor a line that offered optimum possibilities for defense. Their line might be too far to the rear from a political point of view. I suggested this as a partial explanation of our difficulties in Korea, resulting from decisions taken prior to the communist attack in 1950.

I did not think it wise to say so flatly at the time, but I had no expectation that the United States would commit itself to assist directly in the defense of Tachen. As I hinted to President Chiang, there would be too many objections from a technical military standpoint. If the Chinese wanted to defend the islands, their only course was to prepare for the best possible defense with their own resources. Before our conversation ended, the President told me that he was prepared to follow the recommendations in the MAAG report. A regular infantry division was dispatched to strengthen the Tachen garrison, and intensive work was begun on fortifications.

XI

Assistant Secretary Robertson had arrived in Korea on June 25, the third anniversary of the war, and spent much of the succeeding two weeks, together with Ambassador Ellis O. Briggs, in negotiating with President Syngman Rhee. The United States had offered Korea a mutual security pact as well as economic and military aid, and President Rhee finally was persuaded not to obstruct the implementation of an armistice.

Toward the end of May the Chinese communists had renewed their attacks against the United Nations positions in Korea on a considerable scale. At the cost of several thousand casualites on either side, the enemy gained three to four thousand yards over a rather wide front. Their attacks subsided after June 18 but were resumed on the night of July 13, with no less than three divisions assaulting one portion of the central front held by South Korean units. By skillful dispositions General Maxwell D. Taylor, who had succeeded General Van Fleet on the latter's retirement, was able to preserve his line and contain the enemy advance. United Nations forces counterattacked on July 17, and three days later the situation was well in hand. Enemy losses had been tremendous in this final effort. Probably no less than 25,000 Chinese communist troops were killed and twice that number wounded. They had gained some more ground but without seriously affecting our defensive position. When the failure of their offensive was evident, the communist negotiators at Panmunjon became more reasonable and on July 19 agreement was reached on all important points. Within a week the boundaries of the demilitarized zone had been fixed and the armistice was signed on July 27.

The United Nations had thrown back the aggressors and compelled them to agree to an armistice. The communists had made some last-minute gains, which they could represent as a victory. The Republic of Korea had been rescued, its provisional northern frontier restored, and the United States had committed itself to help in case of new aggression. These accomplishments had been accompanied by great sacrifices in blood and treasure. For its part, the Republic of China on Taiwan could now expect to be subjected to increased communist pressures. Also it would have to reconcile itself to the loss of any hope that the Korean War would bring about the downfall of the Peiping regime.

☆☆☆

7: Treaty

WITH THE end of actual fighting in Korea, several of our chronic problems again came to the fore. One of the most serious of these, of course, was the prospect of Red China's being welcomed in many quarters as a reformed character, simply because its hundreds of thousands of "volunteers" had stopped shooting at the United Nations forces in Korea. Wishful thinking about a possible breach between the communist Chinese and the Kremlin also reappeared. On July 29, 1953, I wrote to Ambassador George V. Allen in India:

> Thank you for your letter of July 16 and its enclosures. I think that you and I would agree as to the potentially greater danger to noncommunist Asia posed by Peking as compared to Moscow. Moreover, I believe that many of the more important Chinese officials here would agree with you privately on this score.
>
> I should like to emphasize the word "potentially" in referring to dangers from Peking. In actual fact, there is no evidence to date of any split between Moscow and Peking which would warrant our adopting a policy based upon the assumption of such a development for the foreseeable future. We may speculate about what is going on behind the Curtain, but the obvious facts should not be overlooked in the process. The Soviet Union has done more to build up the military strength of Red China during the past three years than we have done in the same

field for all of our Asian friends put together. With Soviet blessing, communist China has become an open aggressor against its neighbors, and at the same time more than ever dependent on the U.S.S.R. for essential items to support its military machine and civilian economy.

What worries the Chinese Nationalists most, however, is the immediate problem of retaining the support of the United States and trying to avoid or prevent any American action which would imply acquiescence in the communist conquest of mainland China. They are pretty well convinced that the United States is at long last alive to the iniquities of the Soviet Union. But their experience to date leads them to expect us to extend welcoming arms to anyone who shows any sign of avoiding or escaping from the Kremlin's embrace. They firmly believe that the United States would have recognized Red China early in 1950 had it not been for the latter's stupidities in dealing with Angus Ward and with our Consulate General in Peking. They would agree with Edmund Burke when he said, "We have an enemy to whose virtues we owe nothing; but on this occasion we are infinitely obliged to one of his vices." The Chinese Nationalists are fearful that the armistice in Korea will revive this danger, particularly if the communists should play their hand with more finesse this time.

It is also understandable that the Chinese Nationalists are highly sensitive to British and Indian actions, particularly as these influence American policy. They find it difficult to understand why the Indians, whose interests should be the same as theirs, still share with the British an apparent willingness to sacrifice Free China on the altar of appeasement. The Nationalists are convinced—and I share that conviction—that unless mainland China can be liberated in due course from communism, whether of the Moscow or Peking variety, the rest of Asia will eventually go down the same drain.

You were right in distrusting a comparison between Mao and Tito. Another way of putting the matter is that there is almost no basis for comparing China with Yugoslavia. If we should stretch our imaginations sufficiently, it might be possible to suggest that China occupies a position in Eastern Asia roughly comparable to that of France and Germany together in Western Europe. I do not wish to push this comparison too far, but I believe that it gives a fair measure of the precariousness of the free world's position out here. And if India would imagine herself in the position of Italy, with France and Germany in communist hands, it might be healthier than much of the wishful thinking one hears about today.

To sum up, many Chinese here would be afraid that you were right in suggesting that Mao may enjoy a considerable degree of independence from the Kremlin. Whether or not this is actually or potentially true, however, their chief worry is that the United States may accept it as true and, like Britain and India, do the wrong thing about it. Only so long as they are persuaded that Americans continue to regard Mao simply as a Soviet tool will they feel reasonably assured as to our China policy.

II

Admiral Radford had gone to Washington to take up his duties as Chairman of the Joint Chiefs of Staff in mid-1953. We were sorry to lose him from our area, but the appointment was most gratifying to all of us who favored a positive policy in the Far East. Radford's successor at Pearl Harbor was Admiral Felix B. Stump, who arrived in Taipei for an initial visit soon after the Korean Armistice. It was necessary that the mutual confidence and close cooperation established with Radford should continue. I therefore took advantage of my first meeting with Stump to review our common problems, and followed up with a letter to him on August 4:

With reference to our private conversation in my office on July 30, it might be useful if I were to confirm in writing and to elaborate in certain respects on the principal points brought up at that time.

Our directive for MAAG operations, dated April 25, 1951, which is fairly typical of directives for United States government agencies operating here, states that, "United States representatives at country level shall constitute a team under leadership of the Chief of Diplomatic Mission, who is responsible for assuring that United States representatives speak and act in a consistent manner . . . [he] is responsible for the coordination and direction of the entire effort, for ensuring that United States foreign policy is reflected in all operations connected with the furnishing of United States assistance, and for providing coordinated recommendations to Washington."

As you know, we have approximately half a dozen United States government agencies operating on Formosa, each of which reports directly to and receives instructions directly from higher authority in Washington or elsewhere. Altogether these agencies have more than 1,200 American personnel on this island, plus dependents, and including no tactical military forces. My staff at the Embassy consists of only twenty-nine Americans, including seven engaged in purely administrative work and seven Marine guards.

Under the circumstances just described, I am sure you will agree that there is only one practical method of fulfilling my responsibilities: I must in turn hold each local head of every agency responsible for keeping me currently informed and for consulting me in advance of any important action. This method is, of course, open to the objection that practical responsibility is diffused accordingly. The various agency heads on Formosa naturally tend to become absorbed in their particular fields and to regard subjects with which they are dealing as solely political, or purely military, or completely economic, or merely of an intelligence nature. Yet all of us know from experience that every development here of any consequence whatever impinges on all of these fields.

Nearly ten years of experience in operations of this general character have convinced me that there is only one satisfactory standard of relationship between the chief of a diplomatic mission and the heads of other United States government agencies stationed in his territory: in principle, they must have no secrets from each other. I withhold nothing from the Chief of MAAG, for example, and I expect the same from him. Of course, there are many details about which it is unnecessary for us to bother each other, but the principle must be maintained that each has the right to know what the other is doing.

Admiral Stump was a worthy successor to Radford. Relations between the Navy and our Embassy continued to reflect the mutual confidence developed during the two years prior to the Korean Armistice. Recognizing that no rational line could be drawn between American political and military interests in the Far East, we never hesitated to step over into each other's field when there was a practical reason for doing so. Full consultation and basic agreement on policy prevented any serious misunderstandings. Felix Stump proved to be exceptionally gifted, both as statesman and naval officer.

III

The time seemed ripe for another review of our China policy and of the prospects of the government of the Republic of China on Taiwan. I prepared a despatch to the Department, under date of August 20, 1953, entitled, "Prerequisites to a Return to the China Mainland." Excerpts follow:

The present despatch re-examines the logic as well as the conceptional adequacy of present United States aid programs for Free China. The armistice in Korea largely removes any prospect that the United Nations forces now stationed there will again be used offensively in that theater. Such portion of these forces as may be kept in Korea presumably will have no more than a defensive mission, and in due course, no more than defensive capabilities. For the foreseeable future, therefore, the armies of Free China will represent the only ground forces available to the free world in the Far East with actual and quickly expandable offensive power for potential use outside the territory where they are now stationed. Another unique feature of both political and military significance is that of all the countries which have been conquered by the communists, only Free China has been able to retain control of a territory corresponding to Formosa. Considerations such as the foregoing are of particular significance at the present time when there is active support from various quarters for admitting Red China into the United Nations. This step would be accepted throughout Asia as representing acquiescence by the free world in mainland China's definitive loss to the communists. Such official abandonment of any hope that the Iron Curtain might be moved back, almost inevitably would be followed by the expectation that it would move forward and, in due course, engulf what remains of noncommunist Asia. . . .

There are many valid objections to adopting a positive military policy toward the Chinese National Government; there would be many and serious difficulties to overcome. The choice, however, lies between a few difficult alternatives. Of these, a positive policy appears to offer better chances (1) to deter communist aggression and thereby prevent or at least postpone another major war in the Far East, (2) to avoid stumbling into another armed conflict for which the United States is not prepared, and (3) of being in a position to exploit evidences of communist weakness and helping to roll back the Iron Curtain in consequence.

Periodic re-examination of the possibility of a "return to the mainland" by the government of the Republic of China is essential in the development of American policy. This is true for the following reasons, among others:

1. A return to the mainland for the purpose of liberating China from communism is the central aim of all Chinese National Government policy and planning; it is the hope without which morale on Formosa could be expected to collapse.

2. A return to the mainland by the government now located in Formosa is contingent upon support from the United States.

3. The United States cannot commit itself in advance to supporting the Chinese National Government in a return to the mainland, at least not until the prospects for the success of such a project are much clearer and more promising than at present.

4. On the other hand, the United States should not exclude from its planning the possibility of a return to the mainland by the present government on Formosa, or its legitimate successor, under some future circumstances when it would appear to be in the American national interest to support such a return.

If the foregoing numbered statements are accepted, it appears that the United States is justified in continuing its present policy of assisting in the development of military strength on Formosa substantially in excess of minimum defense needs. Only in this way will it be possible to sustain the necessary morale, to obtain the essential degree of cooperation from the Chinese government and its armed forces, and to have at hand a worthwhile margin of offensive military power for various possible uses. . . .

Quite aside from military considerations, the government of the Republic of China is faced with the continuing problems of maintaining its position as the legal government of China and as the regime best qualified to rule all of that great country. This requires astute and strenuous diplomatic and political exertions. It also calls for ever greater and more effective efforts to gain the support of world opinion by establishing its claim to represent the Chinese people. A sustained effort by the Chinese government is essential to improve its fundamental position in this regard, and to persuade public opinion, particularly in the United States, which is supplying political, military, and economic aid, of the extent of its accomplishments in winning a broad base of support among the people of China. Confucius held that of the three essentials of government, obtaining the confidence of the people was the most important, with the provision of food ranking second, and of arms third.

Various criteria have been used by sovereign powers to justify the recognition of another government, including:

1. Whether the government exercises effective control over the territory which its organs occupy;
2. Whether it endeavors to fulfill its international obligations;
3. Whether it enjoys the support of its people.

It may be admitted that the Chinese communist regime exercises reasonably effective control over mainland China. On the second point, however, it has adhered to the well-established communist tradition of ignoring all or nearly all accepted standards of international conduct. The extent to which the Peiping regime enjoys popular support remains, unavoidably, a matter of opinion. Allowance must be made for the presumed fact that a majority of the vast population of China are largely indifferent to political matters. Of those who are politically conscious, however, it would appear that a substantial majority are now in latent opposition, at least, to their communist rulers.

On the basis of the above three criteria, therefore, the Chinese communist regime would qualify for recognition by a foreign power only on the first count at best. The Chinese National Government, however, qualifies for international recognition with respect to the territory it occupies, not only on the basis of its effective control but also by reason of its sincere efforts to fulfill its international obligations, in addition to enjoying popular support to at least as great an extent as any other regime which might obtain control over Formosa and the adjacent islands under present conditions.

There remains the possibility that the communists in Peiping may choose to mend their ways in terms of international conduct, or at least persuade various foreign governments that they are doing so. The immediate practical difference in the positions of the two opposing regimes would then lie chiefly in the ability of each to persuade public opinion, both at home and abroad, that it enjoyed the greater popular support.

Certainly, any considerable expansion of American aid to Formosa, beyond a modest margin over purely defensive requirements, may be expected to be contingent upon evidence of popular support for the Chinese government among the population over which it now rules. If such support is manifestly greater than that available to the communist regime on the mainland, the American government and people may be persuaded that the Chinese National Government could gain the support of the China mainland under certain conditions. The United States could not be expected to favor such action in this direction, however, unless it were satisfied that in returning to the mainland the Chinese National Government could gain the support of the Chinese people to a distinctly greater degree than any alternative regime. Without such popular support there would be little prospect of its ultimate success.

In working toward its chief goal—liberation of the China mainland—it is evident, therefore, that one of the most urgent tasks of the Chinese government is to let the American government and people know more about its actual and potential claims to popular support. This is not a doctrinaire approach to determine the progress of "democracy" in Free China. It may be regarded as simply a realistic precondition to obtaining the amount of American aid and support which Free China desires.

Popular support cannot be measured convincingly by mass demonstrations, parades, banners, slogans, or the editorials of a controlled press. On any such basis communist states easily surpass all others, but the free world knows that these manifestations can be arranged on an imposing scale by governments which are detested by a great majority of their people. Similarly, the population of a country may be peaceful not because they enjoy obeying their rulers but because of the existence of a harsh and oppressive police system. Fortunately, however, there are adequate and practical ways to measure popular support which are applicable to Formosa at the present time.

This despatch covered a broad front and posed more questions than solutions. I invited other officers of the Embassy to draft comments on what I had written. These were considered before the basic paper was put in final form. Some suggestions were incorporated; four of the memoranda prepared by my associates were sent to the Department with the despatch in question. This was a rather unusual procedure, but the subject seemed to warrant it. There was agreement in most cases, but on certain points officers for whom I had a high regard did not share my views entirely. Our differences related chiefly to the degree of optimism or pessimism with which the prospects of the Chinese government on Taiwan could be assessed. Perhaps I was more optimistic than most, but had no wish to underestimate the stupendous difficulties ahead. At the same time, as stated in the despatch, it was evident that the practical task was not to find an ideal solution for China, but to choose between less-than-perfect alternatives.

IV

At the same time I wrote still another brief despatch on that hardy perennial, the question of China's representation in the United Nations. It was forwarded under date of August 24, 1953, and is reproduced here in part:

This despatch is forwarded with considerable diffidence in view of the specialized nature of United Nations' activities, regarding which various persons in the Department and in New York have expert knowledge far beyond that possessed by officers of this Embassy. Technical treatment of the subject has been avoided, and only the broad lines dealt with as they appear from Taipei.

After describing the peaceful Purposes and Principles of the United Nations in Chapter I, the Charter of that Organization states in Chapter II (Membership), Article 4: "Membership in the United Nations is open to all other peace-loving states which accept the obligations contained in the present Charter and, in the judgment of the Organization, are able and willing to carry out these obligations." Experience since the Charter was signed in 1945 has established conclusively that no communist state associated with Moscow qualifies for membership in the United Nations under the clearly stated provision of the Charter. In fact, several of this group of states have, by their actions, made themselves liable to suspension or expulsion under the terms of the Charter.

The question arises whether it would be in the spirit of the Charter and would contribute to the purposes of the United Nations, either to admit additional communist states to membership, or to expel such states as are now members and have qualified for expulsion. Whatever may be said for or against expelling communist members, it may be stated without fear of contradiction in noncommunist circles that, based on past experience, the admission of additional communist states would be more likely to hamper than to help the avowed purposes of the United Nations. The arguments in favor of such admission would, if stated honestly, relate to hopes of appeasement and of economic benefit to the supporters of these arguments rather than to furthering the clearly stated principles and purposes of the United Nations Charter. . . .

It has seemed natural and proper to the United States that

communist governments should be excluded from the United Nations by procedural methods as long as these were effective. When there is indication that they may fail, however, it would appear to be a clear obligation of the United States to oppose such admission on substantive grounds. This obligation becomes of particular importance in the case of (Red) China, the first major country to undertake a deliberate attack upon the United Nations with its armed forces and to be formally branded as an aggressor in consequence. It would require the most convincing evidence of a very tangible character, and over a long period of time, genuinely to persuade the members of the United Nations that the Peiping regime has experienced the fundamental transformation which alone could qualify it for membership in the organization.

There is also to be considered the effect on the remaining noncommunist states of Asia in the event of Red China's admission to the United Nations Organization. Certain of these countries appear to favor such action; others oppose. But all would accept it as representing acquiescence by the free world in mainland China's definitive loss to communist conquest. Depending upon their individual circumstances, all would either seek a larger degree of accommodation with Peking, or prepare to be overwhelmed by force when the communists got around to them.

If, despite all efforts of the United States, Red China were finally admitted to membership, it would generally be accepted in the Far East that the United Nations as such could no longer be expected to function as an agency of collective security. These responsibilities might then be expected to pass definitively to the field of mutual defense pacts and to the regional arrangements foreseen in Chapter VIII of the Charter.

To offset in part the tremendous impact of Red China's success in shooting its way into the United Nations, it would be necessary for the United States to negotiate additional mutual assistance pacts with noncommunist states in the Far East, including Free China. This would best be done quickly, if possible before the formal entry of Red China into the United Nations, since the purpose of these pacts would be largely psychological. More important for the longer term would be the necessity of a speedy and substantial expansion of American military aid programs in the Far East. Nothing short of such measures would have any appreciable effect in keeping hope alive among our friends and in maintaining respect for the United States among both friends and foes. It would also be highly desirable to make clear at the earliest possible moment whether American policy toward communist states is to be one of containment or of liberation.

In pursuing a policy of nonrecognition of Red China and of opposition to its acceptance into the United Nations Organization, the United States government must expect to find itself recurrently in the position of explaining the circumstances under which it might modify this policy. Obviously, a great danger lies here. The exploitation by communist propaganda of the most measured statement on this subject, and the alarm among various noncommunist countries of Asia at any suggestion of accommodation between the United States and communist China, make it of transcendent importance that American policy be stated in the simplest terms.

Technically, of course, there is no necessary connection between the question of American recognition and the membership of Red China in the United Nations, but in the public mind these two are closely related, if not to all intents and purposes identical. In explaining the American position, it may be fortunate that this is true. A case can be made out for extending American recognition to the Peiping regime on the same grounds adopted by the United Kingdom and several other countries. American traditions are somewhat different in this respect, but from both substantive and legal standpoints, the case against Red China's acceptance into the United Nations Organization appears stronger than that against recognition. The United States is in a position to say that it opposes and will continue to oppose the entry into the United Nations of any and all regimes which fail to qualify under the express terms of the Charter. The various counts under which Red China must be excluded could then be detailed in such fashion that all could understand.

It might appear implicit in the foregoing policy that the

United States would acquiesce in Peiping's entry into the United Nations Organization, and presumably extend recognition, at such time as that regime could establish itself as qualified. There would be grave danger in positive statements to this effect by high American officials. But there could be a tacit acceptance of this implication. To qualify fully for United Nations membership under the clear terms of the Charter would require such far-reaching changes in Red China's relationships with Moscow, with the free world, and with the Chinese people, that the China problem would be well on its way to the kind of solution which the United States desires. The Curtain, whether of iron or bamboo, would have been rolled up, and a friendly, stable China would be at hand. The United States should accept no less.

From the propaganda standpoint, there would seem to be considerable merit in representing what now appears to many as a negative position—objection to Red China's acceptance in the United Nations—in the positive light of firm support for the Charter. To place one's opponents in the position of seeming to attack the Charter has the same advantages as making them appear to oppose "peace."

v

Apparently the Department had made no public use of the draft statement on policy toward China which had been submitted in 1951 (see chapter on Consolidation, pages 101–4). It now seemed appropriate to revise this draft slightly, in the light of subsequent events including the Korean Armistice, and to elaborate at the end on present and future United States policy. This was done in a despatch dated September 14, 1953, which included the following proposed summary:

The policy of the United States is to use every effective method of further enlightening the Chinese people on the true nature of Soviet aims, as opposed to those of the free world, while actively extending all practicable assistance to them in regaining their full independence and their administrative and territorial integrity. Meanwhile, the United States will continue to oppose by every feasible means any and all acts of aggression against China's neighbors to which the communist regime in Peiping may lend itself. . . .

The United States intends to pursue these courses of action until peace and security have been re-established and the threat of aggression against the free world has been removed.

VI

At this time a copy of the University of Chicago Round Table Bulletin of September 6, 1953, arrived on my desk. China and Korea had been discussed in some detail, and I was delighted with the cogent remarks of Robert Aura Smith, Far Eastern expert and editorial writer of the *New York Times*. On November 5, 1953, I wrote congratulating him, and added the following:

It is difficult to understand how any honest person can read the Charter of the United Nations (Purposes and Principles; Membership, with reference to entrance qualifications and grounds for suspension or expulsion) and then support Red China for UN membership. . . .

Does anyone honestly believe that the admission of Peking would further the avowed purposes of the United Nations? Isn't there more than ample evidence, based on the consistent behavior of the U.S.S.R. and other communist states, that exactly the opposite should be expected? Why, then do some of our friends support the entry of Red China? I cannot believe that they really want to wreck the United Nations. The explanation seems to be that appeasement, by whatever name it may be called, appears to them the only course remaining.

It probably is true that most of the San Francisco signatories thought that they were establishing an organization which would become universal in due course. There are still arguments in favor of such an organization, but the experience of the past eight years should have made plain to everyone that it would have to be very different from that envisaged in the San Francisco Charter. Unless, of course, we are ready to acknowledge defeat in the great semantic war, and to accept the Kremlin's definitions of "human rights," of "justice," of "social progress," of "tolerance," of "peace," and of other aims set forth in the

UN Charter which still mean something worth-while to many of us.

"Honesty" means something too. Keep up the good work!

Commenting on his reply, I wrote again on November 24:

. . . we should keep Red China out of the Organization by any and all means available to us. . . .

Certainly, neither the wording of the Charter itself nor the intent of the great majority of the signatories foresaw a situation whereby one member of the UN would sponsor the overthrow by force of arms of the recognized government of another member, and then insist that the successor regime be accepted in the organization after it had made a mockery on an unprecedented scale of the purposes and principles set forth in the Charter. Even more astonishing is that some of our best friends concur in what seems to me nothing more than insistence that might makes right.

You are much closer to the UN scene in New York than I and must have a correspondingly clearer idea of the practical effect on the organization itself of the acceptance of Red China into the fold. Out here I am sure that the effect would be to destroy whatever confidence remains in the UN as an instrument of collective security. Even more serious would be the inevitable interpretation that the free world had definitively acquiesced in the communist conquest of China. "Liberation," by whatever means, would have been abandoned as a goal.

You are obviously correct in stating that on the ground of compliance with the Charter the Soviet Union could not be admitted as of now. The same would apply to most if not all communist states. But it does not necessarily follow that the U.S.S.R., or others who are members, should be expelled at the present time. When the Soviets next indulge in some completely scandalous violation of the Charter, which they may be expected to do eventually, I believe that the question of their expulsion should be given active consideration.

It all depends upon what kind of organization we want the UN to be, and whether we should have the courage of our convictions in case the organization takes the wrong road despite our best efforts.

VII

Developments since the Korean Armistice had further confirmed me in the opinion that only by a formal treaty of mutual defense could we expect to maintain among our Chinese friends the morale essential to a long-term program of cooperation. United States support for Free China in the event of military attack or similar threat to its existence was implicit in our actions since mid-1950. Our legal position, however, was unilateral. The aid and support we were giving could be terminated at any time, however unlikely such a reversal of policy might appear. I was convinced that only by a formal bilaterial agreement, which need not go beyond what the United States actually would do in any case, could optimum results be expected from our large-scale aid to the Republic of China.

I knew that the Chinese had been studying our recently initialed treaty of mutual defense with Korea and the text of our earlier agreement with the Philippines. They were keenly aware of the negotiations for a similar treaty between the United States and Japan, which opened in Tokyo in July, 1953. One day the Chinese Foreign Minister remarked to me that they had prepared a draft for a bilateral treaty with the United States, following rather closely the provisions of the Philippine-American agreement. I suggested that their ambassador in Washington give a copy to the Department of State. This was done in October, 1953. Although formal negotiations began several months later, the project of a treaty of mutual defense began to take form from that time.

VIII

In contrast to the custom of earlier years, Taipei was now on the regular route for American officials touring the Far East. Almost every week brought at least one planeload of important civilian or military officers, many of whom had never seen the island before. The most important of these visits in 1953 was that of Vice President and Mrs. Richard M. Nixon. They remained for five days and followed a most strenuous schedule.

I had never met the Vice President and was uncertain how the

186

Chinese public would respond to his well-known informal approach. Moreover, he was to make several speeches during his stay which inevitably would touch upon sensitive topics. We were under instructions to prepare drafts for the Vice President's use on these occasions, and did so with some diffidence. He went over the drafts after his arrival, and we hoped that they were of some use to him. However, he preferred to speak without a written text or notes. Each of his addresses appeared to be extemporaneous, but it also was evident to us at the Embassy that Mr. Nixon had prepared himself assiduously before undertaking this trip and that he gave considerable prior thought to his remarks on each public occasion. There was no other explanation for his carefully balanced encouragement to all resisting the threat of communism and his invariable avoidance of any statement that might give needless cause for worry to his Chinese audiences regarding the precarious state of their country.

Vice President Nixon's handling of crowds on the streets was no less successful than his other public appearances. In my experience, Chinese and other Oriental crowds rarely are spontaneously demonstrative. Of course, they can be organized to put on a big show or incited to violence by fanatics, as elsewhere in the world. It was particularly gratifying, therefore, that in the absence of any organizing effort, thousands of friendly people thronged the streets to see the Vice President of the United States and to shake his hand when offered. Bursts of applause were frequent and evidently spontaneous.

Not even during the few days of Nixon's visit were we to be spared one of our frequent flurries over United States policy toward China. Some remarks by Secretary Dulles were reported in the press and misconstrued in certain quarters as signaling a new and softer line toward the Peiping regime. The Vice President agreed that he must say something before his departure from Taiwan. There was no time to consult Washington, and several of us participated in drafting a brief statement. The final wording and thought, however, were his own. The text was handed to the press on November 12, 1953, the day before he left:

> Secretary Dulles' remarks as reported in the press state nothing new as far as United States policy is concerned.

☆ *China Assignment* ☆

The Secretary discussed two problems—the question of recognition of Red China by the United States and the question of its admission to the United Nations.

On the question of recognition, he says that the United States cannot consider recognition as long as the Red regime: (1) continues to be an aggressor in Korea; (2) promotes aggression in Indochina; (3) conducts itself not in accord with the United Nations Charter.

In effect, what he has said is that the United States will not consider the question of recognition unless Red China quits following communist policy, and quits taking orders from Moscow.

As far as the question of admission to the United Nations is concerned, the Secretary merely stated the regulations affecting membership in the UN. He did not announce any change in the United States position with regard to the question of admitting the Red Chinest regime to UN membership. That position is that the United States will continue to oppose vigorously admission to the United Nations of a government which has waged war against the United Nations, which has on its hands the blood of over 150,000 men from members of the United Nations who were fighting to carry out a United Nations policy, and which at this moment defies and obstructs the United Nations in its efforts to bring peace in Korea.

Altogether, the Vice President's visit to Free China was most successful. His public appearances, his long and frank talks with President Chiang and other Chinese officials, his informed interest in their problems, and his manifest sympathy for their cause all contributed greatly to Chinese confidence in the United States.

IX

The new year, 1954, began auspiciously. Three-quarters of the 20,000 Chinese prisoners of war captured by United Nations forces in Korea chose to come to Taiwan rather than return to Red China. The number was large enough to warrant further conclusions as to what the Chinese people thought of their communist masters. The United Nations Repatriation Commission in Korea had leaned over backward in avoiding any pressure to defect; if anything the encouragement had been in the other direction. Moreover, the soldiers themselves were largely from the interior province of Szechuan. They knew little of politics and less of Taiwan, with which only a handful had any direct connection, but they were quite sure that life under a communist regime was not for them. I met them on their arrival in the port of Keelung and welcomed them in a brief statement (January 27, 1954).

The question of one or more multilateral pacts of mutual defense in the Pacific area was being raised with increasing frequency. Most of the Asian countries potentially concerned seemed to have only one clear-cut concern in common: the fear of new communist aggression. Unfortunately, there also was continuing if somewhat vague distrust of Japan, notably on the part of Korea.

On political and economic grounds it obviously was desirable to present a united anti-communist front, including as many Asian states as possible in association with those Western countries that retained significant interests in the area. Militarily, however, only four of the countries concerned had more than purely local significance: the Republic of Korea, the Republic of China on Taiwan, the United States, and, potentially, Japan. A pact including all four of these countries still would fall far short of counterbalancing communist ground forces (Chinese, North Korean, Soviet) in East Asia; and the air power of the United States and its friends in the region also was quantitatively inferior. Without Japan there could be little prospect of redressing this imbalance in a regional defense pact.

A further complicating factor was that the Asian countries actually or potentially threatened by communist aggression remained divided as to which Chinese regime should be recognized. Whatever second thoughts they had experienced as a result of the Korean War, those who previously had established diplomatic relations with Red China were unwilling to admit their mistake. Fortunately, however, these two groups were located in more or less distinct geographic areas. In the Western Pacific, historically and actually the region of greater American responsibility, the countries that remained outside the Curtain also continued to recognize the regime on Taiwan as the legal government of China. South and west of Thailand, but not including Australia and New Zealand, the Peiping regime was accepted.

At least until confidence could be established between Japan and Korea, therefore, and until Japan was ready and willing to contribute substantially to noncommunist military power, it was evident that bilateral pacts with the United States offered the best hope to peace in the Western Pacific. In Southeast and South Asia, on the other hand, there remained possibilities for regional defense arrangements of limited military significance but of potentially major political importance.

x

In the comments from our various posts in the Far East I was impressed by what seemed to me a tendency to accept as hopeless any prospect for a Pacific Pact, as we were then calling it. Following are paraphrased excerpts from a message that I sent to the Department on February 15, 1954:

> I am prompted by several thought-provoking telegrams regarding a Pacific Pact from various Far Eastern posts to supplement our two previous communications with arguments which might be advanced somewhat in opposition to what appears to be the rather widely accepted view. I agree with most of what has been said, particularly regarding the difficulty of arriving at a satisfactory pact in view of the present relations among the Asian countries concerned; but assuming the United States policy is to regain and retain the initiative, I am reluctant to recommend a negative conclusion in this situation.
>
> In the first place, almost every objection to a Pacific Pact would apply against the European Defense Community, which we support. For a variety of reasons, United States policy in the Far East since the war has generally lagged perhaps three years behind our policy in Europe, but eventually has tended to take a similar path. This should be taken into consideration when describing the Pacific Pact idea as "premature," as has been the custom almost ever since 1945. . . .

☆ *Treaty* ☆

At the end of the war, when the United States held a predominant position in the Far East, it might have been possible to start immediately with a "regional arrangement" as foreseen in the United Nations Charter. If this had been done purposefully but diplomatically, with a clear understanding of the communist threat, which was already quite evident, I believe it is not inconceivable that some or all of the following might have happened:

1. The China mainland or an important portion of it kept outside the Curtain.
2. Great Britain and other noncommunist states prevented from recognizing communist China.
3. The troubles in Indochina kept within Malayan proportions.
4. The Japanese occupation shortened materially and the rearmament of Japan advanced correspondingly.
5. Much better relations today between noncommunist states of East Asia, especially in their attitudes toward Japan, had suitable provision been made for its inclusion, in due course, in the regional arrangement.
6. The war in Korea avoided.

Although admitting freely the highly speculative character of the above, and that it smacks of Monday morning quarterbacking, I consider our present position in the Far East to be so precarious that we cannot afford to overlook anything which offers hope. . . . A start at the present time toward a Far Eastern regional arrangement, to include Japan eventually, should also bring improved relations between the countries concerned. . . .

XI

President Chiang's six-year term of office was drawing to a close. The Chinese Constitution adopted in 1946 provided that the President should be elected by the National Assembly, which in turn was to be chosen by universal suffrage every six years. Of slightly more than 3,000 delegates popularly elected in November, 1947, approximately 80 per cent voted for Chiang Kai-shek in the first presidential election under the new Constitution on April 19, 1948. The new unicameral legislature, or Legislative Yuan, was elected by popular vote in the same year for a term of three years.

The southward sweep of communist conquest made impossible further free and popular elections in all of China. However, more than 500 of the 700-odd members of the original legislature found their way to Taiwan. Their terms of office were extended annually, by decree, beginning in 1951, and the Legislative Yuan continued to carry out its constitutional duties in Taipei. Certainly, it remained the most representative governmental body in all of China.

Obtaining a quorum of the unwieldy National Assembly, which had not been convened in a number of years, was anything but simple. Yet it was necessary, under the Constitution, for the election of a new president in 1954. Extraordinary efforts were made to bring members from various points abroad, and a conscientious study was undertaken to determine how alternates could be chosen for those who were dead or unavoidably absent. A quorum finally was obtained. Minor parties also put forward candidates for the presidency and vice-presidency, but the result was never in doubt. On March 22, Chiang Kai-shek was re-elected for a second six-year term. Chen Cheng was elected Vice President, an office effectively vacant since Li Tsung-jen went to the United States early in 1950.

During March there was an increase of air and naval activity over and around the "offshore" islands held by our Chinese friends. A piston-engined Thunderbolt of the Chinese Air Force on patrol over the Formosa Strait was shot down by a Chinese communist MIG-15, a jet aircraft. The Chinese Air Force had as yet no operational jet squadrons, and this otherwise minor skirmish received greater attention in consequence. Quite aside from technical military considerations, however, I felt that we continued to give insufficient attention to these islands and the surrounding waters. On April 21 I wrote to the Department:

. . . I agree that the Chinese Reds are unlikely to act against Formosa except on their own timetable, but the offshore islands lie outside our announced defense perimeter. These islands undoubtedly are on their list for conquest, and the date may be subject to determination in the light of future events. In any case, it is almost certain that the offshore islands are ahead of Formosa on the list. As matters stand today the communists can take all of those islands if they wish, unless we are prepared to help defend certain of them, which are of particular importance, with U.S. naval and air forces. Are we prepared to do this, or shall we simply dare the communists to attack them and risk their loss in the near future, with consequent damage to the defenses of Formosa and serious loss of face by both Free China and the United States? . . .

Returning to my main point, I realize that a chain of small islands along the Chekiang and Fukien coasts may seem unimportant today in comparison to Indochina and Korea. But they are a part of the same picture, and we in Formosa regard them as having considerable significance for good or ill.

XII

Meanwhile matters had been going from bad to worse in Indochina. Our government had warned that the armistice in Korea must not be allowed to provide opportunity for communist aggression elsewhere in Asia. Yet this was exactly what happened, with Indochina the victim. The situation finally was dramatized before the world by the heroic but unsuccessful stand of French forces at Dienbienphu. It was a widely held opinion among American military experts that the immediate situation could have been salvaged at no great cost. Air support from the United States Navy and other categories of assistance not involving the use of American ground forces, coupled with more active and flexible operations against the communist guerrillas and their supply lines from Red China, offered reasonable prospects of turning the tide.

Apparently, however, the French government had had enough of fighting in Indochina, and others who had been our allies in Korea insisted on peace at almost any price. Obviously we could not go it alone in this case. Dienbienphu fell, and one more communist state came into being by right of indirect aggression in the rich Tonkin delta.

XIII

The idea of a Southeast Asia pact was beginning to take form, urged on by the new and major communist success in Indochina. The

193

Philippines was to be included, logically enough, but not Taiwan. This was no surprise to the Chinese government; British and even French opposition had been anticipated. However, with the Philippines taken care of in another regional grouping, Taipei was concerned lest Manila should lose interest in a more substantial military pact with its northern neighbors. This, in turn, might affect American interests and policy, the Chinese feared. In a message to the Department on May 18, I mentioned once more the greater advantage of an East Asia pact as compared to one based on the "disunited area currently referred to as Southeast Asia." But it was evident that we would have to take second best.

A few days later Secretary of Defense Charles E. Wilson arrived for a visit to Taiwan, accompanied among others by Under Secretary of the Navy Thomas S. Gates, Jr. Military and industrial establishments were inspected and the visitors had three lengthy talks with President Chiang. The President urged that the United States should develop and pursue a policy in East Asia independent of old colonial influences; otherwise failure was inevitable. This was not in contradiction to what I had been advocating, although in my opinion Chiang consistently overestimated the extent of British influence on United States policy.

President Chiang used the occasion of Secretary Wilson's visit to raise the question of a mutual defense treaty between China and the United States. He observed that lack of progress on such a pact was being widely interpreted, particularly in Japan, as indicating that the United States was keeping the door open to future recognition of Red China. The Chinese Foreign Minister interjected that a pact between his country and the United States was prerequisite to a collective security arrangement among the four Asian countries most directly concerned: Japan, Korea, the Philippines, and the Republic of China. However, he recognized that relations between Japan and Korea were such that ten years might be required before they could work together.

Among other topics discussed during Wilson's visit were Chinese proposals to enlarge and strengthen their military establishment, the defense of the offshore islands, and essential clauses in the proposed bilateral defense pact to meet the problems of China, which had no exact counterparts when the United States concluded similar agreements with the Philippines, Japan, and Korea.

Both before and after the visit of Secretary Wilson, the Van Fleet mission spent some time in Taiwan. General James A. Van Fleet, now retired from active military service, had been given the rank of ambassador, with instructions to study and report on our military position in the Far East. He was accompanied by Assistant Secretary of Defense Wilfred J. McNeil, two prominent advisers from business and academic circles, and a staff of senior military officers from the Pentagon. The real purpose of this mission was not entirely clear to us in Taipei, but its presence provided opportunities for much stimulating and useful discussion. The portion of the mission's report dealing with Free China did not become available to us until early December. My initial thoughts were then set down in a letter to General Chase which will be mentioned later.

XIV

Fragmentary information reaching Taipei from Washington at this time indicated that action on a Chinese-American pact was being delayed chiefly because of three problems. The first was that of territorial "scope of application." In other words, the United States would undertake to assist in the defense of Taiwan and Penghu (Pescadores), as it was doing already, but what about the more than thirty Nationalist islands along the coast of mainland China? Secondly, there was the question of former territory of the Republic of China that might be regained, by whatever means, in the future. Foreign Minister Yeh proposed to cover these two points in the pact by a clause corresponding to that in the 1952 treaty between China and Japan, which applied ". . . to all the territories which are now, or which may hereafter be, under the control . . ." of the government in question. Washington considered such a provision too sweeping under the circumstances. They recognized, however, that a pact narrowly and specifically limited to the territory of Taiwan and nearby Penghu would have unfortunate political repercussions throughout East Asia. It would suggest the abandonment by Free China of all hope that the mainland ever would be freed from the communists and might also be taken to imply that the door was being left open to American recognition of the Peiping regime as master of the huge China mainland.

The third troublesome question arising in connection with the proposed pact also stemmed from Free China's great hope and aim of liberating the mainland from communism. The United States shared that hope, but obviously did not wish to commit itself to be drawn into military action as a result of offensive operations initiated by our Chinese allies.

On June 22, 1954, I addressed a letter to Secretary Dulles from which the following paragraphs are taken.

. . . While fighting continued in Korea, of course, Free China had certain offensive capabilities relative to available communist strength. As you know, the military effort of Red China in the Korean theater represented nearly the limit of its capabilities. While maintaining large forces in other areas, the Chinese communists possessed neither the military equipment nor the supply facilities to carry on sustained combat outside Korea, except on a very minor scale. During that period it was quite feasible and desirable that Free China should mount raids on communist-held territory for diversionary and other purposes. Formosa could not only have spared the three divisions, without equipment, which were offered for Korea, but could have undertaken larger offensive operations against the mainland, had the United States been willing to provide naval and logistic support.

During the past year, however, the picture has changed more than most people realize. Communist military strength on the mainland opposite Formosa has grown faster than that of Free China. Future raids on Red territory are liable to be very costly, except for small-scale intelligence and sabotage operations. In fact, it seems prudent to assume that total Chinese communist military strength today is not only greater than that of our friends and allies in this area, but that it is growing faster. Any possibility of significant offensive operations by Free China, therefore, would seem to be contingent upon one or more of the following:

a. Involvement of Red China in large-scale hostilities in another theater.

b. Development of serious internal weaknesses behind the Curtain.

c. Modification of American policies and amplification of aid programs.

The Chinese communists doubtless are aware that **Free China** presents no serious military threat to them under present conditions and that there is no indication of any change in this situation which would be other than to their advantage. . . .

My conversation with the Foreign Minister on June 17 seemed an appropriate occasion to stimulate Chinese official thinking about a possible further commitment on their part not to initiate major military action. . . . The Minister raised the question with President Chiang and later told me that the President preferred to discuss this point only after the conclusion of a bilateral treaty was substantially assured. I am confident, however, that guarantees could be obtained on this point in the event that we should decide to give **Free China** offensive military power, or a bilateral security pact, or both.

A few days later, on June 28, Foreign Minister Yeh informed me that if a mutual defense treaty could be concluded President Chiang would agree to seek the prior agreement of the United States before undertaking any important military action. This was reported to Washington.

xv

At the end of June a telegram brought word that my father had suffered a heart attack shortly after his eighty-sixth birthday. Not long before, William P. Cochran, Jr., had replaced Howard P. Jones as counselor of Embassy in Taipei. Again, I was most fortunate in having an exceptionally able officer to whom I could relinquish charge. With the Department's approval I flew home and found Father resting comfortably in a hospital, but with little prospect of full recovery. After a few days in Maine I went to Washington for what was expected to be a very brief stay. So great was the interest in China, however, that only after three extremely busy weeks was I able to get away. Talks with literally dozens of senators and representatives were on my schedule, in addition to calls on most of the principal officers of the Departments of State and Defense. All of the topics that had occupied us during recent months in Taiwan were reviewed and reviewed again.

In looking over my Washington schedule later, I seemed to be thumbing through the pages of *Who's Who in America*. On one occasion, Admiral Radford and I were the only "outsiders" at a luncheon given by Senator H. Alexander Smith in the Capitol, where thirteen members of the Senate Foreign Relations Committee and eleven members of the Armed Services Committee were present.

The Chinese and all friends of China were greatly heartened at this time by the strong stand taken by both our Senate and House of Representatives. On July 15 the House unanimously adopted a resolution reiterating its opposition to seating Red China in the United Nations and supporting President Eisenhower "in his expressed determination to use all means to prevent such representation." Two weeks later the Senate took equivalent action in approving the foreign aid appropriation bill, by unanimous vote, with a declaration opposing United Nations membership for communist China.

XVI

Eventually I returned to Maine for a week with my father and then took off by air for the Far East. Pauline met me in Tokyo, and we went to Nikko for a few days' rest. Looking from our hotel windows across the valley at the magnificent cryptomeria forest surrounding the Tokugawa Shrine, I was at last able to ponder with some detachment the experience of recent weeks. Here are a few extracts from notes drafted at Nikko and later sent to the Department:

Washington opinion appeared to share that of the Chinese in Formosa that recent developments in Indochina represented a severe defeat for the free world. The loss of Tonkin to the communists, with its highly productive delta and its large population including many thousand Chinese, is looked upon as sufficiently serious. But more important is the psychological effect upon all Asia of seeing militant communism again on the march and the free world in retreat. Of course, the Chinese Nationalists might gain some satisfaction from being able to say, "We told you so." For several years they have predicted that the communists would gain control of all Indochina—without open participation of Chinese communist forces—and eventually all of Southeast Asia and more, unless the United States and France adopted other policies. But any such sense of self-congratulation on Formosa is more than offset by alarm over so obvious an example of the widening gap between communist and noncommunist strength in East and South Asia. Particular concern is felt over the effect on neutralist thinking in Japan, and on fence-sitters everywhere. . . .

The Chinese government on Formosa does not expect an American commitment, either direct or implied, to sponsor its return to the mainland. Rather, it seeks a confirmation of United States intent to assist in the defense of Formosa on a longer term basis, if only by implication, than has so far been admitted. No less important to the Chinese would be the political support implicit in a bilateral pact, irrespective of its exact provisions, which would place them on a par with Japan and Korea in this respect. The Chinese firmly believe that a pact with the United States is prerequisite to their inclusion in any regional security arrangement for the Western Pacific. Without it they would not have the "face" or influence necessary to deal with Japan and Korea. . . .

President Chiang has therefore expressed his willingness, in return for a bilateral treaty, to forego any offensive operations against the communists to which the United States might object.

While in the United States, I noted a revival of suggestions that a line be drawn over which the communists could step only with the certainty that they would be met by armed force. Such action doubtless is appropriate in certain circumstances. Under other conditions it may prove a serious handicap. . . .

In certain regions . . . a defense "line" probably should be indicated only in terms of a general area. The islands in Nationalist hands along the China coast opposite Formosa are a case in point. It is highly desirable that they be kept out of communist control, yet the United States presumably should not commit itself in advance to war with Red China over, say, White Dog Island. Public statements and military action in such connection should be calculated to deter the enemy from aggression to the maximum degree possible without involving unnecessary advance commitments by the United States. . . .

During my recent visit to Washington I was impressed by gloomy predictions from many sides that we were now about to lose the rest of Asia to the communists. With this I disagreed, pointing out that in all probability we should be at war again in the Far East long before communism had taken over completely in that region. . . .

Under the circumstances, I said that the most important and urgent practical step for the United States was to give offensive capabilities to reliable anti-communist Asian ground forces. Eventually Japan, and to a much smaller degree the Philippines, could contribute in this connection. Something might be done in Southeast Asia as well, but none of these areas would have significant military strength in the immediate and vital future. Only Korea and Free China could produce quick results in the form of ground forces which, with American air, naval, and logistic support, could defeat communist China if war should come. Moreover, I believed that the early creation of such anti-communist Asian strength offered the best hope of avoiding another large-scale war in the Far East. No more effective way could be found of influencing developments behind the Curtain. And if war should come anyway, we would be ready.

Influenced apparently by our experience with President Rhee, I noted some concern in Washington lest our Asian friends misuse such offensive power as we might give them and thereby involve us in unnecessary hostilities. I pointed out that not only could we obtain commitments in this connection but that we also should retain in our hands the means to enforce them, such as through the control of ammunition and supplies in general, as well as the possibility of withholding essential air and naval support. In any case, I pointed out that the Soviets had given their satellites offensive power and seemed able to exercise effective control. If we were unable to do the same with our friends, then the future of our country was dark indeed and our entire foreign aid policy should be reconsidered. . . .

It has been widely assumed that the Chinese Nationalist

forces on Formosa and nearby islands possess substantial offensive capabilities. This, of course, is not true. Conceivably they could transport, with their own facilities, one division at most for operations outside the area now under their control. The Nationalist military establishment today is, basically, that which happened to be located on Formosa and several small islands when the Korean War broke out in 1950. These forces have since been reorganized and given additional training and equipment. They have received only about half of the equipment programmed for them on the basis of their size. In effect, therefore, although perhaps twice as large in numbers as would be necessary for a purely defensive mission on Formosa and the Pescadores, the Chinese Nationalist Army is little more than half equipped. Nevertheless, this army, along with the Chinese Air Force and Navy, constitute the best balanced anti-communist military force in the Far East.

Potentially, the Chinese Nationalist military establishment could be given very considerable offensive capabilities within the critical period of the next one to three years. Good manpower is available on Formosa to increase the present establishment of about 625,000 by at least 50 per cent, in the form of ready reserves or otherwise. When fully equipped and trained, this force could provide up to three Chinese field armies of 150,-000 men each for overseas operations, and still leave one field army behind for defense. Such an expeditionary force would be supported by relatively small but efficient Chinese air and naval forces. Obviously, however, so large an operation would be dependent upon American logistic support, as well as the provision of any necessary United States air and naval assistance.

A Chinese military establishment such as that just described presumably would have the capability of defeating any force which the communists could support in South China within the next few years. Similarly, the Koreans probably could be given the capability of at least pinning down any force which the communists could support in North Korea while engaged with the Nationalists in the south. Under such circumstances, American naval and air power could be decisive in defeating communist China without committing United States ground forces.

☆ *China Assignment* ☆

"Would the Formosans fight on the mainland against the Chinese communists?" This question has been asked frequently, since three-fourths of the manpower on the island is Formosan. No definitive answer can be given before the event, but experience and facts are available for a reasonably confident estimate.

The population of Formosa is over 98 per cent Chinese, of whom nearly 80 per cent were born on the island and are therefore called Formosans. A majority of the latter were born under Japanese rule but have retained their predominantly Chinese characteristics: language, customs, etc. The chief distinctions between the average inhabitant of Formosa and of the China mainland today are that the former is in better physical condition, has had more education, and enjoys a higher living standard. Basically, Formosans are simply the Chinese of one of the provinces of China.

Past experience has shown that Chinese soldiers from Manchuria sometimes fought well in South China and sometimes badly. Cantonese have at times distinguished themselves on the battlefields of Central and North China; sometimes they have not done so. In either case, the explanation appears to lie in the quality of leadership, training, and equipment rather than in place of birth. It seems reasonable to assume that the same considerations would apply to Formosans. . . .

Given sufficient time, it is to be anticipated that under communist rule mainland China will build a military machine powerful enough to overawe any and all of its neighbors. On a comparatively short-term basis this development can be offset in large part by sufficient American aid to Formosa and Korea. Unhappily, there is little prospect of correspondingly adequate accomplishments in Japan. Assuming, then, that no major war will intervene, what kind of a Japan does the United States envisage, economically and militarily, three, or five, or ten years hence? A reasonably adequate answer to this question is prerequisite to corresponding answers for Formosa and Korea.

The plain fact seems to be that no satisfactory long-term solution is available for the military and economic problems of Japan, Korea, and Formosa as long as mainland China stays in communist hands. Only when Japan can resume her appropriate economic role on the China mainland—obviously impossible under communism—and when the threat of military aggression in East Asia can be at least substantially reduced, would it appear that a healthy economic and social life can develop in the Western Pacific without massive and continuing American military and economic aid.

As regards Chinese representation in the United Nations, the Secretary's July 8 statement to the press was excellent and should serve as a basis for any further official pronouncements on the subject. . . . Along the lines of the Secretary's statement, the United States might eventually find it necessary to indicate its willingness to consider a revision of the Charter which would make the United Nations a truly universal body, but it could be pointed out forcefully at the same time that the experience of recent years amply proved the futility of expecting such a body to foster collective security.

In the case of China, it is not impossible that a government may come into power on the mainland with which the United States could develop satisfactory relations. There is no present indication of such an event, and it would be a serious mistake to expect it. But the possibility should not be excluded. How, then, can it be determined whether a sufficiently profound change of regime has taken place? Vice President Nixon suggested, "When they stop being Communists." President Chiang Kai-shek once proposed, "When the Iron Curtain has been rolled up." Certainly, until some such drastic change has taken place the United States must exert the greatest care neither to give comfort to the Peiping communists nor to undermine the position of the government on Formosa.

Possibly the determination as to whether a new Chinese regime can be dealt with in normal fashion will appear from its attitude toward the government now established on Formosa. General Marshall's mission was soundly conceived with one important exception: it overlooked the nature of all that communism had come to mean. An honorable regime on the mainland, genuinely devoted to peace and the welfare of humanity, should have no great difficulty in coming to terms with the government of the Republic of China which the United States continues to recognize.

Unfortunately, the great encouragement given to the Chinese Nationalists and others by public statements such as that of the Secretary on July 8 is largely vitiated by other authoritative pronouncements from time to time which include qualifying phrases such as "under the circumstances," or, "for the time being." American assurances have thus come to be looked on by the Chinese as little more than reprieves; they have come to regard the eventual American acceptance of the Peiping regime as even probable. Thus, the "two Chinas" scheme would come first, followed by the withering away of the government on Formosa unless a general war should intervene. Hence the great interest of the Nationalists in a bilateral treaty with the United States which would extend, at least by strong implication, longer than "for the time being."

The larger aim of liberation obviously must be handled with circumspection, but there is no evident reason why the United States should evade this issue. Certainly the communists have not been shy about announcing their goals, and they have gained strength in the process. While assuring the rest of the free world that the United States does not intend to initiate a war in the interest of liberating enslaved peoples, or for any other purpose, it is essential also to avoid reassuring the enemy that he need have no fears whatever. . . .

In the particular case of China, it would seem wise for the United States at the present time neither to underwrite nor to exclude the return to the China mainland of the Nationalist Government now on Formosa. It should be sufficient in a political sense for the United States to share with that government the desire that China should be united under a democratic, stable, peaceful regime, genuinely anxious to maintain friendly relations with the free world. No communist regime would meet these qualifications.

XVII

On September 3, 1954, only a few days after our return to Taipei, my father died. On the same day the communists began a heavy artillery bombardment of the islands of Kinmen (Quemoy) and Little Kinmen. Two United States Army officers, members of our Military Assistance Advisory Group, were killed—our first casualties from enemy action since the Chinese government moved to Taiwan. The Chinese Air Force replied to the Red bombardment by bombing communist artillery positions on the mainland. In addition to our telegraphic reports, I wrote as follows to the Department on September 5:

Rightly or wrongly, I do not take the present fracas around Kinmen very seriously from a purely military standpoint. I may be wrong, and certainly no one can be entirely sure of what is going on inside communist heads at any given moment. But my guess is that they are simply trying us out, taking advantage of the coincidence of the Manila Conference and the summer "invasion season." If they can make it appear to all and sundry that the United States is unable or unwilling to do anything about these offshore islands, the Reds will have won another round.

The Kinmen bombardment called world attention to the hostile intent of the Chinese Reds more effectively than anything else they had done since the Korean Armistice. The Manila Pact or Southeast Asia Collective Defense Treaty, signed on September 8 by the United States, the United Kingdom, France, Australia, New Zealand, Pakistan, the Philippines, and Thailand, was given more meaning and urgency. The potential as well as the actual dangers confronting the Chinese offshore islands were brought forcibly to high-level attention in the United States. Clear and careful thinking resulted. We could hope and believe that our two officers on Kinmen had not died in vain. Their bodies were flown direct to the United States; we held a simple memorial service for them in Taipei.

On his way home from signing the Manila Pact, Secretary Dulles, accompanied by Senator H. Alexander Smith among others, stopped over in Taipei. There was a lengthy session with President Chiang. Secretary Dulles was in good form, as usual, and gave a remarkably clear exposition of recent events, particularly in connection with the new Manila Pact. The Secretary seemed to me at his best on such occasions. His delivery left something to be desired and, at times, it was not easy to catch his words; but the breadth and logic of his presentation were no less impressive than his concurrent sensitivity to the thoughts of his principal listeners. President Chiang also was in good form. He put Free China's case in such reasonable terms that no fair-minded man could have seriously objected. I am sure that the two men parted with even greater mutual respect than they had enjoyed before. Excerpts from my letter of September 13 to the Department are given here:

As you know, Secretary Dulles visited us for five hours on September 9. The time was very short, but the visit was extremely valuable nevertheless. I had no opportunity to see the Secretary alone, and such briefing as I was able to provide was limited to conversation in the presence of others while driving to and from the airport. What the Secretary was able to glean from the visit I cannot say, but the fact that he came here directly from the Manila Conference, together with the sympathetic and considerate attitude which he showed toward the Chinese at all times, served our cause in Formosa very well. . . .

When we left the President's house to return to the airport, I asked Senator Smith and General Chase to exchange cars so that the latter could brief the Secretary on the military situation at Kinmen, which so far had been mentioned only incidentally. As a result, Chase and I were with the Secretary during a thirty-five minutes' drive to the airport. Chase gave him a full and rather optimistic description of the military situation, and added the recommendation that we announce our intention to help the Nationalists defend the offshore islands. I remarked that of course this would entail certain difficulties; for one thing some of the islands probably were indefensible militarily. I thought that it would be best simply to keep the communists guessing, and to give authority to United States military commanders to extend assistance wherever it was considered necessary and desirable, most likely in the form of air support from carriers. General Chase added that naval gunfire also would constitute very valuable support under certain conditions.

Referring to what had been said in conversation with President Chiang about the scope of application of a bilateral treaty, I remarked to the Secretary that it should be possible to find a mutually satisfactory formula. For example, I thought that the treaty might specify only Formosa and the Pescadores by name, but could extend also, "subject to mutual agreement, to any territory which is now or may hereafter be under the control of the government of the Republic of China."

As regards the desirability of tapering off Nationalist (air) attacks in the Amoy region as soon as enemy action permits, I believe you will agree that this is a matter which conceivably could represent the difference between a continuation of the present situation and the involvement of our country in open war with Red China. Last week, prior to the Secretary's arrival and entirely on my own initiative, I expressed to the Foreign Minister on two occasions my concern lest the Nationalist attacks be carried further than could be justified. He took up the matter with the Acting Chief of the General Staff, who remarked that he understood our military representatives to be taking quite a different stand. I then discussed the question with General Chase, and some two days after the Secretary's departure MAAG received instructions from Admiral Stump to follow much the same line I had taken. Fortunately, our government now seems to speak with one voice in this important case, although I have heard nothing from the Department.

XVIII

I continued to believe that the communists had no intention of mounting a major attack against the offshore islands for the foreseeable future. Repetition of this opinion was not always easy to harmonize with my desire to keep Washington's attention focused on the islands as an area of continuing and major psychological importance. The Chinese, it seemed to me, were exaggerating the military danger, both to be on the safe side and to gain maximum support from the United States. On September 30, 1954, I wrote to an officer of the Department of State:

First, let me say that I am highly gratified by what I have

seen of Washington's handling of the (offshore islands) matter since things began to warm up again late last month. Whatever else the communists may have had in mind, it seems obvious that they were probing for signs of weakness on the part of the United States and/or the Nationalists. That the first major artillery shelling coincided with the early stages of the Manila Conference was no accident. Nothing would have pleased the Reds more than to have some United States spokesman come out with a statement that under no conditions would the Seventh Fleet go to the aid of Kinmen, etc. One may imagine the effect this would have had, not only on the Chinese Nationalists but also on other noncommunist Asian countries who were and are watching to see whether we mean business.

On the other hand, a formal, public undertaking to help defend any and all of the 30-odd islands in question may be unwise. Many of them probably are indefensible militarily against a determined attack, due to geography and topography. This, however, is no reason for "writing them off" publicly, either explicitly with reference to all of the islands collectively, or by implication in a public statement of our interest in certain islands which the communists would interpret as meaning that they could attack the others with relative impunity.

The six islands mentioned in my telegram (Kinmen and Tachen are both "double" islands) are those on which regular Chinese military forces are now stationed; they are in general the most important. I believe that the Seventh Fleet should have authority to give any practicable support that might seem necessary to hold these islands. This would mean air support and bombardment by naval guns; as matters stand, it presumably would not mean flying American aircraft over the China mainland except, perhaps, in "hot pursuit." If, however, ships of the Seventh Fleet were attacked by Red aircraft, which is most unlikely, our planes obviously should be free to bomb the communist air base concerned. Judging by our Korean experience, and that on the offshore islands to date, the enemy will be chary of using his aircraft over the islands in question, let alone attacking the Seventh Fleet.

While I favor extending any necessary and worthwhile help

to the six islands mentioned, we should not limit our interest to them. Moves by the enemy, including possible air activity in new areas, might make other islands important to us. This would seem particularly likely if one or more of the six were lost to the Reds; positions on others nearby might take on much greater importance in consequence. All of this favors the course of action we have taken publicly to date: keeping the enemy guessing but maintaining a firm front. . . .

In conversation with several recent visitors, including Admiral Pride of the Seventh Fleet on September 25, President Chiang has expressed much concern over possible heavy losses resulting from a campaign of attrition by the Reds against the offshore islands. He does not expect them to use their air force against Kinmen, he says, but rather to employ a series of mass seaborne attacks. The communist losses would be very heavy, but the President notes that they do not mind losing men. Ground forces available to the Nationalists, however, are limited and the necessity of continuously reinforcing Kinmen, or other islands, might constitute a serious drain. Quite a different kind of attrition was foreseen recently by Foreign Minister Yeh. He thought that Red air attacks on the Chinese Navy in the Tachen area could inflict grave losses on the latter. Tachen is too far from Formosa for the Nationalists to provide effective air support; the supply and defense of the island, other than against actual landings, is largely a Chinese Navy responsibility. Carrier-based aircraft from the Seventh Fleet could, of course, change this picture completely.

So far there is no tangible evidence to support the President's opinion, except the negative item that the enemy air force has not appeared. The Red artillery fire recently directed at Big and Little Kinmen has been heavy at times but poorly directed and ineffective. Nationalist casualties have been all but negligible. However, as Admiral Pride admitted to the President, we guessed wrong in Korea in November, 1950; now we must try to be ready for anything.

Military opinion here seems to be that Big and Little Kinmen could be taken by the communists at any time of year, without the use of their air force, if they were willing to lose enough men. Various other islands, however, such as the Tachen group, are surrounded by so much water, which is rough so much of the year, that we refer to the "invasion seasons." By this is meant the weeks immediately before and after the typhoon season, usually May-July and a short period in October.

Frankly, it does not seem likely to me that the Reds will put forth a major effort to take any of the more important islands in the near future unless their probing should reveal serious United States or Nationalist weaknesses, psychological or otherwise. They have the advantage of the initiative, however, which always works against the side tied down to defensive positions. The communists may have a go at some of the minor islands, of course, and it probably would be well for the Nationalists to play the same game, if only for psychological reasons.

XIX

As it turned out the offshore islands were receiving rather more serious attention at that particular moment, in the Department and elsewhere, than we in Taipei had either anticipated or desired. It was proposed to submit the question to the United Nations Security Council, as a matter of urgency. The plan was for New Zealand to introduce a resolution, with the support of the United States and the United Kingdom, calling for a cessation of hostilities in the Formosa Strait. It was hoped that the Chinese government, as a member of the Security Council, would go along with whatever course of action we might propose, on the assumption that the Soviets would oppose such action in any case. The communists would thus be placed in the wrong once more before world opinion, and another procedural victory gained for our side. The Chinese had not yet been informed of this project when my views went to the Department on October 5, 1954. Paraphrased excerpts from my telegram follow:

Although it is difficult to foresee all aspects of the Chinese reaction to this proposal, I feel it is only prudent to expect a violently unfavorable reception. My own comments follow:

(1) The Chinese probably will believe that the primary motive of the United States is to appease Great Britain—to them

almost synonomous to appeasing the communists—which could have an all but disastrous psychological and perhaps military effect upon Free China and correspondingly benefit the Chinese communists.

(2) It is unlikely that the Chinese government will be attracted by the alternative of a possible procedural victory in the United Nations (should the communists reject the proposal), when placed against the almost inevitable opening of new opportunities for the communists to exploit the whole situation both within and without the United Nations.

(3) The Chinese are likely to interpret the placing of the question before the United Nations as not only intended to appease Great Britain, but also as evidence of the desire of the United States to evade direct responsibility for these (offshore) islands. (The communists may be expected to take a similar view.)

(4) The conquest of some or all of the islands by the Chinese communists might be precipitated if the initial effect of the proposal is to encourage the communists and discourage Free China. While the question is before the United Nations, the Chinese would not expect the United States to take effective action and they could look to no one else for help to hold or retake the islands. . . .

Apparently, the proposal in question has already been agreed upon (with Britain and New Zealand). There remain only considerations of timing, and possible previous or concurrent action which might mitigate the effect of the proposal or, over the long run, tip the balance in favor of the United States and Free China. It is in this sense that the following recommendations are made:

(a) The Chinese government should be informed as soon as possible of the proposal to take the question of the offshore islands before the United Nations, prior to the occurrence of a leak, and in a manner which suggests consultation rather than ex post facto notification. However, this should not be done before the two suggestions listed below are acted upon.

(b) Immediate allocation of increased aid to Free China for FY 55 (over FY 54) which would be sufficient to permit significant expansion of the military program (reserve training, etc.), at least comparable to Korea, would best convey . . . reassurance. . . . So far, all official information given to the Chinese suggests a cut in aid for FY 55, with a depressing effect which would be compounded by the impending action in the United Nations.

(c) Nothing less than an immediate undertaking to sign a mutual security pact covering Formosa, the Pescadores, and in appropriate fashion, other areas under the Chinese government's control, could serve to reassure the Chinese that the (New Zealand) proposal does not forecast a lessening of the determination of the United States to help defend Free China.

I recommend that action on the (New Zealand) proposal be postponed until November, when the weather here is more favorable to defense, and in any case until action has been taken upon the two above suggestions. This is on the assumption that the proposal is more likely than not to precipitate successful communist operations against the islands. Since the course of events probably will compel the United States to take the above steps (b and c) eventually, why not now?

It appears implicit in United States agreement to submit the question of the islands to the United Nations that (Nationalist) guerrilla activities must be completely liquidated beforehand. In my opinion, the development of significant offensive power on Formosa, which it might never be necessary to use, will have far more influence on the China mainland, on the offshore islands, and in the Far East as a whole, than any feasible guerrilla or commando operations or bootleg blockade conducted from the (offshore) islands by the Chinese government. I am already on record in the Department as being unenthusiastic about guerrilla raids against the mainland since the Korean Armistice ended their diversionary value.

Since the Department was already committed to the "New Zealand Resolution," as it was being called, a major effort was decided upon to persuade the Chinese not to oppose the scheme. I was not authorized to discuss it with them; Assistant Secretary Robertson and Walter P. McConaughy, Director of the Office of Chinese Affairs, flew from Washington to Taipei in a special Constellation aircraft. I joined them at talks with President Chiang and other Chinese officials during a total of seven hours, while the New Zealand project was explained. The Chinese reaction was what I had predicted, and the whole plan came to nothing. In addition to other factors, the Chinese were concerned lest the communists should fail to oppose the resolution, although with no intention of abiding by it. This could help Red propaganda to represent the government on Taiwan, assuming that it also failed to oppose the resolution, as having abandoned all hope of seeing China liberated, and hence without any adequate reason for continued existence. Fortunately, however, the Soviet and Red Chinese reaction was so uncompromising that any criticism of the Republic of China, because of unwillingness to participate in what it considered spurious cease-fire negotiations, was avoided.

XX

Foreign Minister Yeh traveled to Washington for the first stage of the treaty negotiations. The most troublesome points already had been resolved in principle. Scope of present and future territorial application was to be covered by specific mention of Taiwan and the Pescadores (Penghu), with an added sentence providing that other territories could be included by mutual agreement. In a separate exchange of letters the use of force by both parties from the areas in question would be a matter of joint agreement, subject to emergencies involving the inherent right of self-defense.

However, there were numerous other hurdles to be negotiated before the agreement could be signed. With the exceptions noted, the existing draft resembled closely the treaties of mutual defense that we had concluded with other countries in the Western Pacific. It was provided that in the event of an armed attack against the specified territories of either party, each would act to meet the common danger in accordance with its constitutional processes. The nature of the action was unspecified in this case, since the draft treaty necessarily was somewhat vague on several points. Although it was important to do the best drafting job possible, many of us considered the details as incomparably less important than that a treaty should be accomplished. The presence of Foreign Minister Yeh in Washington during this period, therefore, was invaluable. The able collaboration that he received from Assistant Secretary Robertson, Walter P. McConaughy, and others in the Department was no less gratifying. Similarly close coordination was maintained in Taipei between our Embassy and Acting Foreign Minister Shen Chang-huan. Chinese and American communications personnel, both in Taipei and Washington, were the principal sufferers as our radio traffic mounted steadily.

The Mutual Defense Treaty between the United States and the Republic of China was signed at Washington on December 2, 1954. Accompanying letters were exchanged on December 10, by a vote of sixty-four to six the Senate gave its advice and consent to ratification of the treaty on February 9, 1955, the President ratified it on February 11, and the ratifications were exchanged with China on March 3, thereby bringing it into effect. The Republic of China had its treaty at last, and the United States now had, among other things, a substantial basis for a positive and continuing China policy.

☆☆☆

8: Problems

I

No ONE expected the conclusion of a treaty of mutual defense between the United States and China to solve all of our problems. In fact, it had the effect of shifting emphasis to several long-range questions that previously had been overshadowed by current events during our somewhat *ad hoc* course since 1950. Now that there was a basis for greater mutual confidence and a better opportunity to look ahead, we could expect to be plagued anew with proposals to "solve" all of our remaining problems by such seemingly simple means as formal acceptance of "two Chinas," both of which would be represented in the United Nations, or by abandoning the offshore islands and their 80,000 civilian inhabitants to the communists. There was also the chronic difficulty of harmonizing hopes for liberation with the renunciation of force.

In all of this complex picture, large sections of the world press would be unhelpful, not at all due to ill will in most cases, but because the all but unprecedented problems of China did not lend themselves properly to casual and sporadic journalistic treatment. Many questions about China, by their very nature, could not be answered honestly by a simple yes or no. Neither Chinese nor Americans nor anyone else knew all the answers. One of our chief concerns, of course, was that the net effect should not be defeatist and isolationist.

There was a continuing and natural tendency to center attention on the locus of the most excitement at a given moment. When the communists were temporarily quiet in the Middle East or Southeast

Asia, for example, and chose that time for a bombardment of the Chinese offshore islands, prominent press correspondents would converge on Taipei. For a few days we would make the front pages. Politicians and editorial writers in various countries would point to the dreadful situation in and around Taiwan. Drastic and urgent proposals would be advanced, often if not usually at someone else's expense. Then the shooting would stop and the Reds would push a button elsewhere. The Fourth Estate would pack their bags and fly away. Their editors would forget about Taiwan, except for incidental references to the "relaxation of tension" in our region, which misled many into believing that there had been a basic change for the better.

On November 17, 1954, I wrote to a friend in the United States:

I have been intending for months to acknowledge your thoughtful letter of April 10 and in particular to comment on the two books about China which you mentioned, Ted White's [*Thunder Out of China* (New York: Sloane, 1946)] and Jack Belden's [*China Shakes the World* (New York: Harper, 1949)].

As you know, books on China are legion, but most of them reach a relatively small reading public. In general, the best sellers in recent years seem to have been the products of journalistic pens with what many would call a leftist slant. In fact, efforts have been made to show that certain prominent American book publishers, as well as various newspapers and periodicals featuring book reviews, have played up publications on China which favored or at least paralleled the communist line, while trying to discredit Chiang Kai-shek and the so-called Nationalists.

All of this is important if it resulted from a deep-laid Red plot; it is far more important that, whoever was behind it, the American public appears to have been misled and our foreign policies influenced in the wrong direction. I shall not attempt to prove that any particular book was communist inspired, nor shall I call anyone a communist simply because I happen to disagree with him. Meanwhile, it may be profitable to look for other possible explanations.

Probably few Americans today would admit to being isolationists, but the tradition is still strong in fact. It is easier to strike a sympathetic chord by criticising foreigners than by praising them. The mess in which so much of the world finds itself today is therefore most popularly and convincingly explained by blaming the various foreign governments in power, whether communist, "fascist," or what have you. None of this, of course, could be in any significant degree the fault of the United States—except temporarily and not too convincingly during an American election campaign. It is all due to those corrupt and otherwise rascally foreigners!

In books such as White's and Belden's the American reader finds in combination a highly readable journalistic style, the attraction of a slumming expedition which makes him feel superior but in no way guilty, and just enough vague idealism to persuade him that the Chinese people would work things out eventually if we were to stop mixing into their affairs. This brings us full circle back to isolationism: seeking excuses for taking no action.

What is missing from this picture? First and foremost there is an almost total lack of recognition of the nature and danger of the global communist conspiracy which threatens us. Something of a case might be made for our leaving a given country alone if the Soviet Union would do the same. Very cleverly, communist propaganda ever since World War II has persuaded important segments of American opinion that we were mistaken in supporting this or that foreign government; it was too reactionary, too corrupt, too backward. Conditions were hopeless and there really was nothing we could do but get out. But the moment we show signs of weakness and uncertainty the communists step in. They are not inhibited by any fear that their well tried formulas of regimentation and terror will fail to control a situation once the Western world, and particularly the United States, has abandoned a positive role in that region. The communists do not admit to being so incompetent in world affairs as many American writers and lecturers would have us feel.

There are, of course, books on China by journalists and others which are at least as accurate in detail as White's and Belden's, yet lead to diametrically opposite conclusions. As regards Formosa in particular, I might mention Henry Bate's *Report from Formosa* [New York: Dutton, 1952] and Geraldine Fitch's *Formosa Beachhead* [Chicago: Regnery, 1953]. On the more substantial side are Herbert Feis' *The China Tangle* [Princeton, 1957] and John L. Stuart's *Fifty Years in China* [New York: Random House, 1954], which last I recommend especially. But I fear that none of these has the qualities mentioned earlier which would make it a best seller.

I believe that White's *Thunder out of China* and his recent *Fire in the Ashes* were both Book-of-the-Month Club selections. That means, presumably, that they have been read by several hundred thousand thoughtful Americans. In so far as these books contain significant and accurate information, which both of them do to an important degree, they serve a useful purpose. But it is most unfortunate, in my opinion, that the conclusions and recommendations parallel so closely just what the communists would like to have Americans think and do. Circumstances may force us to adopt certain of these courses of action, but in general I believe that we should follow a strong and positive policy of our own, which in most cases would be quite contrary to communist desires. When an American recommends otherwise under present conditions, I question his judgment.

II

The first major testing of the treaty came within a few weeks after its signature, and before it had been approved by the United States Senate. On January 10, 1955, Chinese communist aircraft bombed the Tachens, the most northerly of the offshore islands held by Free China. They were garrisoned by an infantry division, reinforced by various special units, and the natural defensive position was strong. I had visited the two principal islands in May, 1954; since then elaborate defensive works had been completed. Undoubtedly the two largest islands could have held out for many months under heavy assault, but there were serious difficulties. The distance of two hundred miles from Taiwan made it impracticable for the Chinese to provide satisfactory air cover, either for the islands themselves or for the ships that kept them supplied. Then there were several smaller outlying islands which were untenable against large-scale attacks, particularly by an enemy with local air superiority. Finally, the considerable civilian population, chiefly fishermen and their families, could be given little or no protection from bombing.

On January 18 the Reds staged a strong amphibious assault on Ichiang, a small island several miles north of the principal group. Ichiang was defended by a light force of a few hundred men with small arms and mortars, but without artillery. They resisted bravely for two days before being overwhelmed. Without air cover, the relief of the island was considered impracticable. It was a classic example of limited war intended to test United States and Free Chinese intentions. On the next day I telegraphed (paraphrased) to the Department:

This afternoon Minister of National Defense Yu Ta-wei called on me and stressed the "extreme gravity" of the situation which is developing in the Tachen area. Repeating substantially what he has recently told General Chase and what General Chase has passed on to Admiral Radford and Admiral Stump, Minister Yu predicts the offensive action of the Reds in the Tachen region will unavoidably produce a chain of mutual retaliation and a consequent expansion of the war. Minister Yu considers it is perhaps already too late to stabilize the front and break this chain, but he believes it is important to try, and that in this sense only the United States is capable of effective action.

Minister Yu feels he has shown great restraint in withholding retaliatory action while awaiting United States concurrence, which has been denied after delays of a week or two. United States approval was received quickly, however, in the case of yesterday's attack on Ichiang and the Chinese Air Force today bombed shipping at Swatow, Pintang, and Amoy. Minister Yu noted his restraint was again evidenced by the absence of a request for United States agreement to bomb targets on the mainland.

The only chance of stopping the spread of the conflict would be an official United States statement to the effect that the Seventh Fleet would extend appropriate air support in the Tachen area against further communist attacks. The Chinese

Navy could, with the prospect of United States air cover if needed, again command the Tachen waters. But Minister Yu is convinced that, failing some positive action by the United States, the Reds will push southward with their command of the air and the consequent ability to use their otherwise inferior naval power, taking Nanchi, Matsu, etc., in due course. By that time, due to the nearness of enemy air activity, frequent alerts in Taipei would be unavoidable and direct involvement of Formosa in the conflict must be expected.

Comment: Conflicting military views on the importance of the offshore islands provide no satisfactory basis for me to express an opinion except from a political or a psychological standpoint. In the latter connection, I believe the loss of Tachen or others among the more important islands would, by undermining confidence in United States strength and determination, have a most unfortunate effect on Chinese and other Asian opinion. I therefore recommend, subject to the opinion of United States military authorities, most sympathetic consideration of Minister Yu's request for a statement regarding air support.

If, on the other hand, it is now definitely decided that the islands in the Tachen area are not particularly important, I believe the United States should so inform the Chinese and assume formal responsibility for advising their evacuation before excessive losses of men and materiel have been incurred. Such advice should be considered in the light of earlier United States urging that "all feasible steps should be taken to strengthen" island defenses.

Often overlooked in this complex situation is the further consideration that present communist attacks represent a clearcut case of new aggression against a UNO member with which the United States has just signed a defense pact. Simply calling for a cease-fire, without at the same time branding the aggressor, would therefore encourage world opinion to assume the sponsors of the cease-fire proposal find little to choose between two belligerents in the present case.

III

The result of the attacks on the Tachens was a United States proposal to assume the responsibility for evacuating both civilian and military personnel from the Tachens, some 30,000 in all. Intensive consultations with President Chiang and his principal advisers inevitably brought up the question whether similar American recommendations for retreat could be expected whenever our Chinese allies were hard pressed. If so, the future for the Chinese seemed very dark indeed. Further telegraphic exchanges with Washington reassured the Chinese somewhat, and on January 24, President Eisenhower sent a message to Congress together with a draft resolution to give him emergency powers in committing United States military forces in the defense of Taiwan, Penghu, and related areas. The Chinese had hoped for the formal inclusion of Kinmen and Matsu in this defense area, but they had to accept second best in the shape of informal assurances as to firm intentions.

On February 5 the Chinese agreed to evacuate the Tachen Islands with American assistance. A telegram from Under Secretary Hoover complimented me on my efforts, but I was far from happy about the whole affair. I decided to see at firsthand how the operation proceeded, and sailed on a United States Navy transport which was to bring back evacuees. The extent and readiness of our Seventh Fleet's resources were never more impressive. While Admiral Pride's flagship was anchored between the two principal islands, the fleet carriers and other combat vessels were spread over a large area, ready to give mutual support at any moment. Transports were picking up 14,000 military personnel and some 16,000 civilians, with their pitiful belongings. Bomb damage had not been serious, except for the sinking of one Chinese LST, but the gambit had worked exactly according to communist plans.

Tachen was a sad place in contrast to the hopeful atmosphere at the time of my previous visit. I climbed around on the rocky main island and watched the Chinese preparing to blow up the fortifications so laboriously constructed during the preceding months. An interval at luncheon with the Admiral on his flagship took me temporarily to another world. That night I returned to Taiwan on a small converted destroyer, from which I sent the following message (paraphrased) to the Department (February 10):

The evacuation of the Tachens is proceeding better than expected. In particular, the United States Navy and the Military Assistance Advisory Group, also the Chinese military and civilian organizations handling troops and refugees, are all doing splendid jobs. However, this is not an operation to be repeated if Formosa and other areas of Asia are to be saved from communism. Tachen may not be particularly important militarily, but the psychological effect of a new communist advance evidently is most damaging to the United States cause.

A bad psychological effect would be compounded and also serious military disadvantages to Free China and the United States would be brought about by still further enemy advances. The Reds are evidently once more moving their military strength south, this time along the coastline. Air bases are being developed to control the sky over coastal areas and eliminate any serious interference with coastwise shipping, which is essential to supplying those bases and for any other military buildup close to Formosa; this is in view of the absence of any prospect of significant communist naval power in this area as well as the totally inadequate internal communications in Fukien and Chekiang. Elimination of the Nationalists from offshore islands evidently is intended to secure a coastal supply route and permit eventual dispute of air control over the Formosa Strait. This would be a prerequisite to securing their flank during communist adventures farther south while Formosa is being saved for future attention, or to an attack on Formosa itself.

As jumping off points for possible Nationalist invasions of the mainland or as springboards for a Red attack on Formosa, the offshore islands have little significance in themselves. But they are extremely important to the defense of Formosa. It seems to me the only valid military argument for evacuating the Tachens is that the distance from Formosa makes air support and supply costly and difficult. Nanchi (or Nanki), the next significant island group to the south, is seventy-five nautical miles nearer and correspondingly easier to support. Our Military Assistance Advisory Group is restudying the defense of Nanchi as a matter of urgency, but tentative conclusions are that it can and should be held, along with the Kinmen and Matsu groups.

"Groups" include nearby positions essential to the defense of the main island in each group.

When the Nationalist Air Force and Navy have received the additional equipment already scheduled for delivery in the next few months they should be able to assume full responsibility for the defense of the offshore islands against anything short of a major Red attack; and even Nanchi, the most distant island, presumably can be given adequate air cover from bases in northern Formosa, thus eliminating the need for carrier support. Meanwhile, I believe the commander of the Seventh Fleet should have orders to extend any necessary air and naval support to the defenders of the three principal remaining offshore island groups.

I still do not believe the Reds intend to provoke a large-scale conflict in the near future, but it may require some military engagement to convince them of our firm intentions. If such an engagement should occur, then Nanchi might well be as favorable a location as any, since in all probability the action would be over in a few hours; it would be around friendly rather than enemy territory; it should give us a much longer breathing spell than any new withdrawals; a communist move southward would be interfered with more than one hundred miles north of the Formosa Strait to the advantage of Formosa itself and points south.

Essential steps to implementing the above include making clear to the Chinese Nationalists what kind of effort we want them to make in holding the offshore islands; also that the United States is undertaking to replace, within reason, military equipment lost by the Nationalists in carrying out our wishes.

On February 22 the Chinese were informed that the United States would not assist them in the defense of Nanchi. They decided that holding the islands would place too great a strain on their own resources, and immediately began evacuation. The Chinese Navy carried out the operation, and within three days had brought to Taiwan the 4,000 troops and 2,000 civilians who had occupied those islands.

IV

It had not been a good show. True, our government, including the Congress, had shown resolution in reaching decisions quickly, while the Seventh Fleet had done an admirable job in carrying out the evacuation. The power and efficiency which our Navy had demonstrated and its evident readiness and capability to crush any interference had impressed both friend and foe. But we had retreated in the face of new communist aggression. Should this have been foreseen and provided for? Need it have happened at all? What should we do next time? Such were the questions we asked ourselves. One of our American admirals, thinking out loud, said to me, "It would have been so much easier to defend the Tachens than to evacuate them."

Only the Associated Press, the United Press, and the *New York Times* normally maintained full-time correspondents in Taiwan, and frequently they were away on special assignments in other parts of the Far East. The Tachen affair suddenly raised our foreign press corps to a figure approaching forty. As may be imagined, we had to devote some time to them. I gave one of my very rare press conferences for the group. The facts in the case were well known, with very few exceptions, and I was able to give frank answers. When opinions were asked for, or loaded questions were put, I replied as fully as I could with the understanding that there would be no attribution. In only one minor instance was this understanding disregarded.

V

Early in March I attended a Chiefs of Mission Conference in Manila. The Chinese offshore islands were discussed in various connections at our sessions there, and the subject was reviewed further during the flight to Taipei with Secretary Dulles and Assistant Secretary Robertson. The instruments of ratification of our Mutual Defense Treaty were ready at this time, and we used the occasion of Secretary Dulles' visit for the formal exchange. A ceremony attended by many leading public figures among the Chinese, and by the senior Americans on Taiwan, provided opportunity to emphasize the importance of the event to a greater extent than would have been possible without the Secretary's personal participation. On March 13 I wrote to Robertson:

At the first opportunity after my return to Taipei I questioned George Yeh as to what he had told you and Secretary Dulles in Washington regarding the prospective effect on morale here if the offshore islands were lost. He confirmed your impression that he had presented the matter in most pessimistic terms, apparently to the extent of indicating that his government's control over its own military forces would be jeopardized, and its basis of popular support among Free Chinese perhaps irreparably undermined. Yeh stated his case on instructions, presumably from President Chiang; he did not suggest the extent to which it represented his own views.

I return to this subject because of the evident impression it had made on you and on the Secretary, which first came to my attention during our discussion in the plane flying up from Manila to Taipei on March 3. Obviously we are dealing here with intangibles which do not lend themselves to exact measurement or prediction. I most certainly would not depreciate the psychological factors stressed by George Yeh; but while considering the possibility that he may have exaggerated their importance, I believe other factors are no less significant. Taken altogether these could well place a substantially greater value upon retaining Kinmen and Matsu than would result from giving primary emphasis to upholding morale on Taiwan.

In my brief review of the Chinese situation at the afternoon session in Manila on March 2, I expressed the view that the loss of the offshore islands would be "very serious but not necessarily disastrous." The precise effect, of course, would depend in considerable degree upon the circumstances under which the loss occurred, and the events which might follow in its wake. Subject to this obvious condition, however, I continue to hold the opinion just quoted, which is the same that I expressed to you and the Secretary on the following morning. This is repeated here in the first instance because I believe it to be true, and secondly because the present is not a time to burn bridges. I see no adequate reason for losing Kinmen and Matsu, but if by some ill chance they should be lost, whether by defeat or default, I should not want it to serve anyone as a reason for pronouncing hopeless the cause of Free China.

Probably much more serious to Free China's morale than the loss of additional small islands would be any formal steps toward the "two Chinas" project. From the Chinese point of view, these might include the entry of the Peiping regime into the United Nations and/or its recognition by the United States. Any cease-fire, except possibly of definitely limited duration, would have similar implications to them. Obviously, anything which would indicate definitive United States acquiescence in the communist conquest of the Chinese mainland would represent irretrievable disaster in Free Chinese eyes. The loss of offshore islands as such undoubtedly would be less important to President Chiang than the danger of the two Chinas idea which he considers implicit in drawing a line down the Formosa Strait. I believe that this must have been very much in Chiang's mind, and also in George Yeh's, when the matter was first presented to you and to the Secretary in Washington. This may explain the forcefulness of his presentation.

Among the most important arguments for retaining Kinmen and Matsu, it seems to me, is the psychological effect on the enemy. It is almost impossible to overestimate the danger of confirming the Reds in a belief that, despite recent strong statements by the Secretary and others, we are for peace at any price. Withdrawal from the Tachens undoubtedly strengthened them in this belief. I have expressed to the Department my opinion that a military engagement may well be necessary to convince the enemy that we mean business. Such an engagement might have been risked at the Tachens or at Nanchi. Resolutely handled, it presumably would have been a localized affair, and might have given us several months of peace in this area—a prospect which we do not now enjoy after the Tachens and Nanchi have been given up and 20,000 more refugees created. We still have opportunity to prepare for positive action at Kinmen and Matsu.

On purely technical and immediate military grounds the surrender of the Tachens probably was wise. Unfortunately, however, almost as good a case could be made out for giving up

Matsu and Kinmen, as Admiral Spruance and others, in effect, have pointed out. It is true that our Navy had planned to occupy the Amoy area, including Kinmen, as a base for operations against Taiwan in World War II. On the other hand, it has been stated recently that we would not bother with the Tachens if engaged in a full-scale war against Red China. But for somewhat similar reasons we also decided to bypass Taiwan itself in World War II! And again, largely on technical military grounds, we withdrew from South Korea, thereby making the Korean War more or less inevitable.

All of which seems to confirm once more that major policy decisions should not be based solely or even primarily upon technical military considerations. Otherwise, in the interest of peace with all concerned—including our own less imaginative military experts—we might find in due course that the ramparts we watch in the Pacific had been re-established on a meridian through Hawaii. Much more likely is that we should be at war again—on a large scale but not necessarily World War III— because we finally found ourselves compelled to make a stand somewhere west of Pearl Harbor against the aggressor whom our successive withdrawals had made increasingly bold. In the present case I believe that we should stop him at Kinmen and Matsu.

VI

On my return from Manila the Embassy undertook a discreet survey of Chinese morale, making direct and indirect inquiries in many quarters. The results were more encouraging than we had dared hope for. The loss of the Tachens undoubtedly had been a severe blow to the higher levels of the Chinese government, particularly among the military. In general, however, the recent signature of the Mutual Defense Treaty had given an increased feeling of security to the civilian population of Taiwan itself. Seemingly this had offset in large degree the effect of the Tachen withdrawal.

Personally, I was not dissatisfied with the immediate situation. We had a treaty that permitted us to help defend territory designated by mutual agreement. The Seventh Fleet was strong and President Eisenhower had the overwhelming approval of Congress to use it in the defense of such Chinese territory as he considered necessary. The Chinese were reinforcing and improving the defenses of the remaining and far more important offshore islands so that they could repell all but the heaviest assault. We would work ever more closely with them in their military planning, and be better prepared ourselves in consequence. All in all, it seemed to be the best we could do under the extraordinarily complex and difficult circumstances.

VII

The following memorandum of conversation is dated May 4, 1955:

Upon receipt this morning of the Secretary's telegram of May 3, authorizing me to advise President Chiang that "we understand his position" with reference to the defense of the offshore islands, that Admiral Stump would shortly be conferring with him on the subject, and that he would continue to enjoy strong United States support, I immediately called on the Foreign Minister. He telephoned to me half an hour later that President Chiang would receive me at 5 P.M. today. The Foreign Minister suggested that, if I felt that I could do so, my opinion expressed to him last Friday that there had been no fundamental change in the situation might be repeated to President Chiang.

I arrived at Shihlin at 5 P.M. and, after a few pleasantries, remarked to the President that in my opinion the recent exchanges with Washington had produced no fundamental change in the situation as it had existed since the Korean Armistice in 1953. Prior to that date Chinese communist strength had been very largely tied down in Korea. Subsequently they had been able to redeploy their forces and to build up the military strength in Fukien and Chekiang which now threatened the offshore islands and Taiwan. Meanwhile, the military strength of Free China had been increasing also. No one could be entirely sure of communist intentions, except that they were always bad. It seemed to me that if a Red attack developed it would be either a probing operation primarily for psychological effect against some small island or islands, which the Nationalist forces could handle without our help, or it would be a major offensive involving not only the offshore islands but other areas as well. In the latter event, both of our governments would have to consider the whole picture anew in the light of actual developments. The defense of this or that minor island would be only incidental to the general situation and would fall into proper perspective.

Pursuing my argument, I said that since the shelling of Kinmen last September 3, I had many times expressed the opinion that there probably would be no major communist assault in the near future. Much was being said about the five airfields under construction opposite Taiwan. I understood that they would not all be operational for several months, and that when completed would not provide for more than about fifty MIG-15s each. By that time the Nationalist Air Force would have more aircraft also, and the situation would not be so one-sided. I did not suppose that the Reds would be fully prepared for a major operation before fall—possibly in October—and very likely not until some time next year.

In brief, I considered that there had been no fundamental change and that the actual military situation was not unfavorable to Free China.

I then conveyed the substance of the Secretary's telegram to the President. He asked whether the telegram meant that President Eisenhower would actually commit United States forces to help in the defense of Kinmen and Matsu. I said that I thought not, but suggested if my previous analysis was correct, this might not make much practical difference. President Chiang emphasized the effect on morale, and I remarked that President Eisenhower also had a "morale" problem in the form of a difficult domestic political situation. By request, I then dictated to Sampson Shen a paraphrase of the Secretary's telegram.

President Chiang next reverted to the thesis that the communists would try to destroy his Air Force and Navy by attrition. Once the Reds had assumed local command of the air, the protection of the offshore islands would cause excessive losses to the Nationalist Air Force and Navy. Moreover, the communists undoubtedly would attack air and naval bases on Taiwan in this connection.

In reply I repeated my belief that the military situation was by no means so one-sided, and that any air attacks on Taiwan presumably would be carried out by bombers based in the Shanghai area rather than by MIG-15s from the nearby fields in Fukien. It seemed to me that such a development would open the question of our treaty obligation to defend Taiwan.

In conclusion, I repeated once more that I could not predict communist courses of action with certainty. I had no crystal ball. But I thought we should not jump to the conclusion that the current Red build-up in Fukien was directed solely against Taiwan. It seemed to me that the five airfields were being constructed as part of a general plan to gain control of the air along the China coast. This could serve various purposes, including the support of a supply line for new adventures in Southeast Asia now that the port of Haiphong was passing into communist hands. The Reds knew that an attack on Taiwan would bring them into conflict with the United States. But if incidentally to the general development of their military strength in this area they could use it as a threat, thereby obtaining possession of Kinmen and Matsu with little or no actual fighting, they could be expected to do so.

President Chiang indicated agreement with much that I had said as to communist intentions. He said that he would reserve comment on the Secretary's message until he could discuss matters with Admiral Stump. He hoped that the Admiral would come to Taipei as soon as possible.

VIII

Meantime the military operations around the offshore islands had created some nervousness in the large American colony on Taiwan, particularly among those who had their families with them. We had been visited in January by a group of evacuation experts from the United States Embassy in Manila. Frankly, I was more immediately concerned about the possible effect of this visit on the morale of the Chinese, should they learn of it, than about any present danger to Americans. I used the occasion (January 18) to prepare a list of questions and answers for discreet oral use by American officials on Taiwan, and sent copies to Washington and Manila:

Q. Does the Embassy have a plan for evacuating Americans from Formosa in an emergency?

A. Yes. Such plans have existed for many years and for many countries, particularly those around the periphery of the Iron Curtain, and are subject to periodic review and revision.

Q. What is the nature of these plans?

A. The details necessarily are secret. Efforts are made to provide for a number of contingencies, and it would be unwise to encourage public discussion of various conditions which might never arise. Moreover, certain plans impinge upon military considerations which must be kept secret. Arrangements have been made to inform all Americans here, as necessary, in an emergency.

Q. Does the Embassy consider it likely that Formosa will be involved in a war?

A. Certainly the United States has no intention of initiating a conflict and will use all of its influence to prevent one. Moreover, it is generally believed that the communists have no present intention of provoking open hostilities with the United States. The possibility of such an outbreak, however, whether as a result of accident or design on the part of our enemy, should not be excluded.

Q. Could the Chinese Reds take Formosa?

A. The considered judgment of the Embassy is that the Chinese communists are not now and for the foreseeable future will not be capable of defeating the available American and Chinese Nationalist forces defending Formosa. In other words, this island could be attacked, by air or otherwise, but not taken.

Q. Under what conditions would the Embassy issue a statement advising Americans to leave Formosa, as was done in the past on the China mainland and elsewhere?

A. No situation is envisaged which would justify the issuance of such advice. The position on Formosa today is quite different from that on the mainland several years ago. Internal order is good and the defensive position against outside attack is strong. Moreover, the United States has assumed definite responsibilities for the defense of Formosa. One of the important factors in making this defense effective is the maintenance of morale among the Chinese here. The presence of some 3,500 Americans, men, women and children, is highly reassuring to the Chinese population. Contrariwise, the issuance of official American instructions for evacuation would be a severe blow to Chinese morale. It could be interpreted not only as reflecting lack of confidence in the general Far Eastern situation but also as presaging an abandonment of the American policy to support Free China.

Q. Under what conditions would the Embassy issue a statement advising the evacuation of American dependents?

A. Again, no situation is envisaged which would justify such advice, and for the same reasons. Decisions as to evacuating individual American citizens, including dependents, must rest with the various private organizations and individuals concerned. There is no intention of ordering the general evacuation of dependents of American officials, but to be guided as far as possible by the wishes of the individuals involved. Only in this way can Chinese morale be safeguarded.

Q. Does the course just described subject American nationals to unjustifiable risks?

A. No. With very few exceptions the Americans on Formosa are engaged in constructive activities of one kind or another. Presumably they came here with full knowledge of the delicate situation existing throughout the Far East as a result of past and possible future communist aggression. These Americans would not wish to weaken the position of Formosa by giving primary consideration to their personal safety. Actually, Formosa may be one of the safest spots in the Far East today.

Q. In the event of air attacks on Formosa, how would the Embassy assist in facilitating the departure of dependents or others who might wish to go?

A. The Embassy has plans which should be helpful in such a contingency, and Americans are welcome to get in touch with the Embassy in this connection at any time when regular transportation facilities may be temporarily unavailable. It should be obvious, however, that airports and seaports would be among the primary targets of any large-scale air attacks, and that considerable improvising might be necessary to evacuate an appreciable number of persons under such conditions. Any organization or individual unwilling to face such eventualities might be well advised to quit Formosa and the Far East immediately, and in an unobtrusive manner which would avoid damage to paramount American and Chinese interests.

A subsequent communication from Manila took issue with some of my answers on evacuation. My further comments (February 16) included the following paragraphs:

I hold no particular brief for the replies which I drafted earlier, but they represent an attempt to give straightforward answers which would strike a reasonable balance between undue alarm and unwarranted reassurance.

The probability is that in the event of heavy bombing of airfields and seaports, whether in Formosa or elsewhere in the Far East, American officials responsible for evacuation would find most of their previous planning to be of little use. They would have to improvise, and it seems to me a mistake to allow anyone to gain the impression that we have some highly secret and miraculous schemes to assure his safe evacuation, and that we are therefore ready to tell him just what to do under any and all circumstances.

IX

On June 6 the Embassy forwarded a symposium entitled "The 'Two Chinas' Concept." As we had anticipated, discussion of this problem was becoming even more active since the conclusion of our Mutual Defense Treaty with the Republic of China. Our series of despatches went into the history of the subject in considerable detail. The related questions of recognition for Red China and of a possible trusteeship for Taiwan were treated incidentally. The following paragraphs are from my contributions to these despatches:

☆ *China Assignment* ☆

After the Korean Armistice in July, 1953, those countries which had so hastily followed the Soviet lead in recognizing the Peiping regime began once more to look for company. Only seventeen of the sixty members of the United Nations had recognized Red China, and these included several members of the British Commonwealth. The three Scandinavian countries and Switzerland also had followed the British lead, but since mid-1950 the gallant band had received no recruits. As far as most of them were concerned, the Korean War was over; "business as usual" was their slogan for the area of East Asia, or the Western Pacific, where of all the Western powers only the United States retained substantial responsibilities in any event.

There was, however, an important new element in the situation which had to be considered. Taiwan and the government of the Republic of China, which the United States had virtually written off in 1949, were very much in the picture again. A new formula for the recognition of China was required. Hints and feelers which had preceded the Korean Armistice in July, 1953, were replaced by more open advocacy of promoting peace by accepting the facts of life. There were, in effect, two Chinas. (The British have maintained consular offices on Taiwan and diplomatic relations with Peiping at the same time. The British business colony on Taiwan has continued to be appreciably larger than the corresponding American group.) Why not recognize both and carry on from there? This approach has a wide appeal, particularly among the great majority of people everywhere who were unfamiliar with the problem in detail, but who were genuinely interested in promoting peace. The two Chinas were separated by salt water, and preservation of the *status quo* presumably favored peace.

In general, however, advocates of two Chinas have chosen to overlook the actual and prospective attitudes of the Chinese regimes in question. Both have repudiated the idea; neither has given any indication of willingness to accept it in any form, even tacitly. It is possible, of course, that the United States could exert such pressure on the Nationalist government as to compel its acquiescence, or at least its avoidance of open and formal refusal. It may be possible that the Peiping regime could be persuaded to give some vague undertaking about the use of force, etc., which wishful thinking in the free world would accept as a basis for recognizing two Chinas. . . . Neither action seems likely, however, and judging by all past records a communist promise would be lived up to exactly as long as convenient to Peiping and Moscow.

It seems improbable that the Chinese communist regime would continue to maintain diplomatic relations with the United Kingdom, even on the present Son-of-Heaven basis, if the British were to recognize and establish diplomatic relations with the present government on Taiwan. Whitehall, at least, must be fully aware of this difficulty, and it may be wondered whether informed British officials really believe that the two Chinas project could possibly materialize, even assuming its acceptance by the United States. Or do they regard it simply as a scheme which would be desirable if it could be realized, and which sounds plausible to much of the free world, but which is being advocated with a more immediate and promising purpose in mind: the weakening of both the morale and the international position of the government of the Republic of China, involving a compromise in American policy of firm support for that government?

Trusteeship for Taiwan is another project which appears quite impracticable, but which might serve other than its ostensible purposes. International discussion of the subject, particularly if the American position were permitted to appear as less than adamant, could not but weaken the internal and external position of Free China. Moreover, the latter's uncompromising opposition to the scheme could, at some future time, be used as an excuse by certain countries for modifying their present opposition to turning Taiwan over to the communists. To those thousands of miles away, a trusteeship for Taiwan may suggest peace and justice. To those in East Asia it would mean appeasement and surrender.

The three preceding paragraphs are not intended to suggest the existence of a diabolical plot, developed methodically over a period of years, by which certain nations hope to liquidate the government of the Republic of China now established on

☆ China Assignment ☆

Taiwan. Earlier portions of the present despatch should have made this clear, at least. The two Chinas and trusteeship projects are being brought forward simply in an effort to make the best of a difficult and developing situation in the interest of the advocating countries. Moreover, both schemes would have the effect of rationalizing much that has gone before and of covering up the policy mistakes of others by leading the United States down the same garden path. In this way, while world attention continues to be focused on Kinmen, Matsu, Taiwan, and the smaller states of Southeast Asia, some or all of which might be sacrificed piecemeal in the process, Hong Kong, Malaya, Singapore, etc., would stand a better chance of surviving into Phase III of the Atomic Age.

The very practical question arises as to what might be gained by accepting Red China into the family of nations. Does past experience give hope that communist states will behave better if formally recognized and admitted to the United Nations? Have relations between the United States and the Soviet Union been better since recognition in 1933 than in the preceding decade and a half? Have British relations with Red China since 1950 been appreciably better than those of the United States, after allowing for the fact that Britain is no longer feared along the China coast, while only respect for American strength and determination is keeping the remaining free nations of East Asia out of Red hands? Will communist China improve on Soviet Russia's record of breaking almost every international agreement which it has ever made? Would two communist vetoes in the Security Council be no more dangerous than one? At most, answers to such questions seem unlikely to produce more than a negative conclusion that international acceptance of Red China might not make the general picture any worse than it is today.

At least two important questions remain to which the United States requires judicious answers: (1) How can the recognition of Chinese governments be handled to the greatest benefit of American relations with its Western allies; and (2) What course of action is likely to affect most favorably United States relations with the government of the Republic of China and with the other governments in the Western Pacific having mutual defense treaties with the United States?

Even assuming that one or both of the two Chinese regimes would refuse to go along with a project calculated to confirm China as 98 per cent slave and 2 per cent free, the argument could be advanced that discussions in that direction between the United States and the United Kingdom might have the advantage of bringing the East Asian policies of the two powers more closely into line. The position of India would be of primary significance in this connection; it is important to the United States in itself and because it continues to preoccupy the United Kingdom.

Of all the major influences which originally impelled British recognition of Red China, only the consideration of India remains unchanged. British investments in China have been lost *in toto;* and trade with a genuinely communist China gives no promise of contributing significantly to Commonwealth economy, even if the restrictions were removed entirely. It is no longer of paramount importance that left-wing Labor elements in Britain should be appeased. The colony of Hong Kong itself, which in 1950 was a strong defensive position, continues to exist only at the pleasure of Peiping's now formidable air force, unless the United States and perhaps Nationalist China should come to its aid.

In retrospect, therefore, it may be seen that British action in 1950 to recognize Red China was taken, not to save the world, but in response to British and Commonwealth political and economic interests. That the future was not more clearly foreseen at the time may be explained as due primarily to the then common belief that the Chinese communists were not real communists. All attempts to bring American and British policy for East Asia into line, therefore, should include consideration of the empirical, accidental, and largely mistaken steps which have characterized the development of such British policy since 1949. The idea has been assiduously cultivated that the United States has made most of the mistakes in the Far East during this period. Britain has been even less inclined than other countries to admit any mistakes in its foreign policy. On careful examination, however, the conclusion seems justified that United States policy in the Far East has shown more consideration for other than purely selfish interests than in the case of the United Kingdom. Any American action in this field, therefore, should be preceded in every instance by a careful examination of the nature of Britain's (and India's) true position. If a friend has fallen among robbers and is found lying by the roadside, it would seem better to help him up and see him on his way than to lie down beside him. Certainly the United States would not wish to pass by on the other side in this case.

In all of this, the position of Free China, the Philippines, Korea, and Japan evidently must be given the most careful consideration. Throughout this area of paramount United States responsibility, the fear of communist strength is very real. Opinions differ in detail among the countries mentioned, but a solid majority in all of them wants evidence of American strength sufficient to offset that of the communists. Anything that appears to them as revealing indecision or appeasement, whether of the Reds or of the former colonial powers, cannot but undermine the generally satisfactory relations which the United States has built up with the free countries of East Asia at the cost of so much treasure, toil, and blood. No thoroughly satisfactory solutions can be looked for until the communists have experienced a genuine change of heart. But remedies are at hand which, applied with firmness, persistence, and understanding, can hasten the day when communists too will see the light. One of these remedies is the Dulles doctrine of the moral nonrecognition of the subjugation of nations such as China.

X

Our home leave, overdue by more than six months, was authorized in June, 1955. Pauline and I both were very tired from the exertions and tensions of the previous two years. Cochran would be in charge; he had my full confidence. We started our vacation by flying to India and spending two weeks on Hadji Butt's comfortable houseboats at Dal Lake in Kashmir. It was an experience which we hoped very much to repeat. Then we flew on to the United States, via Europe. Washington was hot in August, but stimulating as always. Numerous conferences at State, on Capitol Hill, at the Department of Defense, and elsewhere accounted for nine busy days, but brought up little that was new. After six weeks in Maine, Pauline and I were in Washington again for two days only. With his characteristic thoughtfulness, Ambassador Wellington Koo learned that October 3 was our thirtieth wedding anniversary and gave a most pleasant dinner for us at the Chinese Embassy. Next day we were flying back to Taiwan.

By taking a military plane from Tokyo, I was able to arrive at my post a few hours before Under Secretary Herbert Hoover, Jr., and his party. The visit was brief but useful, and particularly satisfactory because of our close agreement on policy.

On October 20 I telegraphed (paraphrased) to the Department:

The first engagement on October 15 between jet aircraft of the government of the Republic of China and of the communists along the China coast was presumably more or less accidental, but it provides a useful occasion for an assessment of probabilities. Obviously no one can predict the future in detail, and accidents can happen any time. However, based upon what is known in Taipei of Red policies, capabilities, and activities, the following courses of action appear not improbable:

1. By such means as occasional shelling of Matsu and Kinmen, and by gradually increasing air activity, the communists will maintain varying degrees of tension in the Formosa Strait. Their purposes will include the promotion of friction between the United States and its Asian and Western allies, including the government of the Republic of China.

2. While the Reds are capable of assembling forces for a large-scale assault on the offshore islands in a relatively short time, no evidence exists of active preparation for such an attack. This appears to support the opinion long held by the Embassy that an attack on a scale sufficient to promise Red success probably would be undertaken only as a part of wider operations, or as a result of what they interpret as significant weakening of the United States position and the consequent undermining of the determination of the government of the

Republic of China to resist. The communists presumably believe the islands eventually will fall into their laps without the heavy losses which would be involved in a direct assault under present conditions. . . .

As seen from Taiwan, indispensable courses of action on the part of the United States to meet the above situation for the immediate and foreseeable future include:

a. Maintenance of decisive atomic air superiority in the China area, without which the success of United States policy cannot be expected, even though this power may not be used.

b. The development of the defenses of Nationalist China, both in the air and on the ground, with maximum rapidity and to the maximum extent practicable.

c. The provision at the earliest possible date of adequate air base facilities to accommodate USAF combat units when deployed on Taiwan. (Current plans call for seven fighter squadrons in case of need, but there are no adequate places to accommodate them; hence the urgent need for Kung Kuan Air Base.) Steps b. and c. appear the most promising deterrents to the undertaking of the Reds to dispute air control over the Strait.

d. The maintenance of the position of the United States toward Red China [in a manner] which [no one] . . . can regard as other than firm and devoid of any inclination toward appeasement.

XI

The annual sessions of the United Nations General Assembly were particularly trying periods for Free China and its friends. Aside from the perennial question as to which regime should represent China in the United Nations, other problems arose at intervals which were no less difficult. At the time, those intimately involved in a minor crisis in New York or Washington might feel, understandably, that the heavens were about to fall.

An example of the difficulties which took place from time to time arose late in 1955, involving consideration of Outer Mongolia for membership in the international body. A common joke at the time was that if by some slip of the tongue a vote on lower Slobbovia had been called for, most members of the United Nations would not have noted the difference. As a matter of fact, except for the prospect of one more invariable vote for the Soviet bloc in the General Assembly with Outer Mongolia admitted, only two countries had any actual or historic interest in the matter: China and Russia. Now, however, it was to be part of a package deal whereby the United Nations would gain eighteen new members, including Italy, Spain, and Japan. My telegram (paraphrased) of November 28, 1955, included the following:

From such information as is available in Taipei at the present time, the situation regarding the package deal for the admission of new members to the UNO appears to be a Soviet maneuver abetted by Canada and Great Britain to put us and Free China out on a limb. President Chiang's reply to President Eisenhower is specific in that the government of the Republic of China is unable to avoid vetoing Outer Mongolia's application for membership "unless some other solution can be found." This suggests the existence of one or possibly two alternatives.

For more than thirty years China has not exercised effective control over Outer Mongolia. Therefore, President Chiang's interest in the question is one of prestige or face (he would call it "honor") rather than of substance. His reply to President Eisenhower suggests his primary interest is to prevent the recognition of Red China in and outside the United Nations. If the UNO can stomach the admission of Outer Mongolia in its present state, with the record of ruthless Soviet action there in 1921 and again in mid-1930's, then it would seem to require no more than a gesture by the Peiping regime toward Korea to obtain acceptance for itself. . . .

What seems particularly disturbing to the Foreign Minister is what he regards as the abrupt change in the position of the United States since the Lodge statement on November 13. He continues to believe that if the United States exerted itself there should be no insuperable difficulty in lining up five abstentions in the Security Council as regards Outer Mongolia, which would avoid the question of the government of the Republic of China veto. The fact that the United States is suddenly pressuring the government of the Republic of China on Outer Mongolia leads to the inevitable suspicion here that the United States has made a deal with the Soviets behind the back of the government of the Republic of China.

If it is true that the Canadians and British have maneuvered us into the present impasse and if no other solution can be found, if we have not already done so we might express extreme displeasure at their having placed us in this position, adding that we are nevertheless prepared to go along with them to the extent already indicated, provided they make a firm commitment to join us in opposing the acceptance of Red China by the United Nations as long as we continue to oppose it; that Canada, which is apparently the prime mover in the package deal, furthermore undertake to not recognize Red China unless and until we do; and that we agree, on the basis of their undertakings, to attempt to persuade the government of the Republic of China to instruct the Chinese delegation not to use the veto against the admission of Outer Mongolia.

Scarcely helpful are the news despatches from the United States reporting President Eisenhower's message to President Chiang and speculating regarding United States pressure on the government of the Republic of China, including possible withholding of aid. Whether inspired or not, we may expect recriminations in the local press.

XII

At this time President and Madame Chiang were vacationing at Sun-Moon Lake. The President evidently had instructed his Foreign Minister, and through him the Chinese delegation to the United Nations, not to yield on the question of Outer Mongolia, and to exercise the veto in the Security Council if necessary. Beyond that, the President apparently was taking advantage of his absence from Taipei to avoid direct involvement in one more unpleasant matter. At this moment the Far Eastern Sub-Committee of the House Foreign Affairs Committee arrived in Taipei, including Representatives Clement Zablocki and Walter Judd. They traveled to Sun-Moon Lake to spend a few hours with the President. Inevitably the question of Outer Mongolia came up and was discussed in detail. The committee returned to Taipei generally sympathetic to

President Chiang's viewpoint on the issues implicit in the package deal.

I had suggested earlier that I might go to Sun-Moon Lake to see the President, but had received evasive replies. On December 7, however, word came that he would receive me. The Foreign Minister and I flew to Taichung and thence motored to the lake. I was conscious of being ill prepared to meet the President on this occasion, since my information as to why the United States apparently had reversed its position on Outer Mongolia continued to be based largely on hearsay. I recalled hearing someone suggest a "voluble explanation" under such circumstances, and acted accordingly. The following paragraphs are from my memorandum of conversation dated December 8, 1955:

> The Foreign Minister also referred to a statement in Koo's telegram quoting Robertson as having observed that Yeh and Rankin were not taking the present matter seriously enough. Minister Yeh then cited a meeting which had just been held at the Vice President's house as evidence of the gravity with which Chinese officials looked upon the dilemma facing them. Not only was early withdrawal from the UN envisaged at the meeting, but also the possible cessation of United States aid and even the eventual closing of the American Embassy in Taipei.
>
> We arrived at the Evergreen Hotel at Sun-Moon Lake about 10:30 A.M. Shortly afterward the Foreign Minister and I joined the President and Madame Chiang in their apartment. The President apparently had just been reading the Koo telegram mentioned above. He immediately remarked upon Robertson's reported statement that the present situation was not being taken seriously enough at this end. He was astonished at this, adding that on the contrary the Chinese took a graver view than did the United States, which seemed concerned solely with the question of UN membership. The problem was a far bigger one, he believed.
>
> President Chiang then asked me to state our case. . . . I had nothing of an authoritative character to add except that I was under instructions to emphasize strongly to him the seriousness with which the United States regarded the current problem of

admitting eighteen new members to the UN and the avoidance of a veto. I took occasion to review recent developments in this connection insofar as they were known to me. The United States had opposed the idea of a "package deal," and in particular had considered Outer Mongolia as unqualified for UN membership. Then, apparently about mid-November, events had occurred on which I had no detailed information. We were no happier about a package deal and Outer Mongolia than before, but we were suddenly in a most difficult position, seemingly as a result of Soviet intrigues among some of our friends. I felt sure that the United States had done its best in supporting both its own interests and those of Free China. Unfortunately, however, both our countries were now confronted with a distressing and complex situation.

I then touched upon certain developments in the history of the United Nations, first referring deferentially to Foreign Minister Yeh's much greater knowledge of the subject, and emphasizing that I was expressing my purely personal views. I recalled that the original conception was a universal organization. Before the ex-enemy states of Germany and Japan were ready for membership, however, the Soviet Union had taken a course contrary to the Charter. If the latter were to be enforced, probably the Soviet Union and certain other states should have been ejected from the UN long ago. This seemed impracticable at the time, and events had since overtaken the question of revising the Charter, which would be a slow process in any case. In the Korean War, the UN had put forth its first and possibly its last major effort on behalf of collective security. Responsibility in the latter field had been assumed more and more by multilateral and bilateral defense arrangements, while there was also a renewed move in the direction of universality. In the light of these developments, unhappily, many provisions of the Charter could no longer be taken literally. The government of the Republic of China had an excellent legal case, based upon the Charter, but the pertinent provisions were already largely outdated by events, and no one would enforce them.

I thought that the President's government also had a good moral case from its point of view, but there was another moral case as well. All of the free world, including the Chinese government, wished to see a number of qualified states admitted to the UN. I mentioned Spain, Japan, and Italy in particular. Many of our friends among the countries of the free world, including Latin America, had strong views on the subject. Unfortunately, however, there was no such general interest in Outer Mongolia, which concerned only China and Russia directly. Most people did not know where Outer Mongolia was. To a great majority of countries in the free world, therefore, bringing into the UN such important and deserving nations as the three I had mentioned was a much bigger moral issue than that of Outer Mongolia.

It seemed to me, in brief, that the UN had given up much of its responsibility in the field of collective security and was moving toward universality of membership. Mme. Chiang commented that the backbone had been removed. I replied that it had been shifted elsewhere, but that I believed the UN would continue to be very important nevertheless. I cited the strong desire of many additional countries to join. The United States wanted the government of the Republic of China to remain in the UN, I said, both because we valued its presence and support for the free world and because it was a block to the entry of Red China. In summary, the United States had done its best in the present case but had not been able to avoid the package deal. We were asking Free China to go along in its interest and ours, making the best of a difficult situation.

President Chiang said that he was impressed by my presentation, which was the best statement of our case he had heard. If we had used this approach considerably earlier, he noted, there might have been time to prepare the members of the Legislative Yuan and the Chinese public. But the situation had developed suddenly without warning, accompanied by wide publicity which had prompted many to take a public stand from which it was now difficult to withdraw.

President Chiang went on at some length about the importance of a consistent policy and the necessity of adhering to principle. His government had made the mistake of yielding claims to Outer Mongolia in the Chinese-Soviet Treaty of 1945. They had hoped to buy thirty years of peace in this way; instead they had lost Outer Mongolia and all of mainland China as well.

Referring to a remark that President Chiang had made about our putting a tacit seal of approval on Soviet vetoes for United Nations membership, my memorandum of conversation continues:

> . . . I reminded him of the statements which our representative in the UN had made and intended to make, expressly disassociating ourselves from the objectionable features of the package deal. But the overwhelming majority in the UN favored the package, and it was very important for both China and the United States to retain the friendship and support of as many countries as possible. I thought that the outcome was unlikely to be very happy in any case, and that the events we were discussing quite likely were bringing war nearer. The point was, however, that we were all in an extremely difficult situation for which there was no ideal solution. We were not starting from scratch. We were in a tight spot and the question was how best to get out of it.

On December 13, China vetoed Outer Mongolia for membership in the United Nations and the Soviet Union retaliated by vetoing Japan. The other sixteen countries were admitted, and Japan came in just a year later. The heavens did not fall in, and Outer Mongolia remained out until 1961.

XIII

The purpose behind the abortive New Zealand Resolution, calling for a cease-fire in the Formosa Strait, continued to be pursued by the United States and others. Prior to August, 1955 there had been occasional and informal contact on a few practical questions between our consulate general in Geneva and communist Chinese officials stationed in the same city. In particular, the United States sought information about a number of its citizens who were being detained on the China mainland. The Reds suggested that matters could be facilitated if these informal contacts were raised to an "ambassadorial level." Their intent was transparent: to obtain a measure of diplomatic recognition from the United States.

While making it clear at the outset that ambassadorial talks did not imply any recognition of the Peiping regime, the Department considered that no possibility should be overlooked to obtain the repatriation of American citizens held in China, or to clarify "other practical matters now at issue." Several meetings were held in Geneva with the American ambassador to Czechoslovakia representing the United States, and on September 10 the communists agreed to release the American civilians in question.

The Chinese government on Taiwan regarded these Geneva sessions with grave misgivings. Our solicitude for United States citizens held on the China mainland was appreciated. But were these contacts with the communists to continue in a manner that would lead to formal recognition of Peiping? Many people in China and elsewhere could not be expected to differentiate between continued ambassadorial meetings and regular diplomatic relations. The alarm in Taipei increased when, after the announcement that our nationals would be released, the United States raised at one of the Geneva meetings the question of renouncing the use of force, specifically in the Taiwan area. Did this presage an American deal with the Chinese Reds behind the backs of the government on Taiwan, or was it simply window dressing to placate our peace-loving allies in Western Europe? Our Chinese friends were somewhat relieved when the Reds rejected the proposal, but further continuation of the talks was a recurring source of friction and suspicion. The Chinese government believed that it was not being kept fully informed as to what was going on at Geneva, and speculation was encouraged in consequence.

Despite the communists' agreement, a number of Americans continued to be held in China after the initial releases. One of the reasons given was that the United States was holding Chinese citizens in American prisons. In fact, a painstaking and lengthy American survey revealed that as of some date in 1956 a total of thirty-four Chinese citizens were in jails in the United States. It was a tribute to the law-abiding character of the Chinese that the number was so small, and most of them were serving short sentences for minor crimes. Moreover, available information indicated that none of them wanted to go to Red China. They preferred to serve out their jail sentences in the United States.

In our understandable anxiety to substantiate publicly the facts about the thirty-four Chinese imprisoned in the United States, essential advance consultation with the Chinese government on Taiwan was overlooked. Someone suggested that the Indian Embassy in Washington be requested to verify the circumstances. As it turned out, the British, the Chinese, the Indians, and the press all learned about the matter at more or less the same time. The Chinese government in Taipei was furious. In effect, we seemed to be proposing that the Indians, who recognized Peiping, should determine whether Chinese nationals, officially represented in the United States by the Embassy of the Republic of China, wished to be deported to communist territory. Apparently no mention had been made of the possibility of sending them to Taiwan until the Chinese government appeared in the picture and offered to receive them. Nothing came of the whole affair, of course, but further distrust of American intentions was created. I telegraphed to the Department on June 4 that our handling of the case might be expected to confirm Chinese suspicions as to what we were doing in Geneva and to support their growing fears that a change in American policy toward China was imminent. I summarized the situation as I saw it in a letter of July 25, 1956, to an officer of the Department of State:

> I was glad to learn that the case of the thirty-four prisoners at least had not been discussed with the Reds until the day the Department also informed the Chinese Embassy in Washington. Our information in Taipei on this point has been based upon Lincoln White's May 25 statement, which clearly implied prior discussion with the communists. But in any case the Chinese here would not have been satisfied unless we had consulted them in advance. Frankly, I think they are right.
>
> The foregoing raises a point on the conduct of foreign relations which I feel has received insufficient attention. One of the reasons we do not enjoy the full confidence of our allies, particularly the smaller ones, is that they imagine we make a practice of clearing everything with the British, or some other third party, before consulting with the country most directly in-

volved. Frequently—perhaps usually—their fears are unfounded, but this sort of thing has happened often enough to undermine American influence over our weaker friends. The risk of leaks will have to be taken, and in my experience leaks are no more common in most foreign countries than at home. Certainly the Chinese can keep a secret when they try.

You may be right in believing that the talks have held off an an attack on the offshore islands. I do not think so, although I cannot prove it, of course. In the communists' place, I should do just what they are doing. They are steadily building up their military capabilities, in South China particularly, at a substantially faster rate than we and our friends are doing in this region. By next year they will have preponderant power in terms of conventional warfare, from which position they may well engineer yet another Geneva conference designed to give them further victories without fighting. The Reds will count on our reluctance to engage in a nuclear war, particularly over "local" issues, and on our inability to win such a conflict in East Asia with conventional weapons. Meanwhile, the communists are busy undermining the prestige and morale of the Chinese Nationalists and our other close allies in the Far East, increasing their influence over the neutrals by political and economic infiltration, and promoting as much friction as possible between the United States and its friends in general. With things going so well, why should they attack Kinmen or Matsu? . . .

Of course, the Reds may make mistakes, as they have in the past. An attack on the offshore islands now, in sufficient strength to overcome Nationalist resistance, probably would be a mistake not unlike that of June 25, 1950, in Korea. Even so, we do not want them to make that particular kind of mistake. The most hopeful deterrents are, it seems to me, the maintenance of our military strength and that of our Asian allies who are willing to fight, at the same time taking all possible steps to sustain their influence, morale, and confidence in us. With the balance of military power apparently now swinging against us in this region, the intangible factors assume particular importance.

XIV

Perhaps the most delicate aspect of the Geneva talks centered around our efforts to obtain a renunciation of force. In varying forms this conception had plagued us for years. The Chinese government on Taiwan considered that it had gone as far as possible in the formal exchange of letters dated December 10, 1954, by which the use of force would be subject to joint agreement with the United States. Moreover, the Chinese were mindful of their obligations under the United Nations Charter. Any further public commitment, they felt, was not only unnecessary but would be taken as a sign of weakness. Moreover, they had no confidence whatever that the Peiping regime would keep any promises that it might make for propaganda purposes. Finally, all proposals for a new undertaking had excepted cases involving the "inherent right of self-defense." This evidently might be exploited by the Reds, under various imaginable conditions, to render meaningless the whole idea of renouncing force.

The Chinese were particularly disturbed over reports that the United States was proposing at the Geneva talks to issue a joint statement with the Red Chinese on the use of force. My despatch of July 27 included the following:

It is understood that the latest United States draft of a joint statement to be made by the American and Red Chinese ambassadors in Geneva would provide for an undertaking to "settle disputes between them by peaceful means and that, without prejudice to the inherent right of individual and collective self-defense, they [the People's Republic and the United States] will not resort to the threat or use of force in the Taiwan area or elsewhere." It also is understood that the United States does not expect the Reds to agree to this wording, if only because of their insistence that Taiwan is an internal Chinese problem, and that in any event the United States will not trade performance for a Chinese communist promise. Consequently, in fulfillment of its treaty obligations to the Republic of China, the United States will continue to maintain adequate military strength in the Taiwan area to counter the communist threat.

The normal reaction in Free China to any joint declaration by Red China and the United States, however phrased, will be highly unfavorable. It would be widely interpreted as another step toward the diplomatic recognition of Peiping and, more immediately, as constituting American acceptance of communist China's rehabilitation as a peace-loving nation. Neutralists and and others should be expected to consider this step as removing the major obstacle to Peiping's acceptance into the United Nations.

In case a joint declaration should materialize, the Free Chinese reaction might be influenced markedly by an authoritative American statement issued at the same time. If, for example, it were made clear that the United States placed no confidence in communist promises as such, but had joined in the declaration to make clear to all its own genuinely peaceful intentions in the present situation, and to place the Reds on record in a manner which would leave no doubt as to their guilt in the event of new aggression, the unfavorable impact in Free China might be substantially lessened. If such a statement were supplemented by formal assurances that no change of policy toward Taiwan was involved, either as to the fulfillment of its treaty obligations by the United States and its continued readiness to veto if necessary any move to seat Red China in the United Nations, or as to the scope of American military and economic aid, the harmful effects would be further mitigated. If a further step were taken at the same time, by which the United States avowed its aspiration for the liberation of the mainland by peaceful means and the reunification of all China in freedom, the net reaction might well be favorable.

It would be of paramount importance to consult the Chinese government as far in advance as possible and to invite its suggestions as to the kind of statement by the United States government that would be most helpful. At that time, the nature of any public statements to be made by Chinese officials on the same occasion could be discussed.

A joint declaration by Peiping and the United States could, of course, be allowed to speak for itself on the American side. Neither Taipei nor Peiping should be expected to show such reticence, however. The Reds presumably would play for neutral and particularly British opinion by representing the agreement with the United States as a definitive step involving American acceptance of a permanent communist state in control of mainland China, which had given proof of its peaceful intentions. Entry into the United Nations and universal recognition of the Peiping regime should follow as a matter of course. A similar renunciation of force might be demanded from Taipei which, if it were obtained, the Reds would represent as presaging capitulation. There would be no further excuse for large-scale military aid to Taiwan, or for the presence of important American forces in the area. So much for the probable Peiping line, which would be echoed with approval in New Delhi and elsewhere, while still other neutrals would hasten to reappraise their positions.

As for Free China, it would be prudent to prepare for a stream of anguished invective from Taipei in response to a joint Red-American declaration for which inadequate prior consultation and agreement with the Republic of China had taken place. Repudiating any suggestion that it had renounced force (which would be equated with a renouncement of its great aim of returning to the mainland), the Chinese government presumably would feel compelled to issue bellicose statements for internal political consumption and to impress its Asian neighbors. An accompanying increase in military activity around the offshore islands, initiated by Free China to demonstrate its determination, should not be excluded in examining the possibilities. In any event, Chinese-American relations would be seriously strained, a grave decline in morale on Taiwan should be anticipated, and intensified communist efforts to exploit this situation should be taken for granted.

xv

I followed up with a letter of August 3, to an officer of the Department to emphasize my opposition to joining in a statement with the communists, however worded or subsequently explained:

I state here and now my opinion that such a joint statement would be highly dangerous to our interests. Moreover, I believe that the Geneva talks should be terminated; in fact, that they should have been terminated long ago.

☆ *Problems* ☆

My point in the despatch was simply that if we should find ourselves confronted with communist acceptance of our proposal to renounce force, there was a possibility of taking the curse off by advance consultation with the Chinese government and an agreement with them on the issuance of statements which would make clear to all that so far from having reached accommodation with the Reds we were more than ever determined to oppose them and to support our friends.

The Geneva talks continued and later were transferred to Warsaw, but the Chinese Reds failed to renounce the use of force. That no further harm was done must be credited in large part to our successive representatives, Ambassadors U. Alexis Johnson and Jacob D. Beam, for their skillful handling of this thankless business.

XVI

In March, 1956, Secretary Dulles again made a brief stop in Taiwan and had a reassuring session with President Chiang and Foreign Minister Yeh. The Secretary took full and personal responsibility for misunderstandings that had arisen during the previous year over the offshore islands. He was too generous; any blame should have been apportioned in many directions, among both Americans and Chinese. Chiang knew this as well as anyone, but he appreciated Mr. Dulles' willingness to accept responsibility. It was the kind of gesture he understood and could make himself.

Chiefs of Mission from all major United States diplomatic and consular posts in the Far East gathered in Tokyo for a conference in March, 1956. Ambassador and Mrs. John M. Allison, together with Minister-Counselor and Mrs. J. Graham Parsons, took good care of us as usual. The commander of our Far East Air Force, General Laurence S. Kuter, and Mrs. Kuter invited us to be their house guests. They had made brief visits to Taiwan, but now occasion was provided to get better acquainted. In addition to their being delightful hosts, I was struck once more with the broad understanding and high caliber with which our country is favored in so many of its senior military officers.

During our sessions at the Embassy, we were joined by General Lyman L. Lemnitzer, then Commander-in-Chief of the Far East

Command. Again, I was deeply impressed by one of our outstanding military leaders and his presentation of the Far Eastern situation from the military point of view. It was no surprise to me when General Lemnitzer later became Army Chief-of-Staff and then Chairman of the Joint Chiefs of Staff.

The conference furnished still another occasion to emphasize to officials from Washington and from other Far Eastern posts the issue that seemed to me most important in dealing with Chinese. The concept of two Chinas was first on my list, and after stating the basic problem I went on to say:

> Expressed in such terms the parallel with Germany, Korea, and Vietnam becomes clear. As in their case, the so-called two Chinas scheme is simply an easy formula for accepting a *status quo* which almost no one believes could endure. It would contribute to peace no more than formal Western acceptance of a divided Germany.
>
> The Chinese are concerned over what they regard as our basically different approach to Asian as compared to European problems. How would the German Federal Government look upon our holding ambassadorial talks with East Germany? And what if these negotiations were prolonged over a period of many months, with no end in sight? What would be the effect on our other European friends, on both sides of the Curtain? Informed officials may or may not accept at face value our assurances as to the strictly limited character of the present Geneva talks. But no one else in Asia should be expected to do so. To the great majority these talks represent no less than *de facto* recognition of Red China and proof positive of American determination to reach a general accommodation with the communists at almost any cost. . . .
>
> I have suggested in the past that we imagine Europe with Germany and France already communist, with Britain disarmed like Japan, and Spain splintered as is Indochina today. That is not far from the present position in East Asia. When I used this comparison in talking with Admiral Radford last summer, he remarked that under such circumstances in Europe some-

one no doubt would propose surrendering the Channel Islands
to the Reds as a means of bringing peace.

The Kinmen and Matsu groups, with a few scattered positions
making twelve "offshore" islands altogether, constitute Free
China's front line. That line is one hundred miles west of Taiwan,
and I believe we should keep it there. The islands have little or
no military significance for offensive operations against the
mainland, as the communists well know, but they are important
to the defense of Taiwan and the control of the Formosa Strait.
It is generally accepted in military circles that the communists
would not attempt an amphibious attack on Taiwan without
first removing the obstacles presented by Kinmen and Matsu.
Moreover, as long as the offshore islands are strongly held by
the Republic of China, and the Reds are kept in doubt as to
American reaction against a serious attack, so long will the
enemy hesitate either to risk a major amphibious assault or to
attempt the establishment of air supremacy over the Strait.
Modern radar installations on the islands and the maintenance
of supply lines and patrols in the Strait by the Republic of
China also are important factors in the defense of Taiwan.

For the time being, at least, the danger to the communists
of heavy losses at the hands of the Republic of China, plus the
risk of war with the United States, probably more than offset
any possible gain fron conquering the islands. Once they were in
Red hands, however, the enemy would be bolder. Full control of
the air over the Formosa Strait would make it a communist lake,
and would move the front line eastward to the Pescadores and
the coast of Taiwan. If only because of the provisions of our
Mutual Defense Treaty, direct American involvement in hostilities would become more likely in consequence.

In any case, the Republic of China is determined to hold the
principal offshore islands. It seems to me they are right in doing
so, and that this is also in our own larger interest. . . .

If it could be established with any certainty that surrender
of the offshore islands would bring peace in Asia, we might find
it difficult to argue against such action. I recall a conversation
with Wilbur Carr, our minister in Czechoslovakia, just before

the Munich Conference. The British, influenced by Runciman's reports, evidently were about to press the Czechs to meet Hitler's territorial demands. I asked Carr whether he thought this would satisfy Hitler. "Of course not," he replied. In the present case Red China does not even pretend that the offshore islands represent a last territorial ambition. The communist aim obviously is to weaken the Republic of China, politically and militarily, in preparation for final conquest. It is the case of Czechoslovakia and the Sudetenland all over again.

Unfortunately the United States failed to blockade all of Red China when its armies attacked in Korea. Nothing less would have permitted us to compel the eventual withdrawal of Chinese forces beyond the Yalu after stopping them in the field. As matters stand today, controls on communist China's trade are ineffective from an economic standpoint. . . .

On the other hand, present trade controls have considerable political and strategic importance. Red China finds it more expensive and otherwise more difficult to obtain certain strategic items. Still more important is the political or psychological factor. Much face would be gained by the removal of trade controls which now brand communist China as even more of a pariah than the Soviet Union. Trade in Red eyes is a strategic and political instrument from which mutual economic benefits are neither expected nor desired. Any relaxation of controls at this time would only enhance communist China's prestige and power among its neighbors.

So far from easing controls on the overseas trade of Red China, I believe we should be prepared to tighten them at a moment's notice in case of new aggression. For example, we recognize the legal right of Free China to the offshore islands. A serious attack on them, by sea or air, unquestionably would constitute aggression and a threat to peace in general. The United States is not obligated to assist directly in defending the islands, but we have every practical interest and moral obligation to stop aggression. After inviting action by the United Nations, we could at once institute a blockade of the China coast from the mouth of the Yangtze south to the port of Swatow. Our Navy could operate at a distance from the coast; the close-in patrols would be maintained by our Chinese friends. Meanwhile, the Reds quite likely would draw in their horns, particularly if our reaction were quick. In any case, a blockade would give us time to determine whether the communist offensive posed so dangerous a threat to peace as to require some form of active military intervention on our part. . . .

Remember, we are dealing with morale. What people believe can be more important than the facts behind their beliefs. Our official assurances are discounted as of no more than short-term value. Our actions during the past year are seen as evidence of a clear intent to make a deal with the communists. . . .

What, then, can the United States do about our first line of defense in Asia: the morale of those friends who remain on our side? First, we must maintain our own military strength in the Western Pacific at a level adequate to deter open aggression. This I hope and believe we are doing. Second, we must pull our military and economic aid programs out of the morass of red tape and delay which has threatened to engulf them during the past year. They must be made more purposeful, and first things must come first. Third, we should consult more fully with our Asian friends in the earliest possible stage of every international project affecting their interests. Finally, we must keep hope alive.

As matters stand, it often seems to our friends in Asia that the United States either refuses to take a position on a given issue until a crisis forces us to do so, or else we present them with a cooked dish—take it or leave it—which we and one or more of our European allies have prepared. It is all too easy to pass from impatience to arrogance, as we have learned from the experience of colonial powers. Certainly, there is no better way to lose friends and influence people against us than failure to persuade our allies that we fully understand and appreciate their viewpoints, even if we cannot always agree with them on the best course to pursue. The way we handle our foreign relations is scarcely less important than the actions finally taken. . . .

The simple truth is, I believe, that there can be no hope for lasting peace in this region while China remains in communist hands. With atomic superiority we can maintain a temporary and precarious balance of power which may avert or delay a major war. That is extremely important. But we must expect to lose out eventually unless, by active containment or otherwise, profound changes can be induced behind the Asian Iron Curtain. Publicly and repeatedly we should share the legitimate aspirations of our Asian friends, even while restraining them as to method. We must exert continuing efforts to bring about the reunification of China and Korea, in freedom. We should encourage our Asian friends in the belief that this can and will happen. We must keep hope alive and thereby sustain the morale so essential to surmounting the moral crisis facing the whole world today. In this process, confidence in the firm and understanding purpose of the United States will be built.

It is beyond doubt a moral crisis that confronts us. The communists have conditioned the rest of the world to outrageous conduct over a period of many years. Actions that would have provoked war a few decades ago are accepted today as a matter of course. The perpetrator may be criticized, but is then embraced. He need only promise to stop doing what he had no right to do in the first place. Nearly forty years' experience with Soviet communism clearly establishes that every friendly gesture on our part is exploited by the Reds for ulterior purposes. On the other hand, strong action often brings them to reason. While remembering these facts of life, it is also vital that we should not lose our own sense of right and wrong. I discussed this point with Cardinal Spellman during his most recent visit to Taipei. He and I agreed that in international relations today one of our gravest dangers lies in failing to recognize sin or evil for what it is.

XVII

In July, 1956, everyone in Free China was heartened once more by the action of the United States Congress in passing a resolution which set forth the unaltered and unanimous opposition of both Houses to the seating of Red China in the United Nations.

Our schedule for 1956 did not include a trip to the United States. During September, Pauline and I enjoyed a vacation in Indonesia and Southeast Asia instead. This included one more visit to Bangkok, a city we always found most delightful, followed by a flight to Singapore. There we were welcomed by Consul General and Mrs. Elbridge Durbrow in an atmosphere reminiscent in many ways of Hong Kong. I called on Sir Robert Scott, the British commissioner general, whom I had last seen in Washington several years before. We continued by ship to Djakarta, Surabaya, and Bali, which far exceeded all our expectations. Returning, we went by air to Surabaya, motored across Java to the old capital of Djogjakarta, visited the splendid ninth-century Borobudur temple, and flew back to Djakarta. Ambassador and Mrs. Hugh S. Cumming, Jr. invited us to spend a night in their summer quarters on the hills above Bogor. Then we returned by air to Singapore, Hong Kong, and Taipei, with many pleasant recollections of fascinating Indonesia and its friendly people.

☆☆☆

9: Programs

I

THE BROADENING of American foreign relations through official
"programs" appears to date no further back than the end of World
War II. Many of the activities involved were by no means new, but
traditionally they had been carried on by private or quasi-public
organizations and individuals through other than official channels.
Doubtless the magnitude of the problems of relief and reconstruction
facing us in 1945 was largely responsible. But there was also a
growing awareness that we had defeated one set of enemies only to be
faced by another, which might prove even more dangerous: the international communist conspiracy directed from the Kremlin.

The American public came to realize that we could afford to neglect no opportunity to counter the world-wide communist menace.
To further this goal we developed numerous programs in the fields of
information, educational exchange, culture, entertainment, and exchange of persons, among others. All of these programs were pursued on Taiwan with success, largely under the direction of the
United States Information Service and its three successive and able
heads, Josiah W. Bennett, Seymour I. Nadler, and Ralph L. Powell.
The total cost of these activities, however, amounted to no more than
a few hundred thousand dollars yearly.

By far the most important United States programs on Taiwan
were, of course, the manifold operations known collectively as the
Mutual Security Program. The first major foreign economic assistance effort to affect postwar Taiwan was that of UNRRA, financed

up to 72 per cent by the United States. This, in turn, was followed by a so-called post-UNRRA relief and the China Aid Act of 1948. Other forms of economic assistance were made available as well, and in 1950 a small but efficient mission from our Economic Cooperation Administration was working closely with the Chinese in improving agricultural methods and importing essential commodities. Its available funds, however, were small. A measure of Taiwan's financial needs could be obtained by adding the twenty million dollars received through ECA in 1950 to the net loss of gold and foreign exchange by the National Bank in the same year. This total of approximately ninety million dollars proved, in fact, to represent the average amount of foreign economic aid required by Free China in the years 1951-57.

One of the most satisfactory features of our economic assistance to Taiwan was the work of the Joint Commission on Rural Reconstruction, which was responsible for the agricultural portion of the ECA program. Authorized by the China Aid Act of 1948, and under the imaginative direction of Dr. Chiang Mon-lin, former chancellor of the National University of Peiping, the commission contributed importantly to a gratifying rise in agricultural production. Rural health and cooperative marketing activities were furthered, and notable contributions made to the land reform program, which by 1957 had given to 75 per cent of Taiwan's farmers title deeds to all or part of the land they tilled. Subsidiary but very real attractions of the commission were that it was able to operate on a very modest budget and never required as many as twenty Americans among its personnel. The Chinese staff carried by far the greater part of the load, and did so admirably.

With the substantial increase in American economic aid late in 1950, it was clear that we should have to take a more active interest in Chinese financial problems. There were competent economists and financial experts in the Chinese government, including the Minister of Finance, C. K. Yen. Moyer of our ECA mission felt, however, that greater high-level interest in economic affairs was needed among Chinese officialdom. He proposed establishing an Economic Stabilization Board, to include top officials from the more important branches of the government, which would meet periodically to consider all important economic or financial problems. Representatives of the American Embassy and of our economic mission would attend as observers.

Everyone seemed to agree that the idea of an Economic Stabilization Board was a good one, but for various reasons the project had failed to get off the ground. Moyer suggested that I call on President Chiang and ask him to appoint a high Chinese official as chairman of the new board. I did so; it was my first talk with the President on economic matters. He was sympathetic, and early in 1951 he appointed the governor of Taiwan, who was also a member of the cabinet, as chairman. The Board continued to function usefully in succeeding years and played an important part in promoting the economic stabilization for which its name called. Later, members of our military mission, as well as senior Chinese military officers, attended its meetings.

II

Moyer's successor as director of our economic mission was Hubert G. Schenck, formerly professor of geology at Stanford University, and a man of great intelligence and imagination. The mission's accomplishments continued to expand under his direction. Schenck, in turn, was replaced in 1954 by Joseph L. Brent, a former Foreign Service officer. Again, we were most fortunate in having an able American in this key position.

It should not be imagined, however, that economic progress on Taiwan was simple or easy. Within the limits of funds made available from Washington, there was the continuing problem of maintaining optimum distribution among three general categories of expenditures: (1) consumer goods to be sold to the public for local currency; (2) commodities of a nonmilitary character, but intended for consumption by the Chinese military establishment, such as textiles, fibers, and food; (3) capital goods for economic development. Annual aid from the United States averaging ninety million dollars was rather evenly divided among these three categories. There was constant pressure from political and financial circles to import more consumer goods, both to raise living standards and to check inflation. The military, also, was never entirely satisfied with their share. Both Chinese and American economists wanted more investment in economic, particularly industrial, development; they begrudged the money spent for consumer goods and military purposes. Nevertheless, a reasonable balance was maintained.

At times both the Chinese and our economic staff became discouraged or frustrated in the face of innumerable day-to-day problems. I found such a situation on my return from the United States in the fall of 1955. The occasion seemed appropriate for a general review of economic conditions. Besides talking with members of our economic mission in detail (Brent was away at the time), I had long conversations with President Chiang, Vice President Chen Cheng, Finance Minister P. Y. Hsu, Governor C. K. Yen, and others. My conclusions were that nothing was seriously wrong, but that we were beginning to suffer from what someone called "scatteration" in our economic effort. There was also confusion in the use of "counterpart" funds, representing local currency derived from sales of imported consumer goods. My letter of November 4, 1955, to the acting director of our economic mission was written after my preliminary review, and contained the following:

I fear the subject has become so complex that a fresh approach may be called for. Certainly, many of the loose ends mentioned in an earlier paragraph will have to be tied up before we know where we or the Chinese stand. I believe, however, that we should give consideration to the possibility of reverting to an earlier conception of financial aid. This would involve the elimination of any general bugetary support as such by the United States, and the placing of all counterpart expenditures on a strict project basis. I would go even further in an effort to get our fingers out of as many minor pies as possible, so that we might concentrate on the most important parts of our program. This should have the effect of fixing full responsibility, financial and other, on the Chinese themselves in most fields. As a partial offset we might have to assume a somewhat larger share of the burden in economic development, while continuing such technical assistance as seems to promise really worth-while results. On the military side, it may not be feasible for the near future, but I would favor working toward a situation where the Chinese would assume full responsibility for pay, food, clothing, general administration, and maintenance in their military establishment.

The United States contribution would be limited to equipment and supplies not available locally, plus the services of MAAG and the financing of any special projects which we considered essential. The latter would include all counterpart expenditures for military purposes.

In addition to simplifying our own operations, any steps which place responsibility squarely on the Chinese should be beneficial both to them and to the United States. At present, responsibility is so diffused in so many fields that unless the trend toward even greater complexity can be reversed, we cannot hope to deal effectively with the financial problems confronting us. As a part of any program to fix responsibility, it would seem essential that, once a budget had been fixed, no additional outlays at either American or Chinese instance would be undertaken without full prior consultation and the provision of new funds for the purpose. If additional sources of money from current revenues or additional American aid were not immediately available, joint consideration would be given to postponing projects already included in the budget so that the necessary funds could be transferred. As a corollary to the foregoing, Americans and Chinese would have to agree not to resort to additional bank loans except by mutual consent. . . .

At the same time I am convinced that still larger numbers of American officials looking over Chinese shoulders and putting fingers into still more pies do not provide an answer to our problems. In fact, I believe that we have already too many official Americans in most agencies here, with the result that the law of diminishing returns has begun to operate and is responsible for a part of our increased difficulties during the past year. What we need is a simplification of our effort, with greater concentration on what is most important, and a concurrent plan to give the Chinese greater and more definite responsibility.

III

By 1953 the Chinese had been able to increase their total tax revenues, local, provincial, and national, to a level approximating one-fourth of the gross national product. This total was being more or less evenly divided between civil and military outlays; it evidently was about all the economy could bear. Current revenues were sufficient to support the full cost of general government and a substantial part of Free China's expenditure for defense. By the end of 1954 we felt justified in predicting that within perhaps three years Free China's economy should be self-supporting except for what might be called extraordinary military expenditures, although there would be a continuing shortage of investment capital for adequate economic growth. Meanwhile, sales of consumer goods imported under our aid program covered the local currency needs of the Chinese military establishment over and above its normal budgetary resources, besides contributing importantly to economic development projects. The goal of normal self-support was not attained in 1957, but by that year Chinese current revenues were covering both the full cost of civil government and nearly all of the recurring local currency needs of the armed forces. Nonrecurring military expenditures for airfields, barracks, roads, and numerous other items promised to taper off with the completion of many such projects in 1957-58. Remaining to be covered, of course, were necessary imports of military equipment and sufficient foreign exchange or its equivalent to support essential economic development.

Taiwan's rapidly growing population and limited available land made industrial expansion imperative. United States policy was to encourage private enterprise wherever possible, and the Chinese were in general agreement. New legislation was enacted to attract foreign private capital, and shares of enterprises taken over from the Japanese were used, along with bonds, to compensate landowners whose property was being distributed among small farmers. Light industry, notably in the textile branch, expanded rapidly in private hands. It was evident, however, that sufficient long-term investment in power, chemical fertilizers, sugar, metals, and similar products could not be expected from private sources. Public corporations appeared to be the only answer, and United States loans facilitated rapid development in these and other branches. Largely as a result of industrial expansion, in the period 1951-57 China's gross national product rose at least twice as fast as the 3.5 per cent annual increase in population. Living standards climbed steadily in consequence.

A good case could be made for charging to defense all types of American financial support for Free China. The consumer goods supplied and sold for local currency, which in turn supported the military budget, served the same purpose as dollars that otherwise would have had to be furnished directly. Various aspects of new economic development had a direct bearing on the military program, notably in the fields of transportation and communications. Expansion of electric power facilities also was a basic need for the military as much as for civilians. In fact, without the support necessary to maintain a stable economy, no satisfactory military effort would have been possible.

Of course, the United States foreign aid program was supporting many countries under a great variety of conditions. It was natural that efforts should be made to differentiate between economic and military aid in presentations to Congress. Unfortunately, the complex situation described in the preceding paragraph became even more complex when an attempt was made to apply criteria on a global basis. One result was a division of procurement between the Department of Defense and the International Cooperation Administration for the same nonmilitary commodities, depending on who would consume them in Taiwan. Perhaps the most logical, although hypothetical, division between military and economic assistance would have been to call everything military except such aid as might have been needed in the absence of any communist threat to Taiwan, and hence of any necessity for a large military establishment. On this basis, the average annual American outlay for so-called economic aid to Free China in the period 1951-57 might have been considered as made up of two hundred fifty million dollars for military purposes and some fifty million dollars for civilian economic requirements.

With equal logic, it could be said that the entire Mutual Security Program for Free China was directed toward establishing and improving the economic well-being of the people of Taiwan. Without the military features of the program, which provided essential strength in maintaining a strategic balance in the Western Pacific, the economic portion would have been useless. The whole was indivisible.

IV

In its initial stages, our program of military aid for Free China necessarily concentrated on supplying a few essentials, notably ammunition, to deal with a possible communist attack. The needs of the United Nations forces in Korea naturally received the highest priority while fighting was in progress. Taiwan could expect no more than a modest share of such equipment and supplies as were not needed in the north. Nevertheless, our Military Assistance Advisory Group, under Major General William C. Chase, was able to report gratifying progress by the date of the Korean Armistice in 1953. The Chinese Armed Forces had been well trained in basic terms before our military mission arrived in 1951, and a large percentage of their officers and men had battle experience behind them. Our immediate purpose was to improve their firepower and mobility.

By 1954, when it became evident that further fighting in Korea was improbable for the foreseeable future, military equipment became easier to obtain. More thought could be given to improving the training and organization of the Chinese forces. Questions as to size and organization also depended upon the mission or missions contemplated for the military establishment. At the same time, the limiting factors of financial availabilities, suitable manpower, and training and maneuver areas on a densely populated island all had to be considered. No less important were the prospective psychological effects of any substantial increase or decrease in men under arms and the resulting impact of considerable numbers of demobilized men on an economy that already suffered from underemployment among unskilled workers.

There was also the practical matter of Taiwan's geography. No roads crossed the great range of mountains running nearly the entire length of the island from north to south, and the main lines of communication were necessarily along the thickly populated west coast. These were vulnerable to air and even commando raids, making it necessary to maintain strong forces in both the north and the south on the assumption that they might not be able to give each other support on short notice. Moreover, it seemed only prudent to compensate for quality with quantity until the effectiveness of the Chinese forces could be increased by further deliveries of equipment. All troops at least had some kind of weapons, and hence a military capability that could not be spared under the circumstances. The conclusion was inescapable that no substantial change in numbers of men under arms could be envisaged until our military aid program was much further advanced. We reported to Washington in detail along these lines in March, 1954. The Van Fleet Report later that year provided opportunity to comment further. My letter of December 8, 1954, to General Chase, of which copies went to Washington, included the following:

First, I may say that the Report seems to me on the whole of excellent quality and the conclusions generally sound. It will be most useful to all of us for reference and guidance. . . .

At present, I have no particular comments to make on the treatment given to the Chinese Navy and the Combined Service Force. In the case of the Air Force, however, it may be that the recommendation to reduce it in size reflects the need for a more precise statement of its mission. I shall not attempt at this time to draft such a statement; your Air Force officers are more competent to do this, but I might suggest another approach to the matter.

As in the case of the Chinese Army, it would appear desirable to so equip, organize, and train the Chinese Air Force that there would be no need to base combat units of the United States Air Force on Formosa. Provision, of course, should be made to take the latter course under certain circumstances, but both militarily and politically it would seem preferable to have the Chinese Air Force do the job under what might be called "ordinary" conditions. This job evidently would include the defense of Free China against any probable enemy attack, as well as reconnaissance and transport functions. In addition, since we are giving the Chinese "limited offensive" capabilities, it would appear logical that their Air Force should be able to provide tactical air support for the Chinese Army and Marines on any offensive mission which they are likely to be given. Starting with these considerations, I believe that a sound case could be made for maintaining the Air Force at least at its present strength. . . .

In the Report's discussion of manpower (p. II-9) it is estimated that the resources immediately available appear adequate to support forces of 800,000 men for twenty-seven months of combat, or about the same as for the Republic of Korea. It is also pointed out, however, that the annual input to the manpower pool on Formosa is less than half that of Korea. The conclusion is drawn that the twenty-four infantry divisions recommended (330,000 men with half of the divisions at full strength) represent the "maximum feasible mobilization goal." On a long-term basis, I would agree. But it seems to me that our particular problem is the next two or three years, during which the general situation may become somewhat clearer and Japan can begin to contribute substantially to the military strength of the free world. If a large-scale conflict should break out in the meantime, we should have to make maximum use of Free China's manpower. Our present planning should foresee that eventuality. Five years from now will be soon enough to consider basing the Chinese Armed Forces on a normal annual increment of manpower.

I note also that the Report recommends breaking up the Armored Force into tank battalions to be attached to the infantry divisions. I seem to recall that you expressed similar ideas shortly after your arrival in Formosa, but that for political and practical reasons no radical change was made. If you still think this plan has merit, it might possibly be implemented as part of a package deal which would meet some of President's Chaing's wishes in other respects. For example, on a divisional basis the Chinese Army might consist of twenty-one full-strength infantry divisions, each with some armor, and nine reserve divisions, each with a cadre strength of perhaps 1,500 active duty personnel. Such an organization would adhere to the JCS figure of twenty-one infantry divisions . . . ; it would give "face" to Free China by increasing the total number of divisions to that proposed for Korea, it would provide places for a considerable number of officers now in surplus, and it would serve to train a very substantial number of reservists who might go far to meet the needs of [full-scale war] in case the enemy should leave us no other honorable choice.

To put into effect a plan such as the above, we should have to persuade President Chiang to accept nine MDAP supported reserve divisions, and the addition of tank units to twenty-one regular divisions, in exchange for disbanding his Armored Force and giving up the idea of twenty-four full-strength infantry divisions. Properly explained to him, I think he would agree. We also would have to obtain JCS approval. By adhering to their figure of twenty-one infantry divisions, and offering the Armored Force plan as a means of economizing on men and money as well as noting that Van Fleet recommended it, I believe that we might persuade them to support nine reserve divisions along the lines already approved for Korea, NATO, etc.

Of course we should have to be ready with answers to the questions of equipment and economic support for the nine reserve divisions. Here, again, we have the example of General Taylor's plan for a bare minimum of equipment for the Korean reserve divisions. Also we have a certain amount of obsolete equipment here which could be used. Certainly, I would not now recommend the addition of full equipment, costing perhaps $270 million for nine divisions, to our MDA program for Free China. As I have remarked frequently, I believe that the United States should have under its own control an adequate stockpile, somewhere in the Far East, of equipment which could be sent quickly to any point where it might be needed. I understand that something of the kind exists already in Japan; perhaps this should be supplemented by stocks in Okinawa, Guam, or elsewhere. It would not seem necessary to keep on hand full equipment for all of the reserve divisions projected for Korea, Japan, Formosa, and the Philippines. But there should be enough to fill the pipeline until additional shipments could arrive from the United States. In any case, this equipment would remain under our control until we wanted it used.

On the economic side, the suggested plan would cost no more than what is now projected except for some additional support for the reserve program. Indirectly the United States is already paying for the present reserve training scheme, whether the JCS admit it or not. How large the increase should be to meet the goals suggested above, your experts will know better than I. By some target date, enough young men should have had or be under reserve training to bring all divisions up to full strength at least. For some time to come, however, I suspect that the availability of barracks will be the chief limiting factor, since the rate of construction has not kept pace with the availability of funds.

V

The Chinese had been working on more ambitious schemes for improving and enlarging their military establishment. These were called the "Kai Plan" and the "Hsieh Plan." They foresaw an army with thirty-six infantry divisions and expanded reserve training, among other features. My letter of December 29, 1954, to Admiral Radford enclosed a copy of my December 8 letter to General Chase and included the following paragraph:

> You will note that my letter to Chase mentioned an army of thirty divisions. In the first instance this is a "political" figure, since it goes halfway from the existing force of twenty-four infantry divisions toward meeting the Kai Plan goal of thirty-six. Also, it is the total that appears to have been mentioned most frequently for the Republic of Korea (twenty regular plus ten reserve divisions). In addition, the figure of thirty divisions is one with which General Wedemeyer was working on the mainland. Finally, by including the present armored units and the existing reserve training program, even with a modest expansion of the latter foreseen in the Hsieh Plan, and bringing up to full strength the present twenty-one regular infantry divisions for which support has been authorized by the JCS, the number of men on active duty at one time in the Chinese Army should not be materially larger than the 365,000 total now being used as a basis for our MDA Program.

In the following year (1955), when the general conception for the Chinese military establishment as I had outlined it in this letter was becoming reality, General Chase often referred half jokingly to the Army organization in particular as the "Rankin Plan." Of course, I could claim no originality of authorship beyond a modest effort to harmonize and simplify various political and military factors.

VI

General Maxwell D. Taylor, who had been commander of our Far

271

East Command in Tokyo, was appointed Army Chief of Staff in mid-1955. On his way to the United States he stopped over in Taiwan for talks with President Chiang and other Chinese officials, as well as Americans, about the future of our military aid program for Free China. The military situation on and around the offshore islands naturally came up for discussion, and I was not quite satisfied that the matter had been presented to General Taylor in the best possible light. I told him that I hoped to pursue the subject with him further in Washington, which I did a few weeks later. In any event, General Taylor left a highly favorable impression on all the Chinese and Americans whom he saw in Taiwan. There was confidence that our problems would receive most sympathetic attention from the United States Army.

During General Taylor's visit the Chinese put on one of their impressive military displays, of which I saw many during my years in Taiwan. We traveled south to Ping Tung, which had become one of the island's principal military centers, both for Army and Air Force activities. General Taylor seemed most favorably impressed by what he saw, and everything apparently went like clockwork. After Taylor's departure, President and Madame Chiang invited us to fly back to Taipei in their plane. Pauline and I chatted with Madame Chiang on the way, while the President rested briefly and then picked up a book of Chinese classics and read to himself. Only later did we learn of what he had experienced at Ping Tung.

The story never was made public in all details, but a group of relatively junior officers of the Chinese Army apparently had used the visit of General Taylor and the presence of numerous other officials, Chinese and American, to present certain demands to the President. These had to do with promotions and other proposals, which may have had a degree of merit, but the manner of presentation, and the background of certain of the officers involved, suggested that subversive influence was at work. Subsequent investigation by a high-level civilian committee bore out this suspicion, although there was never any official confirmation of the report that the dissidents had machine guns trained on the reviewing stand at Ping Tung where we were sitting with the President.

In any case, the situation was taken in hand on the spot in Ping Tung and the major casualty was General Sun Li-jen, Commander-in-Chief of the Chinese Army, whom we all liked and admired. He was held responsible for the unhappy affair because of his position. Actually, it appeared that while he knew something about the group of dissident officers in question, General Sun had no idea that they would push matters so far on this occasion. It marked the end of his brilliant military career. I visited him at Taichung some time later; he was comfortably installed with his family in an attractive house and enjoying his rose garden.

VII

During my 1955 trip to the United States, General Chase reached the retirement age. His contribution during a period of four difficult years had been invaluable. I had recommended strongly that he be promoted so that he could stay on in Taiwan. Later, he wrote to me from the United States that he was to lecture at the National War College on "The Future of Nationalist China." Did I have any suggestions, and on what points should he be particularly careful? The following paragraphs are from my reply of November 15, 1955:

The possibility of your upsetting our "apple cart" in your talk at the National War College is the least of my troubles. You know the score as well as anyone, and it seems to me there is only one thing you would need to be careful about. That is one of our oldest problems: in giving a balanced presentation, to avoid criticisms that provide any more ammunition than we can help for those who are looking for an excuse to write us off again. . . .

The future of National China, which I prefer to "Nationalist China," is sufficiently obscure to permit predictions on a basis of 60-40 probabilities at best. Even such predictions may at any time be thrown out by some accident. At present, however, it appears that for the next few years the probabilities favor a continuation of the *status quo*—call it a stalemate, if you like. During that period Free China will continue to make tangible progress in the military and economic fields, always assuming sufficient material and moral support from the United States, paralleled by an adequate effort on the part of the government of the Republic of China itself.

In the international field, however, it appears that the position of National China is liable to deteriorate over the next few years in comparison to Red China. The latter not only has enormously greater human and material resources, but a highly purposeful Soviet MDAP during the past few years has developed the Peiping regime into the world's third power in the air and on land. Since the fighting stopped in Korea there have been no serious drains on this expanding strength. Other factors, of course, affect the relative positions of Free and Red China, but military power is a *sine qua non* where communism is concerned.

Under the above conditions, and in view of well-established communist policy, the *status quo* as regards Free and Red China should not be expected to continue indefinitely. . . .

During the period of stalemate it probably will become apparent in due course as to whether the communists or the free world will gain the upper hand in the cold war in East Asia. If the communists pull far enough ahead, then a sizable hot war, involving the United States, will become almost inevitable. If, on the other hand, the free world can strengthen its relative position in this part of the world over the next few years, there should be a 50 to 50 chance of preventing a war, and at least some prospect of an internal collapse or other profound change in Red China which would permit a genuine solution of the China problem. It is these possibilities, along with our desire to prevent the outbreak of large-scale hostilities if we can, which provide the basis for a China policy. . . .

In other words, the "Future of National China," and of all China, will depend in large measure upon decisions taken in Washington. I do not suggest that the United States carries the sole responsibility. That must be shared by the government of the Republic of China, the Peiping regime, the Soviet Union, the United Kingdom, and perhaps others. But our part will be a vital one. . . . We miss you here. I am continually reminded of the grand job you did in Free China.

General Chase was succeeded as Chief of MAAG by Major General George D. Smythe, who in turn was followed by Major General Frank

S. Bowen, Jr. Both officers established creditable records in carrying out their duties in Free China.

VIII

By this time stories were appearing with increasing frequency in the world press about Chiang Kai-shek's "aging" army. The impression given was that these Chinese soldiers were tripping over their long gray beards as they marched. There was a problem, to be sure, but it was in no way so grave as represented by those who wished to discredit Free China. The forces that came to Taiwan from the mainland were aging at the same rate as everyone else; the average age was approaching thirty when we finally worked out a plan with the Chinese to do something about it. Money was needed, and in this respect our help was indispensable.

As an index to the size of the problem, it was noted that a little over 10 per cent of the men in the Chinese Armed Forces were forty-five or older. Many of these, particularly the commissioned and noncommissioned officers, were fit for duty and could expect to give many more years of effective service. But some men under forty-five were no longer physically fit, and it appeared that about 70,000 should be demobilized altogether in the near future. An organization was set up, headed later by President Chiang's elder son, Lieutenant General Chiang Ching-kuo, which sorted out the veterans and helped them to get re-established. Some (about 20 per cent) were able to fend for themselves; others were given vocational training or employed on public works. Still others were placed on the land as farmers or in institutions for treatment of chronic ailments. Their places in the Armed Forces gradually were filled by the young men who had been receiving reserve training, irrespective of whether they were Taiwan-born or from the mainland. The total cost of this operation was kept within modest dimensions. It could be maintained on a continuing basis by the Chinese themselves after our initial help.

Within two years after reserve training had been started systematically in February, 1953, a total of 110,000 young men had completed the basic course. Of these, 16,000 had been incorporated into regular military units. The Chinese operated the reserve training centers entirely on their own and did a splendid job. The camps were

275

clean and attractive, with much attention given to sports and physical fitness in general. Morale was high, and the camps served to bring together the sons of Taiwan-born Chinese and those from many parts of the mainland.

I reported to Washington as follows on August 24, 1956:

Considerable progress has been made during the past year in Army replacement training. Plans are well under way for training nine Reserve Infantry Divisions. The problem of releasing the ineffectives from the GRC Armed Forces has not met with the success which was originally expected. Settlement has been made for only 24,000 (19,800 on an interim basis) of the older and physically incapable men scheduled for first priority discharges from the GRC Armed Forces since the start of Vocational Assistance Commission for Retired Servicemen Program. Although plans have been initiated to release approximately 44,000 additional ineffectives, the arrangements necessary to make them self-supporting or to institutionalize those who require special care are proceeding slowly. Should settlement be effected for the 44,000 ineffectives now being carried on GRC Forces' rolls, this problem would be reduced to a much more modest, if continuing, proportion.

Meanwhile, young draftees are being inducted for two years in the Army and for three years in the Air Force and Navy. Over 80 per cent of the new recruits were born on Taiwan, and within a few years a majority of the men in the Armed Forces will be natives of the island. In addition to bringing down the average age of men in the services, a new element of flexibility will be introduced. Unlike most of the older soldiers who came from the mainland, the young men will be able to return to their homes, after completing their military service, and find places for themselves in the local economy. Thus it should be possible in due course to adjust the number on active duty to practical needs. The present figures of twenty-one regular and nine reserve infantry divisions, for example, might be altered to eighteen and twelve respectively, without working undue hardship on individual servicemen or affecting the total of trained men who could be called up in an emergency.

☆ *Programs* ☆

IX

Meanwhile the Chinese Air Force and Navy, although small, had not been neglected. The Air Force was being equipped with jet fighter-bombers as fast as the pilots could complete their transition training. Five jet combat wings, two conventional transport wings, and one jet reconnaissance squadron were equipped and became fully operational in due course. The Navy was provided with three Benson-class destroyers besides a number of mine-layers, bringing its strength up to seventy-three combat and thirty-seven other vessels. The efficiency of both services increased in gratifying fashion. Technical and general schools, as well as professional academies, were developed and expanded for all. The average Chinese soldier, sailor, or airman was rapidly becoming, for the first time, a literate, technically trained servant of his country. In addition to humanitarian considerations, he was worth in military terms all and more than it was costing to give him training, education, and care after eventual demobilization. By 1957 Free China had the best balanced and the second largest Asian military establishment on the side of the free world. The outlay for the American taxpayer was less than 10 per cent of what it would have cost to maintain in the Western Pacific an equivalent counterweight and deterrent to communist aggression in United States forces.

On August 24, 1956, our Embassy forwarded to Washington a new study of Free China's armed forces. I wrote the more general part, and our military attachés appended detailed outlines of what we could and should expect the Chinese to do, always assuming that we continued to do our part in supplying the tools. At my request, they also undertook a review of possible or probable enemy military action, adding recommendations as to appropriate counter-action by Free China and the United States in each case. We felt that perhaps not enough attention had been given to preparation for immediate steps in an emergency, particularly where coordination between Chinese and Americans would be necessary.

Vice Admiral Stuart H. Ingersoll, heading the United States Taiwan Defense Command, was in full agreement with the need for planning to meet all emergencies and assigned a senior officer to direct the work at his headquarters. We believed that our Chinese friends would feel greater confidence as a result, that the enemy inevitably would learn something of our planning activities and be more circumspect in consequence, that quick reaction was the most hopeful means of localizing any conflict that might break out, and that careful preparation offered the best guarantee of victory in any case.

Detailed planning was continued through 1957 under the direction of Ingersoll's successor, Vice Admiral Austin K. Doyle. Once more we were extremely fortunate in having as our senior military officer one who was not only an able commander but who understood and believed in what our government was trying to do in China. Our program of military assistance for Free China had permitted the Chinese military establishment to reach a high degree of effectiveness. Continuous planning could now be carried on by Chinese and Americans with greater confidence in their ability to meet emergencies.

X

From time to time we were asked about our "political program." If this meant the policy of the United States toward Free China, the answer was not difficult. More often, however, the inquirer had taken more or less for granted that in the first instance, our efforts were dedicated to introducing or expanding American ideas of democratic government among the Chinese. In fact, a pervading if indirect aim of all United States economic, military, informational, and cultural programs was, of course, to attract wider acceptance and understanding of American methods and ideals. Our immediate practical purpose, however, was to promote defense capabilities and the well-being of the population at large as a means of strengthening the free world and thereby supporting our basic foreign policy.

In helping with land reform on Taiwan, in improving living standards by aiding in industrial development, and by assistance in the field of education, the United States contributed indirectly to genuine democracy. The Chinese themselves were no less aware than we of the need for gaining public support for their government and its policies. All progress in this direction had our open sympathy. Elections to public office, based on universal suffrage for both sexes, were introduced for the first time on the island. The most important elective office involved—that of mayor of Taipei—was won by a nonparty candidate, which spoke well for the progress of representative government in what usually was considered a one-party system.

There was no possibility of truly national elections with the mainland in communist hands, and the government on Taiwan could not abandon its strong position as representing all of China by resorting to new "national" elections in the one province fully under its control. Taiwan, of course, had its quota of elected representatives in the Legislative Yuan. One or more native-born Taiwanese usually held portfolios in the national cabinet. Minor political parties also were represented, but the dominant force continued to be the Kuomintang, or National party. Presumably it was inevitable in any case that during a period of civil war, with the communists in control of the mainland, virtually all noncommunists should join forces.

In any event, higher authority has never assigned to Americans the responsibility for developing a new political philosophy for China. It would be both presumptuous and futile for us to attempt it. "Democracy" does not mean the same in Asia as in North America, and probably never will. This is not to say that many ideas and customs that we would accept as democratic are not widespread among the Chinese. But we often confuse matters by insistence on the word "democracy," which the communists already have prostituted so generally for their own ends. "Freedom" is a more useful word; all of our programs for Free China contributed to more freedom for its people and more strength for the free world.

☆☆☆

10: Expansion

GROWING AMERICAN interest in Taiwan was perhaps most dramatically evidenced by visits of ever larger numbers of United States officials. Certainly they were responsible for a substantial part of the foreign publicity that the island received. Virtually without exception these visits were useful and pleasant experiences for the Americans stationed on Taiwan. We hoped that our visitors enjoyed themselves too. Certainly they went away with new knowledge and impressions which, on balance, proved most helpful to us and to the cause of Free China. Often they interpreted current Washington thinking to us in an intimate way that was invaluable in our work. To the Chinese these visits were continuing evidence of American interest in their problems.

During the earlier years of my tour of duty in Taipei, the city's hotel accommodations left much to be desired. The Chinese government operated several guest houses for official use; these were much better than the hotels, but were intended, of course, for official invited guests, both Chinese and foreign. Although almost every American was made welcome by our Chinese friends in Taipei, only a small portion of our official visitors arrived as the result of formal invitations from the Chinese government. In fact, they often arrived with only a few days' or even a few hours' warning. The Embassy was repeatedly in the position of having to ask the Chinese, on short notice, to provide accommodation for American officials in their guest houses. There was no charge for rooms or meals under these circumstances, of course, and finding room often necessitated embarrassing shifts involving visitors of other nationalities.

Usually our travelers came by air, en route between Tokyo and Hong Kong. Compared to those cities, Taipei had little to offer by way of shopping, sightseeing, and other amusements to divert our guests after their business was finished. Particularly in Hong Kong, most of them were glad to be left to their own devices. But in Taipei every official American traveler had at least one or two definite desires: to meet President and Madame Chiang Kai-shek and, if a military man, to see a military review or exercise. Up to a point, meeting these wishes was desirable from every aspect. But we Americans sometimes neglect to follow the old Greek proverb, "Nothing too much."

President Chiang was a busy man. His health was good, but there were physical limits to what he could or should do as he approached his seventieth birthday in 1957. He worked a fourteen to sixteen-hour day, six days every week, but on Sunday the President tried to avoid all engagements other than his regular attendance at Methodist church services. I recall one period of nine weeks when we were visited on eight weekends by parties of official Americans, all expecting to be received, and presumably entertained, by President Chiang. In fact, the President and Madame Chiang did far more for our travelers than courtesy required, but they were doing it for China. As to military exercises, which the Chinese had a flair for organizing, it became a common but obviously exaggerated joke that more ammunition was expended in putting on displays for visiting Americans than would have been needed to repel a communist attack.

II

I had written before on the general subject of official visitors, but the aggravation of our particular problems in Taiwan prompted me to put forward a proposal to the Department. The idea originated in a booklet prepared in Washington some years earlier on the subject of Congressional travel. It had been useful, although in my opinion the booklet had a defect that might have been responsible in part for the very situation which now confronted us on Taiwan. Its requirements, if followed literally, made the Foreign Service into something like a mother hen clucking and fussing continuously over her chicks. Congressmen do not necessarily like to be fussed over any more than other people.

My concern in the present case, however, was not with Congressional visits, as is apparent from the text of a despatch dated October 27, 1956:

> The cover of the *New Yorker* for September 15, 1956, portrays what has become a world-wide phenomenon in recent years; a crowd of people awaiting the arrival of a Very Important Person at an airport. The group at the ramp could well be the senior officers of any Embassy performing what sometimes becomes almost a daily chore, with serious consequences to the performance of their regular duties.

> Considerable attention has been given to the handling of Congressional visits, in view of their obvious significance. . . . Congressmen, however, account for only a minor fraction of the travelers for whom Foreign Service posts have responsibilities. In the case of Taipei, for example, visits from the Executive Departments in Washington are far more numerous than from the Legislative Branch. And the visitors in question expect no less attention, on the average, than do members of Congress. Moreover, private individuals with connections which they consider influential can be equally demanding.

> It seems appropriate, therefore, to broaden the scope of inquiry to include visitors in general, seeking methods of serving their legitimate needs without neglecting other important Foreign Service responsibilities. The present despatch attempts to do this in a very tentative and sketchy fashion.

> In considering the problems confronting the Foreign Service in the handling of visitors, there is no purpose in attempting to turn back the clock. The tremendous expansion in the world-wide responsibilities of the United States, paralleling the extraordinary development of air travel, has made a large increase in such visits inevitable. A continuing rise in the number of American travelers, official and other, must be expected and prepared for. . . .

> It goes without saying that a Foreign Service establishment

has primary responsibilities to discharge its statutory duties in the most effective manner possible, and to present the United States in the most favorable light to the government and people of the country where it is located. Unfortunately, activities in connection with official and other visits have expanded to a point where substantive Foreign Service duties are sometimes perforce neglected, while friction with the local government officials not infrequently results from excessive demands upon their time and finances. Unless corrective steps are taken, this situation threatens to become steadily worse. The national interest will suffer accordingly.

Elementary measures to facilitate official and other travel are widely appreciated. These include advance notice to the posts concerned as to schedules and the desires of the visitors. Wherever possible, notice should be sent out sufficiently in advance to permit posts to comment on the possible undesirability of arriving in a certain country on the date proposed, for whatever reason, or to suggest other changes in schedules and activities. The purpose of the visit should be given in reasonable detail, avoiding broad generalities, which are unhelpful. The wishes of the party as to tight or easy schedules, large or small meetings, days of rest, entertainment, etc., should be given as fully as possible for the guidance of the post abroad. All of these and other similar considerations are well known to the Department and will be of continuing importance.

Tactful means also should be sought to apprise the travelers, in advance, of the fact than many other Americans of no less importance are also traveling, and that American officials abroad, as well as foreign officials, have arduous and important duties besides waiting around airports and giving parties. . . . Many traveling American officials apparently expect to be met on arrival with full honors . . . despite the fact that an equivalent foreign visitor to the United States could expect little or no attention in most cases. This last point is particularly annoying to foreign officials, since in addition to serious demands on their time and funds they are also made to feel inferior in many cases.

☆ *China Assignment* ☆

It is suggested that the Department might find discreet ways to cover various points in a pamphlet prepared for travelers abroad who expect to make more than routine use of Foreign Service facilities. Such a publication could serve the threefold purpose of explaining how visits abroad impinge upon the conduct of foreign relations, what the visitor should expect from Foreign Service establishments, and at the same time it could serve to instruct the posts abroad as to what they should and should not do in such cases.

In addition the pamphlet might make brief reference to travel facilities. Contrary to conditions in wartime, transportation, hotel, and other facilities have become normal in most parts of the world. Often they are better than ever, and there is correspondingly less reason for special assistance by officials and others. Moreover, it should be American policy to encourage the maximum use of commercial transport and accomodation, in the spirit of free enterprise.

When a trip is planned, therefore, it should be on the assumption that normal facilities will be used wherever possible. Foreign governments and Foreign Service posts should not be expected to provide free lodging and meals where suitable hotels are available. In cases of uncertainty, the post abroad should be consulted in advance.

Both the rank of the visitor and the purpose of his trip are important in determining his program in a foreign country. Members of Congress and of the Cabinet, as well as other civilian and military officers of four-star rank or above may be considered sufficiently important to warrant courtesy calls on heads of foreign states and other officers of the highest rank, even in the absence of any definite mission. Americans of lesser rank or importance should expect to make such contacts only if there is a substantive reason for so doing. . . . A common American desire to talk to the "boss-man" may result in harm both to democratic processes and to the project in question. The Foreign Service establishment on the spot is in the best position to judge.

The pamphlet might go on to explain that in view of the large number of official visits abroad, and the pressure of other duties, chiefs of mission and deputy chiefs are forbidden to meet or see off visitors in person at airports, railroad stations, docks, etc., except in specified cases. . . . Other official visitors customarily would be met by one American of intermediate or junior rank, with a local assistant if needed. These requirements would have to be mandatory to be effective, and every chief of mission would have to use his authority to bring into line all United States government agencies represented in his area of responsibility.

In the case of other than official travelers, it is often useful or necessary as a matter of courtesy that their itineraries and desires should be communicated to Foreign Service posts along their route. However, the character of any instructions to the field should be quite definite, and the traveler should be informed accordingly before beginning his travel. It should be understood by all concerned that "appropriate courtesies" ordinarily do not imply entertainment by American officials and an audience with the local ruler. When instructions say simply that the visitor will call at the Embassy if he wishes anything, this should be taken literally and no one should run after him.

The foregoing suggestions are put forward quite tentatively, although they are the result of extensive experience. The matter obviously is one of the greatest importance, in which the maintenance of good relations with foreign countries, and of the efficiency of American operations abroad, are often overlooked.

III

In due course, Madame Chiang took a personal interest in the hotel situation in Taipei. The Grand Hotel—certainly a misnomer earlier—was expanded and refurbished to a point where it became one of the most attractive and comfortable establishments in the Far East. Scarcely less satisfactory was the fact that it paid its own way, despite recurring Chinese offers to official visitors to forego payment or extend a highly preferential rate. Charges were reasonable, and most of our officials were on "per diem" allowances; there was no reason for their being a further drain on the Taiwan economy, which we were trying to make self-supporting. I told the Chinese so. In any case, this hotel and somewhat smaller but adequate establishments, built or remodeled elsewhere on Taiwan, helped materially in placing visits on a more normal basis. Nevertheless, the general problem of official visitors continued to become more difficult, and I returned to the attack a year later in a despatch of October 23, 1957:

The problem of official visitors at foreign posts, dealt with in the referenced despatches and elsewhere, continues to grow more and more acute. Excessive demands upon the time of Foreign Service and other United States government personnel, and consequent enforced neglect of other important duties, is only one aspect. More serious is the unfortunate impact on American foreign relations of excessive demands upon the time and financial resources of officials in countries which the United States is expending much effort and treasure to cultivate. At the same time, these foreign officials are becoming increasingly sensitive to the superior and patronizing air of many visitors, however unintentional.

An American official of no very exalted rank often arrives at a foreign capital in a two million dollar aircraft with a retinue. He frequently expects a guard of honor, a motorcycle escort, and to be received and entertained by the head of state. A foreign official of corresponding rank arrives in Washington—if he is lucky enough to make a rare trip abroad—by commercial means. He is met, if at all, by a comparatively junior American officer, and may be received later by no one senior to a deputy assistant secretary. Actually, this latter treatment is entirely appropriate. The trouble lies in the excessive amount of official American travel abroad and the exaggerated ideas which have developed as to what should be done for the dispensers of Uncle Sam's largesse. The effect is to perpetuate certain of the most objectionable trappings of colonialism, and to undermine American foreign policy in consequence.

Taipei's despatch 168 of October 17, 1956, put forward the proposal that the Department should prepare a pamphlet for the use of officials traveling abroad. The purpose would be to make them aware of the large numbers of Americans traveling, of what they should expect by way of attention from United States and foreign officials abroad, and of the importance of making an optimum impression.

✩ *Expansion* ✩

The present booklet dealing with Congressional travel is not particularly helpful at most Foreign Service posts. If taken literally, it would compel all but the largest Foreign Service establishments to suspend virtually all other operations during the visit of a Congressional group. Statutory responsibilities are seriously neglected in such a process, particularly when it happens frequently, and the impression also is given that Foreign Service personnel have almost nothing to do except provide entertainment for visitors. But since this booklet on Congressional travel appears to be the only one of its kind, there is a tendency to apply its instructions to "distinguished visitors" in general. Thus the difficulty is compounded.

One secondary factor is that the representation allowance in a small or medium-sized post often is almost entirely absorbed in connection with the entertainment which visiting American officials have come to expect. Thus there can be no systematic planning for the most effective use of such allowances.

In view of the Department's overall responsibilities for the conduct of foreign relations, it is urged once more that steps be taken along the lines suggested in Taipei's despatch 168.

IV

The United States business colony on Taiwan remained small, despite the great expansion of our economic activities in general. Aside from a few American executives and pilots connected with commercial airlines, the number of businessmen living on the island could be counted on the fingers of one hand. The British commercial community in Taipei, despite the United Kingdom's recognition of the communist regime in Peiping, remained considerably larger than the American. British consular officers continued to function and to support their country's interests by dealing with the office of the Governor of Taiwan rather than with the Chinese Ministry of Foreign Affairs. We enjoyed cordial relations with successive British consuls and their staffs. Their large and attractive old residence near the sea and golf course at Tamsui was a favorite rendezvous of the foreign community.

In sharp contrast to the business colony, American missionary activities in Taiwan increased phenomenally after the Red conquest of the China mainland. The work of a century and more was abandoned by degrees as the communists put increasing pressure on all missionary work in the territory under their control. This extended not only to worship and religious instruction, but also to educational, medical, and other fields in which Americans had been prominent. Many priests and other clergy were imprisoned.

The old established church organizations that had supported this work in China naturally turned to areas where they might make use of their experienced personnel and extensive facilities. Like the Chinese government on Taiwan, they too were hoping and preparing for an eventual "return to the mainland." Missionaries were welcome in Taiwan, not only because of important Christian influences in the Chinese government and a wide appreciation of the good work accomplished by missionaries, but also because of evident international political advantages to Free China in cultivating the Christian churches while the communists were persecuting them.

Taiwan was by no means a virgin field for missionary endeavor. During the Dutch occupation of a few Taiwan seaports in the seventeenth century, Protestant Christianity was introduced. On his return to Holland, one of their missionaries claimed to have baptized more than 5,000 "heathen." After the Dutch withdrawal, organized Christianity largely disappeared from the island until the nineteenth century. In 1865, missionaries of the Presbyterian Church of England began work in Tainan, then the island's chief city. Medical work was begun almost immediately, and a hospital was opened in due course. The Roman Catholic Church and a very few other Protestant denominations also established themselves on Taiwan, but the English Presbyterians remained the most active. A few Canadians and Americans were associated with their work.

When I arrived in Taipei in 1950 the total American missionary representation on the island numbered perhaps thirty men, women, and children. On my departure at the beginning of 1958, the total was over seven hundred. The church organizations established on the island before World War II had expanded considerably, but much of the increase was due to the activities of Protestant denominations which had worked on the Chinese mainland but never before on Taiwan. More than a score of church organizations, several of them with numerous branches, became active and well established in Free China. The distinctions between various denominations working in so small a territory must have puzzled many Chinese, particularly those native to Taiwan; but both the government and the public followed a policy of tolerance in matters of religion, and the entire missionary development not only was highly salutary, but on the whole harmonious. Church membership grew rapidly, and new churches were established with gratifying frequency. We received surprisingly few complaints from any quarter about relationships between church and state or of frictions among denominations of differing doctrines.

In addition to the periodic and necessarily brief visits of Cardinal Spellman, Taiwan attracted increasing numbers of other prominent churchmen. Usually their stops were short, but Bishop Ralph C. Ward of the Methodist Episcopal Church spent a great deal of time on the island. He was an "old China hand" in the best sense. At the Embassy we always were glad to see him and to benefit by his vast experience and broad understanding of Chinese and world problems.

President and Madame Chiang showed their interest in Christian matters in various unostentatious ways. Prominent religious visitors were often at their dinner table. I recall one interesting evening in particular, during the second visit to Taiwan of the Reverend Billy Graham. All of the guests were engaged in Christian work except Pauline, myself, and one member of Graham's party. Someone raised the question whether it was possible to be saved without a formal profession of faith. One of the more fundamentalist guests seemed to think that it was not. Madame Chiang gently took issue with him, suggesting that many millions had never been given an adequate opportunity to become Christians. At this point Billy Graham intervened, "Isn't that something for the Lord to decide?"

v

The American effort on Taiwan did not await the formal promulgation of Parkinson's First Law to demonstrate its universality. Our first concern was to get essential jobs done quickly with whatever American personnel might be available. But between times I fought a rear guard action to keep as small as possible the number of United States agencies functioning on Taiwan, and the size of their staffs. In most cases I was unsuccessful. Individuals in authority, whether in Washington, Pearl Harbor, or Taiwan, usually agreed with me in principle. The system evidently was too much for any and all of us, but we had to keep on trying. Perhaps at least the process of expansion could be slowed down.

After General Chase's retirement, and Admiral Radford's appointment to Washington, the military command structure on Taiwan was overhauled. Vice Admiral Stuart H. Ingersoll, who replaced Vice Admiral Alfred M. Pride as Commander of the Seventh Fleet, was given concurrent responsibilities for the United States Taiwan Defense Command, which required him to set up a headquarters in Taipei. He divided his time between this headquarters and his flagship. With the Army in general charge of the Military Assistance Advisory Group, and the Navy represented by USTDC, it was inevitable that the Air Force also should establish a headquarters on the island. Of course, there were practical reasons for these steps. The chief advantages, it seemed to me, were that we now had an officer of higher rank available much of the time to deal directly with his Chinese counterparts and that all American military responsibilities for the defense of Taiwan, in theory at least, could be concentrated in his hands. The disadvantages included a further proliferation of United States organizations and a parallel increase in personnel.

Admiral Ingersoll and I saw eye-to-eye on what needed to be done in general, and I give him full credit for keeping his own headquarters as small as possible. Partly in an effort to strengthen his hand, and also to take advantage of the known sympathy and the exalted position of the Chairman of the Joint Chiefs of Staff, I wrote to Admiral Radford on January 3, 1956. My primary responsibility, of course, was for policy coordination and political relations with the Chinese, but these were inseparable from basic military considerations. Although I took full responsibility in writing this letter, I was quite certain that Admiral Ingersoll would not disagree with the following paragraphs:

> You may recall our discussions in the past as to the desirability of setting up more than one United States military headquarters on Taiwan. During the past year we have expanded from one to three such headquarters (Army, Navy, Air Force),

each reporting directly to higher authority elsewhere. In this same period of one year, the number of official Americans assigned to Taiwan has risen from 2,500 to more than 6,000, including dependents. The figure promises to approach 10,000 within the next few months, exclusive of any tactical units which may be stationed here. Housing, office, and other facilities for this official group are being supplied largely by the Chinese.

When anyone mentions the disadvantages of divided authority and responsibility resulting from the existence of three separate commands, the explanation is advanced that if a hot war should break out, everything would fall into place. This I do not accept as satisfactory. In the first place, if we are trying to win a cold war and avoid a hot one, we should be set up in the most effective possible way to further that purpose. Any other approach implies that our current policy is expected to fail and that only in a hot war can problems be solved. Moreover, I am by no means convinced that the present arrangement on Taiwan is best suited either to avoid stumbling into a hot war, or for optimum preparation in the event that such a war should break out despite all efforts to prevent it.

Take the present situation on the offshore islands, for example. The Chinese forces stationed on Kinmen and Matsu have completed their training and are more-or-less fully equipped. The responsibilities of MAAG with regard to these troops would seem to have been discharged, since MAAG has no operational functions. Yet the Americans now on the offshore islands are MAAG personnel, reporting to General Smythe. Admiral Ingersoll is dependent largely upon the cooperation of MAAG and the Chinese in finding out what is happening on the islands; Americans not under his control are called upon, inevitably, to give what amounts to operational advice to the Chinese. As far as can be, this cooperation is on a reasonably satisfactory basis. But I do not see how a fleet commander can count on winning an engagement, or avoiding one if that is his purpose, if he is dependent on the "cooperation" of his screening force.

In all of the foregoing the 13th Air Task Force remains quite independent and not even responsible to Admiral Stump. If Washington should decide, in due course, that the war had risen to a certain temperature, everything might conceivably drop into its proper slot. Meanwhile, however, much could have happened to our great disadvantage and to the utter confusion of our Chinese friends. At no very distant date we must expect the Chinese Air Force to be faced with a grave problem in maintaining local air superiority over Kinmen and Matsu. They will look to the 13th Air Task Force for advice and assistance, ignoring the Air Section of MAAG which already is being overshadowed and supposedly has no operational responsibilities in any case. And where does Admiral Ingersoll come in?

The foregoing are among our major current problems, but related to them are the political and economic aspects of supporting a large and growing American family on Taiwan. Not long after MAAG was established here in 1951, I reviewed with the various organizations concerned their prospective personnel needs, particularly as regards the numbers to be stationed in Taipei. We were all concerned lest Free China's capital should develop an "occupied territory" atmosphere, with all of the political disadvantages which that implies. A prospective figure for Taipei of 250 Americans, plus dependents, was arrived at, based upon military and economic programs substantially as large as those being carried out today. We now have some 3,000 official Americans in and immediately around Taipei, including dependents, with a total of perhaps 5,000 in prospect. We have imported a Little America, and one need only observe the street traffic and the new housing developments, etc., built for American personnel by the Chinese, to see what has happened to our original estimate and intentions. . . .

VI

Three months later we were instructed by the Department to report on how the authority and responsibility of the Ambassador were being maintained over the activities of various United States government agencies operating in Free China. I replied in detail on April 25 explaining that the Ambassador's effective authority was being maintained rather satisfactorily by informal methods. This, it seemed to me, was the only reasonable approach to controlling a situation where official agencies were now reporting to higher authority elsewhere through at least twelve separate channels. The only real alternative would have been a large increase in the Embassy's civilian staff, which as it was represented barely one per cent of the official Americans on Taiwan, even after excluding purely tactical military units. My letter of April 25 included the following:

Under the circumstances just described it obviously is impossible for the Chief of Mission and his staff in the Embassy to keep systematically informed of all the voluminous official correspondence and countless oral transactions which might conceivably involve the need of policy coordination. Considered strictly in organizational terms the problem may seem impossible of solution. If Taiwan were under United States military occupation the present situation would not be tolerated. The headquarters carrying what are now the Embassy's responsibilities would be staffed by several hundred Americans. All correspondence would pass through this headquarters, and the staff of the commanding officer would set up elaborate procedures for policy and other coordination.

A substantial expansion in the Embassy's staff, to a level by no means unknown in the Foreign Service today, would permit undertaking much of the physical coordination which a corresponding military headquarters would employ. But this would not solve the problem unless it were accompanied by an extensive revision of our several military chains of command extending to Washington, sometimes direct but more often via Pearl Harbor, Tokyo, or the Philippines. . . .

Being convinced that . . . increases in Embassy staffs invoke the law of diminishing returns at a very early point, I have taken the alternative course of placing primary responsibility on the local heads of the various official American agencies. It is their individual responsibility to detect matters involving policy and on which the Embassy should be consulted.

The various official American agencies here have responded well on the whole, particularly as they saw that we were trying to help, not hinder them. We make it as easy as possible for the other organizations to consult us. The Ambassador and the Deputy Chief of Mission are always available on short notice.

Two other senior Embassy officers have special responsibilities which take them to ICA and one or more of our military head-quarters almost daily. It is convenient to consult them and experience has shown how helpful they can be to the agencies concerned. Of course, this informal procedure depends for success very largely on the qualities of both the Embassy officers concerned and those in charge of the various other official groups in Taiwan. To date we have been fortunate on this score. I shall continue to insist on quality rather than quantity in Embassy personnel, as the only group for which I am directly responsible in this respect.

In gaining the confidence and cooperation of other agencies I have emphasized repeatedly that in principle we must have no secrets from each other. This is, of course, impracticable in a literal sense because of the extent of American activities here and their highly technical nature in many cases. But intelligent American officials get the idea quickly; they sense what is important to the Embassy and other agencies. They realize that we are all working for the United States of America. . . .

In general, I believe that the United States is conducting its operations abroad with an excessive number of American personnel. The answer to nearly every problem apparently is to send out additional experts from the United States, along with a Little America in the way of facilities to sustain their morale and, incidentally, to separate them as much as possible from the local people with whom they are supposed to work. . . .

VII

I was asked for still another survey of American organizations and personnel. My reply of June 26 listed fourteen lines of authority and a somewhat larger number of organizations. In fact, it was becoming difficult to be certain just how many there were. The total number of official Americans, including dependents, had increased by some 2,000 in the preceding six months. I continued to favor bringing along dependents for a variety of reasons, but with ever larger numbers our problems were multiplying in something like geometric proportion. I recall one of our generals saying ruefully at this time. "They have just sent me another sergeant with a wife and six children. Where shall I put them?"

It seemed essential to emphasize the growing number of lines of authority between official Americans on Taiwan and their superiors elsewhere. One or more individuals connected with a particular Washington agency or sub-agency might be serving on the staff of another organization in Taipei without creating complications. But as soon as they were given a new title, or a separate line of communication and authority, empire building became almost automatic.

Even within the Embassy itself, but more often in other offshoots of the Department of State, there was repeated pressure to set up new "sections" or "units." The usual reason was the need for a specialist to perform a given task. Assigned to one of the four traditional Embassy sections—political, economic, consular, and administrative—the specialist usually could be absorbed and still do his work with little if any corollary expansion of staff. But give him a title suggesting even quasi-independent operation, together with any encouragement from Washington to establish a separate line of communication, and the burgeoning process could be expected to begin. In addition to a secretary, he would soon need an assistant, who in turn would require a secretary, while both would of course need interpreters, and so it would go. Additional office space and housing would be required, and the expanded operation in due course would make almost inevitable further additions to the administrative establishment providing services of various kinds. All of this bore no necessary relation to the amount or character of the substantive work that our specialist had been sent out to do. In fact, these complications tended to divert attention from any consideration of whether the specialist in question was needed on a permanent basis or could have returned to the United States after a period of temporary duty. The larger the organization, the more serious was the problem, and in the armed services such unearned increments were likely to be measured in scores or hundreds of personnel. But the differences between State and Defense were only of degree.

In all of our considerations of personnel problems, a clear distinction was maintained between tactical or combat units of the armed services and all others, military and civilian. In the first place, the numbers in our tactical organizations on Taiwan were never large. We wanted to keep it that way. Secondly, since most of them were present on a rotational basis, they had few dependents on the island. Finally, the political effect was quite different as between combat forces and chair-borne personnel like the rest of us. It was obvious to all that the soldiers were in Taiwan to help directly in its defense, and an increase of a few hundred men, or even a thousand, stationed at Chinese military bases without families, had no other major political impact. Over 5,000 official Americans, including families, living in Taipei, were a different story.

I had no desire to reorganize our effort along military lines, with a single chain of command and channel of communication. Indeed, there were cogent reasons for having more than one line of authority from Taiwan. But nothing more than perhaps half a dozen could be justified. With fourteen already established and more in prospect, the problems of coordination were becoming difficult enough; the administrative headaches and the objectionable political effects were even more serious.

VIII

During Vice President Nixon's brief visit to Taipei in 1956, we discussed the troublesome organizational situation. He appreciated our arguments and subsequently took up the matter in Washington. A further tightening of responsibility for coordination followed, paralleling the result of efforts by Admiral Radford and others to straighten out lines of authority. The Vice President had also had a useful talk with President Chiang and impressed all of us once more with his grasp of Far Eastern problems.

The Nixon party arrived late one day and expected to take off about the middle of the day following. At the last moment their Constellation was found to have a flat tire, with no spare available on the island since our stable of aircraft contained only the work-horse variety. It was a sweltering day, and we brought the Vice President and Mrs. Nixon back to the Embassy where some air conditioning was available in my office. After a short rest, and while a new tire was being sought in Okinawa and the Philippines, we all adjourned to the Grand Hotel for a simple meal of Chinese chow. The first tire arrived by air and was the wrong size, but a second came in shortly afterward and the Nixons took off for Bangkok only a few hours behind schedule.

On November 6 we replied to a request from the Department for a detailed evaluation of our programs in Free China. In conclusion, I gave current figures for the number of official Americans on duty and added the following comments:

> The United States effort in support of Free China since 1950 is something of which Americans may be proud. It is well on the way toward a point when programs can and should be rounded off. One of the tests of success will be the extent to which the Chinese have been trained and equipped to run their own show. A gradual and systematic phasing down is in order for the near future, in which the quality of Chinese-American cooperation will be of paramount importance. The alternative is liable to be a drift into neo-colonialism, which the United States desires no more than China.

IX

With the arrival of General Chase and the first echelon of his Military Assistance Advisory Group in 1951, agreement was reached with the Chinese government to accord diplomatic immunity to all official American personnel in Free China. This applied equally to members of their families, although military dependents in appreciable numbers did not arrive until much later. When the total American colony reached several thousand, however, with even higher figures in prospect, it became apparent to all that diplomatic immunity for everyone was no longer an entirely satisfactory conception.

The United States had no regular military bases on Taiwan and wanted none. Tactical military forces on the island never exceeded a few hundred personnel. These usually were Air Force units, stationed temporarily at bases controlled by the Chinese, which came to Taiwan on a rotational basis intended to maintain maximum flexibility and mobility. A squadron, or other small unit, would arrive from Okinawa, spend a few days or perhaps a month or two in Taiwan, and go on to the Philippines. Other United States military units were responsible for communications, and again the numbers were relatively small. In all cases, the Chinese retained responsibility for security where American units were located. By far the largest proportion of our American military personnel continued to be engaged in advisory, supply, and administrative activities; these were scattered throughout Taiwan.

Under the circumstances, it was neither feasible nor desirable to maintain an American military police force adequate to assume responsibility for discipline. Such a force would have had to be disproportionately large, if only for geographic reasons. Its existence would have been politically objectionable, and its authority over American civilians, including military dependents, would have been at least questionable. Fortunately the United States record of behavior on Taiwan was good. There were traffic accidents, of course, but American drivers had far fewer than the general average. Insurance was carried on all private vehicles, and claims were settled with reasonable promptness. There were some cases of drunkenness and an occasional fight, usually the result of too much liquor, but the Chinese attitude on such matters was tolerant and their police usually were good humored. Chinese and Americans liked each other, and on the whole, we behaved ourselves.

As the American official colony on Taiwan approached 10,000, however, it became evident that quality was being diluted. At first, the majority of Americans were selected specialists, civilian or military, who dealt with their Chinese counterparts on a highly responsible basis. Later, as a Little America grew up on Taiwan, complete with supermarkets, an even larger proportion of our personnel occupied subordinate positions where contact with the Chinese was much rarer. In fact, many of these positions could have been filled equally well with Chinese personnel, at a fraction of the cost to the American taxpayer. At the same time, a sharp increase in street traffic ("sergeants' wives driving Cadillacs"), and American competition for the limited supply of good housing, tainted the hitherto friendly atmosphere.

It was not that official Americans on Taiwan lived in luxury; except that many were able to afford a usually untrained servant, our official family enjoyed no amenities that would have attracted attention in the United States. But Taipei, although temporarily a national capital, remained substantially a typical, provincial **Far**

Eastern town. There had never been as many as one hundred European or American residents before World War II. With more than 5,000 Americans enjoying living standards that seemed fabulous to most Chinese, we became egregiously conspicuous, to say the least. Cars driven by or transporting Americans represented a large part of the street traffic in Taipei and other cities on the island. The adverse effect unquestionably was cumulative; I have suggested that it increased as the square of our numbers.

x

Paralleling action in other countries where large numbers of official Americans were stationed, negotiations for a "Status of Forces Agreement" were initiated with the Chinese government. This was intended to cover all military personnel and their dependents in lieu of diplomatic immunity. At one point the Chinese suggested tentatively that commissioned officers might continue to enjoy diplomatic status, but such a distinction was considered unsatisfactory. The provisions of the proposed agreement usually followed precedents established elsewhere, and there were no serious differences with the Chinese except in the all-important matter of criminal jurisdiction. As it was, the draft agreement went back and forth between Washington and Taipei every few months during 1955 and 1956 without a meeting of the minds on vital points. There was continuing opposition in the United States to making any more of our military personnel subject to the jurisdiction of foreign courts. The Chinese, on the other hand, were unwilling to accept less than we had given to other countries.

There the matter stood, with the draft in the hands of the Chinese, when on March 20, 1957, an American sergeant shot and killed a Chinese. There were no witnesses. As the American told the story, his wife saw someone peering in a window of their house in the late evening. He got his .22 caliber pistol, went outside, and called to the man, who approached with something in his hand, which looked like the iron spit from a nearby barbecue pit. Thinking that the man was threatening him, the American fired. He reported the matter immediately, and a joint Chinese-American investigation was begun. I saw the Acting Foreign Minister on the following day and expressed my regret; it was the first he had heard of the case.

☆ *China Assignment* ☆

Initially the Chinese and American investigators cooperated closely on the case of Master Sergeant Reynolds, who enjoyed a good record and was engaged in medical supply work. It was established at once that the victim, Liu, a minor employee of a Chinese government agency and a reserve officer, was unarmed at the time he was shot, and had only a short stick in his hand. Later, interest in the case seemed to lessen, and the evidence available to the General Court Martial convened in May added little to the information gathered in the first few hours after the shooting. No motive was proved other than intended self-defense. Various Chinese newspapers then took up the affair, spurred on by the Girard case in Japan, which was receiving world-wide attention at the time. (Girard, an American enlisted man, was accused of killing a Japanese woman on a military firing range. Eventually, he was tried in a Japanese court.) In any case, there was no lack of hearsay in the Reynolds case. Under American military law, however, the Court had no alternative to acquittal on the charge of voluntary manslaughter. When the verdict was announced, American spectators in the courtroom applauded.

XI

I returned from one of my periodic trips to our only other "China post," Hong Kong, on May 24, the day following the acquittal. Two Chinese colonels from the adjoining air base met me at the plane. One said something about avoiding correspondents who were waiting for me in the passenger terminal. He drove me across to the military terminal to wait for my car. After trying two or three telephone numbers, I located our naval attaché, Captain Alfred D. Kilmartin, who said that he would come and get me at once. Meanwhile, the Chinese colonel explained that there had been a riot at the American Embassy, and that he was very sorry, but that Americans in the courtroom had applauded Reynolds' acquittal.

Captain Kilmartin told me what he knew about the riot and subsequent wrecking of the Embassy. On the way from the airport into town we met General "Tiger" Wang, Chief of the Supreme General Staff, who was on his way to meet me. He jumped from his car in the middle of the street and ran over to convey his regret at what had occurred.

I went directly to the Foreign Ministry. The Minister received me at once, and I made a strong oral protest at what had happened, demanding full compensation and adequate apologies. I then asked him to accompany me to the Embassy. We left the Ministry in his car, without police protection. I suggested that we stop first at the United States Information Service, since it was on the way. Entering the square where USIS was located, our car was allowed to pass through a thin police line. Hundreds of people were still inside the line and in front of the USIS building, although only a few police were in the building itself. Windows and doors had been smashed, and much of the contents of the offices, notably furniture and books, had been dumped into the street. The crowd showed no hostility toward us, and one man shouted as we passed, "Mr. Minister, save us from this disgrace."

We drove on past one of the buildings occupied by our Military Assistance Advisory Group. A few cars had been overturned in the street and some windows broken by stones, but a Chinese rifle company had kept the crowd out of the building. We were now approaching the Embassy, and it seemed unlikely that we would be able to get through the crowd that continued to fill the street. Stones were thrown at our car. Again, the Foreign Minister was recognized, and this time someone shouted, "Get him; he is to blame for everything." We reached another thin police line at the rear gate of the Embassy. No one was inside the compound except a handful of police, but a large crowd was watching events from across the street on both sides and from a small park at the intersection. As we arrived at the gate, some people in the crowd clapped their hands. A few stones came from the same direction; two struck the Foreign Minister without injuring him seriously.

We walked into the Embassy compound. The buildings were gutted. Everything inside that could be lifted had been thrown out through the doors and windows. The debris included not only chairs, typewriters, tables, and desks, but also file cabinets and small safes. I never before had appreciated how effective this method could be. A number of motor vericles had been overturned; my personal car was on its side, with a safe dropped on it from the floor above.

The police begged us not to stay. There were very few of them, and they feared that a new incursion might start at any moment. I learned that the police had succeeded in getting out the last of our

American personnel and sending them home just before my arrival. We left by the front gate and some of the police joined us in the Minister's car during a roundabout drive to the house of our counselor, James B. Pilcher. The Foreign Minister left me there; he was no less distressed over the course of events than I.

XII

Pilcher had been entertaining official visitors from Washington at the Grand Hotel when the riot started. Liu's widow and a few companions had picketed the Embassy during the morning, but there had been no suggestion of disorder. One of our officers invited her to come inside. She refused and demanded a guarantee from the Embassy that Master Sergeant Reynolds would not leave the island until she had received compensation for her husband's death. Learning that a crowd was gathering outside the Embassy, the chief of the City Police and a colonel from the Provincial Police Administration came to inspect. Apparently Mrs. Liu was doing nothing illegal. They tried unsuccessfully to persuade her either to go home or to take her protests to the Chinese authorities.

During the noon hour the curious but hitherto well behaved crowd was swelled by working people and by students from nearby schools. Presumably a normal proportion of hoodlums were among them. A few police arrived, making perhaps twenty altogether, and closed the Embassy gates. In some way word got around that Reynolds had just been flown out of Taiwan. About 1:30 P.M. the first stone was thrown, followed by a barrage at the Embassy windows of anything the crowd could lay hands on. Our political counselor Paul W. Meyer, and the administrative officer, Howard E. Chaille, were in the Embassy with six other Americans. One of these was the Marine guard on duty for the noon hour. Howard Chaille quite properly instructed him on no account to use his pistol against the mob. At this time Meyer succeeded in telephoning Pilcher at the hotel and an official of the Foreign Ministry about the seriousness of the situation. He advised Pilcher not to come to the Embassy, but to go directly to the Foreign Ministry. Pilcher did so and remained with the Minister, insisting on action, until just before I arrived.

An hour after the first stone was thrown, the mob broke down the gates and stormed into the building, smashing everything in sight on the ground floor. The Americans and a few Chinese members of our staff gathered in the air raid shelter. During the next two hours, successive waves of rioters swept through the buildings; they were made up of different groups and included many who were simply curious. The police did what they could, but it was not much. Evidently they were under orders not to use their side arms under such circumstances, and they had no weapons but their hands. Also, there were far too few of them. The mob saw immediately that they had little to fear.

Not until about 4:30 P.M. did some of the rioters discover the Americans and Chinese in the air raid shelter, which offered no protection in this case. Police tried to escort the Americans to safety, amid a shower of missiles, and eventually helped them to get away in a truck. Several of the Americans, as well as the Chinese police received painful injuries, but none of these proved serious. Two more Americans had hidden in the garage and escaped safely just before I arrived at the Embassy with the Foreign Minister. Pilcher and I could thus account for all of our staff by about seven o'clock that evening. One was in the hospital but out of danger.

The police had been right in urging that the Minister and I should not prolong our stay at the Embassy. It was getting dark; a mob pushed back the police soon afterward and had one more go at the Embassy. There was nothing to save or protect; someone tried to start a fire, which luckily did not spread.

XIII

Pauline had remained in Hong Kong, and a telephone call confirmed that all was quiet at our house on the mountain. After a conference at Admiral Ingersoll's headquarters and a telegram to the Department, I accepted Pilcher's invitation to spend the night at his house in town. Reports kept coming in of mobs threatening this or that point of the city. Fortunately, the Chinese Army had assumed responsibility at the outset for the security of all American military establishments. During the night they finally received orders to take over at the Embassy and elsewhere, as necessary. Pilcher and I were unable to confirm this until very early the next morning, however, when we found that the Army already had righted and towed away our damaged motor vehicles and had started to clean up other debris at the Embassy. We took over immediately, in the interest of salvaging "classified" material.

Order was finally restored and then came a time for more soul-searching. I had the painful duty of calling on President and Madame Chiang immediately after their return to town, and I spared them nothing. The world press descended on us from all quarters, as was to be expected, and I held a press conference. The CBS representative asked for a television interview, of which the following is a transcript:

1. Mr. Ambassador, how do you feel about the attacks against the American Embssy and USIS?

This is a very serious situation. We are greatly disturbed by this attack on American personnel and official property. I have lodged a formal protest with the Chinese government. I have protested both orally and in writing, stating that the United States expects full compensation and adequate apology.

Yesterday evening I called on President Chiang Kia-shek to stress the gravity of the situation. I wanted to be sure that he knew the facts as known to us. He is making a thorough investigation and stated that the guilty would be punished. President Chiang asked me to express his profound regrets to President Eisenhower and Secretary Dulles; also to assure them that the incident does not reflect anti-American feeling but simply resentment at the verdict of the court-martial.

There has been one real consolation. Many, many Chinese, of different walks of life, have called Embassy and USIS officials to express their sincere regrets. I am sure that the tragic action of the mob does not represent the general feeling of the Chinese on Taiwan.

2. Mr. Rankin, do you feel that the Chinese authorities took the action necessary to protect American lives and property?

We feel that the Chinese officials were slow in giving us adequate protection. They have been asked to explain the reason for the delay. An investigation is already underway. Three of the top military and police officials have been removed for failure to prevent or suppress the riots.

☆ *Expansion* ☆

I believe that the Chinese government undoubtedly was taken by surprise, but I do think that the responsible officials could have moved more rapidly than they did.

3. Mr. Ambassador, what long-term effects do you think this incident is likely to have on Chinese-American relations?

That is a most difficult question to answer. I am hopeful that the Chinese government will take the necessary steps to restore American confidence in them, and that in time our relations will be as good as ever.

Free China and the United States have long been friends and allies. We have been shocked by this outbreak of violence. I am sure that the Department of State is giving very serious consideration to this matter, but it may be some time before we can get a full picture.

XIV

In the following weeks a great deal of time and effort was devoted by both Americans and Chinese to determining the causes of the May 24 riot. A considerable number of rioters were tried and sentenced, but the trial revealed nothing new or spectacular.

My eventual conclusions were quite simple. There had been no serious public disorders on Taiwan for ten years, and internal security had become lax. The city authorities were not prepared to deal with a large mob, either in terms of equipment or numbers of police. The Chinese Army had only small tactical units in Taipei, and had no authority to act in defense of civilian establishments in any case. The two persons who could have given orders were not available. President Chiang was on a walking trip in the mountains and the Minister of Defense was visiting the offshore islands. As to the mob itself, there was little difference from mobs elsewhere. We were satisfied that while some of Liu's friends and his widow had planned a small demonstration in the hope of a cash settlement from the United States, the outbreak of violence had been spontaneous. So much for Chinese shortcomings.

The American position toward an agreement on the legal position of our military forces in Taiwan, it seemed to me, had been too inflexible. I am not a lawyer and, recognizing our world-wide problem,

I had hesitated to offer advice. Apparently Chinese law demands that one who kills must be punished, however mildly, and immediate compensation is expected if those concerned can pay anything. A Chinese court might have sentenced Reynolds to no more than sixty days' confinement, but his conviction would have satisfied both their legal conceptions and public opinion. At first such a result might seem repugnant to American ideas of justice, but that an occasional member of our Armed Services should be placed in the same position as a private American citizen, who would also be performing essential functions on Taiwan, might not have been too great a price to pay in our national interest. The Reynolds case was the first of its kind in Free China, and undoubtedly a solution fair to him could have been worked out once Chinese conceptions had been met in principle. A group of Americans was to have gathered at the Embassy on the afternoon of the riot to discuss an *ex gratia* payment to the widow. Perhaps this should have been arranged before the verdict was announced. In any event, we could expect cases such as Reynolds' to be exceedingly rare, particularly if the number of Americans on Taiwan could be gradually reduced. So we come back to what I am convinced was our major fault: too many official Americans.

Once again our Navy came to the rescue. Admiral Ingersoll offered me two attractive rooms at his headquarters. A naval medical research unit, one of the two functioning outside the United States, had leased a wing of the Taiwan University Hospital and was installing its equipment. The commanding officer, Captain Robert A. Phillips, offered us the use of a floor of his building until the Embassy could be restored. With borrowed furniture, we were functioning again after the loss of only four business days. Counselor Pilcher and Administrative Officer Howard E. Chaille produced incredible results in this period and subsequently.

XV

I was highly gratified by everything that I heard of the behavior of all members of our Embassy and USIS staffs, both American and Chinese, during the riot. They had shown courage and restraint. In a sense, they were the innocent bystanders in the Reynolds case. Other Americans did not criticize the United States Army for its handling of the case. The responsibility had been theirs, but **Major**

General Frank S. Bowen, Jr., chief of MAAG, had consulted the Embassy and the interested Chinese authorities at every step. The Army had done its best, and all Americans stood together. Some were simply more fortunate than others because of the Chinese Army's interpretation of its responsibility for security. I recommended several of our personnel for special commendation, and the Department finally approved a one hundred dollars award to one of our Chinese staff for saving a life.

I was particularly grateful to the Embassy wives who volunteered to sort out chaotic records. The results were phenomenal. The "top secret" file had not been violated, and we were able to locate sufficient cryptographic material to establish that our codes were intact. More than 90 per cent of our remaining files were reconstituted in usable form, the remainder being carefully burned. No classified documents of consequence were missing, and almost none had been exposed long enough to be considered as really compromised. We could conclude that no Chinese had raided the Embassy for the purpose of gaining access to files and codes.

An old friend, Deputy Inspector General Edwin A. Plitt, was sent out by the Department to report. His visit was pleasant and helpful. Apparently his report was not too hard on us.

The moment we were squared away, I urged our senior Americans to see what good we might extract from a bad situation. The Chinese were in a chastened mood. There were various important things that we and most of them had agreed should be done, but which for one reason or another had been neglected. Now was the time to get action, particularly in the military and economic fields. Assistant Secretary Robertson expressed some concern lest I push our Chinese friends too hard, but I reassured him in a letter of August 9. It was a fruitful period. Meanwhile, the Chinese repaired our Embassy building and paid for new furniture and equipment as well as settling for all American personal property lost in the riot. At the Foreign Minister's suggestion, a ceremony was arranged when we reoccupied the Embassy. Chinese and United States Marines raised the American flag again, in the presence of most of the Chinese cabinet and a large number of other senior civilian and military officials, Chinese and American. Toasts were drunk, and we could hope and believe that the Reynolds case and the May 24 riot were things of the past.

☆☆☆

11: Policy

I

THE YEAR 1957 was to be my last on Taiwan. I had no intimation as to when a transfer might come through, but after more than six years in one post, orders could be expected at any moment. Again, the time seemed appropriate for reviewing what had been done to date and preparing for what experience had taught us might happen in the future. Going over various papers I had written in the past, Colonel David Barrett's frequent remark came to mind, "I am a man of few words, but I say them over and over again."

There is indeed a danger of hypnotizing ourselves by continual repetition of what we have determined to be valid, and thereby closing our minds to the significance of new developments. But there also is great value in repetition, as the communists and others have taught us. In influencing opinion, we scarcely could find a better method than to simplify and repeat, simplify and repeat. Repetition is easy, but honest simplification of highly complex international issues is difficult. The communists understand this perfectly, but their philosophy does not require them to be honest or sincere. A common rule with them seems to be: oversimplify and repeat.

I had been in Taiwan longer than any other senior American official, civilian or military. Were there some loose ends that I might help to tie up? Were there experiences in the past whose significance we had overlooked while seeking guidelines for the future? One point that concerned us all was what action the United States should take once the Reds began a serious attack on the offshore islands. We

308

might have to act quickly, yet premature action obviously must be avoided lest the United States appear as an aggressor. Our aim must be to stop aggression at the onset, and thereby prevent the outbreak of a serious conflict.

Active military planning for various eventualities was now being carried on, in cooperation with the Chinese, under the able direction of Vice Admiral Stuart H. Ingersoll at the United States Taiwan Defense Command. On January 8, 1957, I addressed the following letter to the Admiral:

> Pursuant to our conversation of yesterday, I would appreciate your frank opinion of the military feasibility of the proposal described below.
>
> It continues probable, in my opinion, that a direct communist attack against the offshore islands now held by the government of the Republic of China would be either a probing operation, primarily for psychological effect and to test Nationalist and American reactions, or part of a large-scale offensive involving not only the offshore islands but other areas as well. Alternatively, communist action, at least initially, might be confined to air patrols in the Formosa Strait, followed by attacks on Nationalist ships carrying supplies to the islands.
>
> Unless they are prepared to accept the risk of open conflict with the United States, which seems unlikely for the foreseeable future, any action taken by the Chinese communists involving the offshore islands presumably would be designed to keep the United States in doubt as long as possible. It would appear desirable, however, that American policy should foresee some positive action at an early point calculated to cause the Reds to cease their attacks without United States forces having become involved in combat of any consequence. With this in mind, the following tentative proposal is put forward:
>
> *Supposed Situation:* The Reds would mount attacks against the offshore islands or supply lines sufficiently serious to threaten their eventual loss if such attacks continued.
>
> *Proposed American Action:* The United States would announce immediately the establishment of a Taiwan defense zone, bounded on the west by the China coast from Swatow

to Wenchow, in which the movement of all communist or "neutral" seaborne traffic of a contraband or war-making character, as well as flights of Red combat aircraft, would be interdicted. Responsibility for enforcement would be undertaken by the GRC (Chinese) Navy and Air Force, jointly with the United States Navy, ships of the latter initially to remain at a considerable distance from the China coast. Such evidence of United States determination and willingness to act quickly might well cause the Reds to cease their offensive operations. In any case, this immediate and positive American reaction would encourage the Nationalists in their defense and give time for consideration of any direct assistance which the United States might extend in keeping the offshore islands out of communist hands.

It should be noted that the action proposed would be taken in response to open and serious aggression against a member of the United Nations with which the United States has a treaty of mutual defense (which is pertinent even in the case of an attack aimed only indirectly at the territory specifically covered by that treaty). The United Nations could be informed accordingly and appropriate assistance from other members invited. As a next move, depending upon circumstances, the United States either could assist actively in the defense of the offshore islands or, if a contrary decision were taken and the Nationalists then became convinced that they could not hold the islands, the United States could offer to protect and assist in their evacuation as was done at the Tachens.

Admiral Ingersoll approved my suggestion in principle. I forwarded it to the Department and later had opportunity to discuss the matter with General Maxwell D. Taylor and Admiral Arleigh H. Burke, then respectively Army Chief of Staff and Chief of Naval Operations. They did not disagree with my proposal; I did not expect offhand concurrence in so important a matter. My purpose was to stimulate thinking about practical steps to be taken in an emergency. I had been concerned for some time with the importance of being prepared for quick action which would impress the enemy and clarify the situation at the same time. Much of our thinking, both military and civilian, leaned heavily on the tacit assumption that we would need and use nuclear weapons in case of war with Red China. But it seemed to me that we would hesitate to take such action until we were finally engaged in a full-scale conflict. Meanwhile we might have lost opportunities to head off such a conflict, or at least to prevent the enemy from gaining important initial advantages. When the communists shelled Kinmen Island on an unprecedented scale the following year (1958), the actual deployment of the Seventh Fleet served much of the same purpose that I had in mind.

II

The Department again called me home for consultation. Before leaving, I saw President Chiang on January 9 and again on January 12. Excerpts from my memoranda of conversation are given here:

Madame Chiang telephoned my wife asking us to have luncheon with them today, only the four of us to be present.

President Chiang opened the conversation by asking . . . whether I thought the United States was now better disposed toward their plan for a "counter-attack." I took the opportunity to say that this word frightened people in the United States. They could understand China's hope of "liberating" or "restoring freedom to" their country; they could even appreciate the aim to "return to the mainland." But to Americans, a "counter-attack" brought visions of bullets flying through the air and the danger of involving the United States in war. At the same time, I said that I hoped and believed that there was today in the United States a growing understanding that China could not remain permanently divided, and that since we certainly did not want it united under communism, it must be united in freedom.

The President then asked me to make very clear to "the Administration," while I was in Washington, that there should be no fear of his government's failing to keep its commitments to the United States. He repeated this two or three times, in different ways, and went on to say that he would never ask anything unreasonable from the United States, that he would do nothing to harm American interests, and that he would always consult us.

President Chiang next remarked that he would ask me something as a friend rather than as an Ambassador. He was writing a book, the title of which was to have been "Peaceful Coexistence?" It covered more than thirty years' experience in dealing with Soviet Russia. He wanted me to read the manuscript before leaving for Washington, and to give him my frank opinion. I said that I would be glad to do so, although my time was short and I would hesitate to criticize what he had written. The President emphasized that he wanted criticism.

Complying with President Chiang's request of January 9, I read the typescript of his proposed book and sent word that I would be glad to discuss it with him at his convenience. He replied by inviting me to tea, with my wife, this afternoon. The only other person present was Madame Chiang, who acted as interpreter.

The President opened the conversation by assuring me once more that we need have no fear of his government's attempting a "return to the mainland" without consulting us in advance. However, he believed that preparations should be made for the event. Otherwise the day would come when the United States would want the GRC (Chinese government) to do just that and would find them unprepared.

He added that Americans also need not concern themselves over the possibility of Soviet Russia going to war; certainly not unless the United States itself became directly engaged. The latter should not happen in Asia in any case.

President Chiang then observed that we would get our jailed Americans out of China if we were firm. But his thirty years' experience had taught him never to trust communist promises.

The President requested me to tell President Eisenhower that his Middle East policy was exactly right.

He then asked my opinion of his book. I replied that time had not permitted more than one quick reading, but that I found it most interesting; the presentation of various major issues was the best I had ever seen on those subjects. However, I supposed that he wanted my opinion as to the probable impact on American readers in general. On this point I suggested that the historical portions either be expanded somewhat or considerably condensed. As they stood, there were many references to Chinese individuals, places, and events which would mean nothing to the average American without some additional details, although this would not be necessary for a Chinese. In actual fact, I thought a condensation which would omit such names, places, etc., as much as possible would be preferable for American consumption.

As to communist methods and the lessons to be drawn, I thought his treatment excellent and had no suggestions to offer other than to attempt some condensation wherever possible in order to attract a larger reading public in the United States. In the final part of the book, which suggests future courses of action, I suggested a shift of emphasis to avoid the appearance of advocating war. . . . I said that the American public is highly sensitive to any kind of "war" proposal, but that his case seemed to me just as good without proposing "little wars." Pressures on Red China, and a "crusade" in the name of Asian nationalism against communist imperialism, could be advocated without suggesting the inevitability of war, large or small.

III

Although I had been in and out of Washington for some forty years, it had never before been my fortune to attend a presidential inauguration. It was an inspiring and heart-warming experience for an American who had spent so many years abroad. Otherwise, my movements during a little more than two weeks in Washington followed the usual pattern of conferences on Capitol Hill, at the Departments of State and Defense, and at the Central Intelligence Agency. Extracurricular activities included two speaking engagements, both connected with my alma mater, Princeton. One of these was an extemporaneous talk, followed by questions and answers, before members of the faculty at the Nassau Club. The other was a prepared address to my classmates of 1922 at their annual dinner in New York on January 18. Again I attempted an honest simplification of our foreign policies with incidental reference to the tiger as Princeton's symbol:

Some years ago, on the day before I presented my credentials as ambassador to the President of China, a large tiger skin arrived at our Embassy with the compliments of the Chinese Foreign Minister. It was a gift in the tradition of China, the ancient home of the tiger, where he was a symbol of strength and valor long before he came to Princeton. The Foreign Minister was not flattering me personally; he was hoping for an American policy of strength.

Unfortunately, we have not only good tigers, as at Princeton, but also some bad ones, as in Peiping and Moscow. Mao Tse-tung summed up the problem very neatly long ago. He said that when you meet a man-eating tiger, either you kill him or he eats you; it doesn't matter whether he is provoked or not. Here we have an important clue to dealing with both tigers and communists, and from very high authority.

I then reviewed our strategy in the Far East, and went on to conclude:

By methods such as I have described, I believe that our country will move forward, in strength, toward the goal of world peace with freedom. The road may be long and certainly will be difficult, but all experience shows us that strength offers the best hope of eventual victory and of preventing or limiting wars in the process. I say "preventing or limiting" rather than "avoiding," which suggests appeasement and accommodation and has no place in a policy of strength. If we are strong enough in every sense, I believe that there is a reasonable chance of keeping the peace we all desire and of placing it on ever firmer foundations.

The Chinese have another saying: "You can't negotiate with a tiger for his skin." Often our conflict with the international communist conspiracy seems much like that. Certainly we cannot negotiate with a tiger for his skin and we do not intend to negotiate for ours. When we seek ways of preventing war and easing international tensions, we can be constructive when we talk from strength. And the day is coming when we can reach the peoples, the human beings, back of the Iron Curtain and talk to them rather than to the tigers now in power. . . .

☆ Policy ☆

In all of this great effort we must so conduct ourselves as to convince friends, neutrals, and foes, not only that our way is better, but that we will persist until victory is won.

IV

I had become increasingly dissatisfied with the way nearly all of us bandied the word "policy." Taken at face value, many official statements suggested that our foreign policy was subject not only to frequent modifications but also to periodic reversals. If so, then it did not deserve to be called "policy." The United States record over the years on this score had been far superior to the aggregate of its concurrent flood of official pronouncements. But it seemed to me that we were handicapping ourselves vis-à-vis the communists, whose basic policies, both actual and avowed, were simple, widely understood, and relatively unchanging. I was increasingly impressed by our need to simplify and repeat, and again in drafting two despatches to the Department I found repetition so much easier than honest simplification.

On March 28, 1957, I forwarded to Washington a paper entitled "The Missing Ingredient in United States Policy Toward China." It followed closely upon still another review of the "return to the mainland" thesis. My attempt was to establish what appeared to be the chief inadequacy, for the longer term, of our China policy: its indifferent success in maintaining Chinese confidence in the future. Excerpts follow:

Since mid-1950 the United States has given military and economic aid to the Republic of China amounting to two billion dollars. In 1954 the two countries concluded a mutual defense treaty, each pledging armed assistance in case of need, and in 1957 nearly 5,000 Americans (not counting families) are engaged in implementing that treaty and aid program on Taiwan. The visible accomplishments are great. A military establishment of some 650,000 men has been equipped and trained to a point where it represents a formidable segment of the free world's strength. Living standards on Taiwan are far higher and economic production has been expanded at a much more rapid rate than in Red China, despite the latter's considerable accomplishment in various fields. Yet today the government on Taiwan seems as far as ever from its great objective of bringing about the liberation of mainland China from Red tyranny. In fact, the disparity between the two protagonists in total military and economic strength is increasing at an accelerated pace, to Free China's disadvantage. Nor is there any real basis, and no desire in informed Chinese circles, for a permanent independent existence on the island of Taiwan. A great people like the Chinese will never accept definitive mutilation of their country.

In recognition of the situation just described, it is not surprising that serious questions are being asked, in the United States and elsewhere, about morale in Free China. It may be accepted that satisfactory morale cannot be bought, even for two billion dollars, although financial support is an important factor. Morale depends no less on confidence in the future than on acceptance of the present. To date, morale has stood up remarkably well on Taiwan, sustained by generous evidence of American support, by faith among the Chinese leaders in their high mission, and by vestiges of the old tradition that time solves all problems. But as the years go by, and particularly as Red China becomes ever stronger, the Chinese on Taiwan doubt increasingly that time is on their side and look with growing apprehension on various possible alternatives to their dream of a "return to the mainland." . . .

Responsible officials of the Republic of China hold that to supply the missing ingredient in American policy toward China the United States need only support the government now on Taiwan in a "return to the mainland." As matters stand, however, they do not foresee such American action except possibly under an extraordinary combination of circumstances which might be hoped for but scarcely counted on. Their sense of frustration is thus compounded. They realize that effective American support for their ambitions would depend in a large degree upon broader United States policies, as yet not clearly defined, toward the liberation of captive peoples and the reuniting of divided countries elsewhere in the communist-infested world. Hence their keen interest in Korea, Germany, and Hungary. But whatever major crisis may next confront the Republic of China, and whatever may be its final resolution, the Chinese government faces the prospect of first learning about it from the daily press and of having its own future decided largely by others. A "pawn complex" is thereby aggravated while confidence and responsibility degenerate correspondingly.

Thus in 1957 the United States is confronted by a revival in Free China of such questions as: Containment or liberation? Actively posed in 1952-53, particularly before the Korean Armistice, this question of course oversimplifies the problem. Containment was a vital first step in any case, while liberation is not an alternative course but an ultimate goal, with many essential measures and an indefinite period of time in between. . . .

The United States has achieved a large degree of success in containing the present enemy and in securing its bases, in the larger sense, including those of its friends such as Free China. This has been done not only at the cost of much treasure but of commitments to use American armed forces in many parts of the world. The question now may be asked: "Has the United States succeeded in convincing its friends abroad that by working together they can survive, to live in freedom, and that the international communist conspiracy is doomed to eventual extinction? American policy development and implementation will be truly responsive to the world situation only when that question can be answered with a clear "yes." . . .

During the coming months, new measures to sustain confidence will be called for increasingly in Free China and other threatened countries. More and more they will ask where the United States is leading them, now that aid programs at levels acceptable to Congress are producing about all the results that can be expected and the Red menace remains as appalling as ever. Is the fate of the free world to depend in the last analysis upon communist mistakes and weaknesses serious enough to prevent their committing new and serious aggressions? What assurance have the more exposed countries, like the Republic of China, that they themselves will survive an eventual Red collapse? Since the communist conquest of mainland China and the outbreak of the Korean War, successive events have raised free world hopes from time to time that a corner had been turned and that communism was at last in retreat. Such hopes so far have proved illusory, and evidently cannot provide an adequate basis for practical policy determination by the United States. A longer term policy and program, with an avowed aim corresponding to the unchanging communist goal of eventual world domination, is required.

I went on to stress once more the increasing importance of action on various recommendations in political, military, and economic fields, most of which have been described earlier. I urged also the need for bringing the Chinese into our planning for the use of American aid at the earliest possible stages, both on practical and psychological grounds. In conclusion, I wrote:

Marxist scripture foresees a day when the decaying capitalist world, surrounded by triumphant communism and facing economic as well as political disaster, will strike out in desperation with whatever military strength it may possess. This should be a sobering thought for Americans who maintain that under no circumstances would the United States ever strike the first blow. Actually, of course, the American spirit would force a resort to offensive action long before the nation found itself at bay. What, then, should be expected of the smaller and more exposed countries around the periphery of the Curtain, like Free China, which the United States has armed and otherwise supported? The danger of their becoming desperate obviously is much more immediate, and the possibility of their taking desperate action is correspondingly greater.

Free China is not desperate as yet, and the vital interest of the United States requires that its allies should never become desperate. A responsible partnership of free nations, possessing identical or complementary objectives and mutual confidence in their attainment, offers the least danger of stumbling into war and the best hope of final victory.

Given a chance, most men everywhere will choose freedom. With this great initial advantage in "the battle for men's minds," the free world can and must go on, by word and deed, to convince friend and foe alike that freedom, not communism, is the wave of the future and that it will surely triumph. . . .

V

The above despatch was followed by yet another, which was to be my final effort, in a long series, to sum up United States policy toward China. The date was April 25, 1957, but the substantive portion differed in no significant degree from that of my despatch of six years earlier (see Consolidation, pages 101–4). Selections that supplement the earlier despatch are given here:

There is need for a new and comprehensive statement of American policy toward China in form suitable for publication. Many aspects of this broad and complex subject have been dealt with in authoritative public pronouncements during recent years; nevertheless, otherwise well-informed people in the United States and abroad often appear confused when discussing a course of action affecting China, even when the individuals in question are disposed to be objective. As a result, American policy toward China is variously described as weak, narrow, captious, emotional, irresponsible, bellicose, legalistic, petulant, vindictive, or sterile. Perhaps the most frequent charge still is that the United States has "no policy" toward China. These adjectives suggest that significant developments in the past are easily forgotten, and that almost everyone finds it difficult to draw a line between policy and strategy, or between strategy and tactics. . . .

United States policy toward China is essentially simple and unchanging. Under existing circumstances, the strategy demanded by that policy derives almost entirely from the necessity of confronting the world menace of communism. Only the tactics involved are necessarily somewhat complex and subject to change in the light of developing events and of American commitments elsewhere in the world.

Ever since the United States began to exert an important influence in the Western Pacific, late in the nineteenth century, its policy has supported the administrative and territorial integrity of China. The United States has opposed the creation of

319

spheres of influence in China by outside powers; it never held or sought colonial possessions on the mainland of Asia. As its closest ally, the United States played a predominant part in defeating China's enemy in World War II, and in 1943 voluntarily relinquished the extraterritorial rights and privileges in China which it had enjoyed along with other powers.

In 1945, after eight years of war and fearful human and material losses, the Republic of China found itself victorious but economically prostrate. The most populous and productive areas of the country has been occupied for many years by enemy forces. Communications—never highly developed over the enormous area of China—were chaotic. Food was woefully scarce; industry and trade were all but stagnant. Currency inflation had reached an explosive stage, and the means to bring it under early control were lacking. Nevertheless, with the economic and other aid extended by the United States in that period, the Republic of China, like other countries whose territories had been overrun by the enemy, unquestionably would have surmounted its postwar difficulties if the Soviets had permitted.

Shortly before the war ended, the Chinese and Soviet governments signed a thirty-year Treaty of Friendship and Alliance on August 14, 1945. The Treaty provided, among other things, for mutual assistance in the war until victory was won, for "close and friendly collaboration" thereafter in peace, for "mutual respect" of each other's "sovereignty and territorial integrity," for "non-interference" in the other's internal affairs, and for mutual "economic assistance in the post-war period." The Soviet plenipotentiary, Molotov, at the same time handed the Chinese a note assuring them that, in carrying out the Treaty, the Soviets would give China "moral support and assist her with military supplies and other material resources, it being understood that this support will go exclusively to the National Government as the central government of China."

The Republic of China subsequently introduced a draft resolution before the United Nations, dealing with the conduct of the Soviet Union in relation to the 1945 Treaty, and on February 1, 1952, the General Assembly announced its findings. These were that the U.S.S.R. had obstructed the efforts of the National Government of China in re-establishing Chinese national authority in Manchuria after the end of the war in 1945, and gave military and economic aid to the Chinese communists against the National Government; also that, in general, the Soviets had failed to carry out the 1945 Treaty with China. The United States supported that resolution.

Defeated on the field of battle in Korea, with United States forces once more playing a predominant role, the communists sought an armistice. One was signed on July 15, 1953, after protracted negotiations, which the Reds have since violated continuously and flagrantly in many ways. An essential provision of the armistice was that it would continue until a political settlement had been reached. No such settlement has been possible, however, owing to the refusal of the communists to consider any terms which the United Nations or the Republic of Korea could possibly accept. A state of unresolved conflict exists, therefore, between the United States and communist China. All trade and financial transactions with Red China are prohibited by United States laws and regulations. Travel in enemy territory invariably is denied to United States citizens in time of war, and communist China cannot be considered as other than enemy territory.

Meanwhile, the government of the Republic of China established a temporary seat on Taiwan early in 1950. More than half a million men of its armed forces were evacuated from the China mainland, and over a million civilians chose life on Taiwan in preference to communist rule. These included many prominent leaders in government, both civil and military, and also large numbers of outstanding personalities from professional and business life. Of the 760 members of the Legislative Yuan popularly elected from all parts of China in 1948, no less than 540 came to Taiwan to continue their constitutional duties.

The repair of war damage and the general economic development of the island were expedited with the transfer of the National Government to Taiwan. The armed forces were reorganized and their training intensified. Other than for the defense establishment, the various agencies of the central government were reduced to skeleton proportions for their sojourn on

Taiwan, and a maximum of responsibility for internal affairs
was left with the regular provincial authorities. By 1951, expanded United States aid, both military and economic, was
playing a major role in Taiwan and nearby islands, often referred to collectively as Free China.

United States support for its long-time friend and ally, the
Republic of China, was placed on a definitive basis by the signature of a Mutual Defense Treaty on December 2, 1954, which
received the overwhelming approval of the United States Senate.
The Treaty commits the United States to assist in the defense
of Taiwan against aggression, following the pattern of earlier
agreements with the Philippines, Japan, and Korea. By 1957
the re-equipped military establishment of Free China once more
constituted a large and vital part of the free world's might in
the Western Pacific. Taiwan became indeed a position of
strength, where United States military bases were unnecessary;
the substantial military capabilities of Free China itself constituted an important deterrent to Red aggression elsewhere in
East Asia.

In economic and social fields, an evolutionary land reform
was accomplished on Taiwan after 1950. Living standards rose
far higher and economic production expanded more rapidly
than in Red China or in most other Asian countries. Notable
progress was made in education and public health, to levels all
but unprecedented in Asia. Last but not least, communist subversion was brought under control without imposing excessive
limitations on personal liberty. With any internal Red influences
thus largely eliminated on Taiwan, the government of the Republic of China was able to accomplish, with the United States
assistance, what the Soviet Union had prevented on the mainland of China.

Free China ranks among the more populous half of the members of the United Nations, which the government of the Republic of China has supported faithfully since its creation. The
United States feels a deep loyalty to Free China and its government, which remained faithful to the Allied cause throughout
the darkest days of World War II, and in the light of all available evidence the government now seated on Taiwan is far more

representative of the Chinese people than the Red regime in Peiping.

Popular support is difficult to measure in a communist police state, but there is no reason to believe that the Peiping regime enjoys the loyalty of more than the usual small fraction of the population on which Red regimes elsewhere place genuine reliance. A highly significant indication was given by nearly 20,000 Chinese soldiers captured by United Nations forces in Korea; three-quarters of them chose to come to Taiwan rather than return to the communist mainland where they were born. Among more than ten million overseas Chinese, particularly in Southeast Asia, the government on Taiwan has retained the loyalty of a surprisingly large percentage, certainly including a majority of the better educated and more influential persons, despite the colossal handicap of its military defeat on the mainland in 1949 and the fact that these overseas Chinese have almost no traditional connection with Taiwan itself.

On one issue the government on Taiwan and the communists on the mainland are in full agreement: there cannot be two Chinas. A great people like the Chinese will never accept the permanent mutilation of their country. This only reinforces the conclusion that there can be no genuine lasting peace in Asia while half a billion Chinese remain under communist rule. Peace will remain in jeopardy and freedom a word of mockery until a reunited China joins the free world. Lenin said that the road to Paris lay through Peiping. In any case, China is half of Asia and Asia is half the world. The fate of China may well determine the fate of all.

At this point I endeavored to sum up in two sentences what I described as "enduring United States policy"—the only policy deserving of the name:

The United States foresees a new China united in freedom, under a government enjoying wide popular support, freed of foreign domination, and fulfilling its international obligations as a peaceful and friendly member of the family of nations. Within the framework of its world-wide commitments, including the United Nations Charter, the United States will do everything in its power to bring about these conditions in China.

In two additional sentences I tried to indicate the general nature of our strategy in confronting and counterbalancing the Red menace in East Asia:

> In support of its policy toward China, the United States contributes to the military, economic and political strength of like-minded countries in East Asia, and specifically the Republic of China established temporarily on the bastion and rallying-point of Taiwan, with the purpose of producing a continuous improvement in the position of the free world relative to the communist regimes in that region. The United States will pursue this strategy until all China is again under the effective control of a Chinese government possessing the qualifications sought by American policy.

With this brief summary of what I considered to be our policy and strategy, I went on to describe in more detail what often was called American "policy," but actually should be termed current tactics:

> Since United States strategy demands a continuous improvement in the relative position of the free world, Red China's entry into the United Nations would require new and heroic tactics to compensate for the prestige, influence, and power which the communists would gain with the seating of their second most important state in the world organization. Such a prospect, together with the inevitable weakening of the United Nations itself which would result from accepting into membership a powerful and unrepentant aggressor dedicated to the goal of communist world domination, warrants every possible exertion on the part of the United States to exclude Red China from the world body. Should Peiping be seated in the end, the United States would have no choice but to redress the balance in favor of its national interest and that of friends and allies who share actively in confronting the communist menace in East Asia. The temper of the Congress, on the various occasions when the

antecedents of this question have been considered, leaves no doubt that the action eventually taken would reflect in full measure the unswerving determination of the United States to pursue its basic strategy to a successful end. Such action should eliminate once and for all the remotest possibility of American recognition for the communist regime in Peiping.

In the military field, the United States Navy commands the seas in the Western Pacific, including the approaches to countries which it is committed to defend, such as Free China. The Air Force and Navy maintain air strength and mobility in the region sufficient to establish air superiority over vital areas on short notice, in addition to possessing general supremacy in nuclear capabilities. Military aid programs assist countries of the free world in East Asia to maintain internal order and to provide in varying degrees for self-defense, according to their abilities and willingness. In the Republic of China and Korea, the two East Asian allies of the United States willing and able to maintain armed forces with capabilities beyond those of pure defense, substantial aid is provided to maintain highly trained and well-equipped military establishments of over 600,000 men in each country. These forces, together with those of the United States, substantially counter-balance communist military strength in East Asia. Such a balance is a basic and minimum requirement.

United States economic programs are designed to support the defense effort of friendly and allied countries, and to promote their economic development. A modest but steady rise in living standards is sought, such as to maintain at all times in Free China and other free countries of East Asia a level appreciably above that of communist China. The ultimate goal, when peace and security are attained and military burdens eased in consequence, is that the free nations should be able to support themselves.

It should be noted, however, that United States strategy calls for improving the *relative* positon of the free nations. The essential corollary to economic aid to allies, therefore, is the denial or limiting of offsetting benefits to the communist regimes which threaten those allies. Existing trade between the free world and Red China, and any further relaxation of restrictions on such trade, obviously serve to undermine basic United States strategy. Purely economic factors are of secondary importance in the well-established communist trade pattern; normal commercial exchanges are held to a minimum, while strategic and political advantages remain the primary goals. While the financial benefit to communist China of increased trade with the free world would be at least as important as to the supplying countries, political and other advantages to the Reds would be far greater and with no compensating gain for the supporters of United States strategy.

The most serious result of relaxing trade restrictions in Red China, however, would be the political effect throughout East Asia. Communists everywhere would gain in influence and arrogance by so clear a demonstration of Red China's ability to attain its ends without atoning for past and continuing crimes, while the free world would be made to appear blind to its fate and interested only in immediate financial profit. If feasible, it doubtless would be cheaper and certainly less hazardous to compensate free world traders for any benefits they might gain from deals with communist China rather than to expand United States aid programs and commitments sufficiently to offset prospective Red gains from such trade. The whole question, of course, is in large measure beyond the power of the United States to control except for the maintenance of a total embargo on any trade of its own with communist China. However, friendly countries and others are left in no doubt that the United States also favors strong, effective multilateral controls on commercial exchanges with the Chinese communists. A modest reduction in their trade is not too much to ask as a contribution from its friends toward the tremendous military and economic burdens which the United States carries for the benefit of the free world in East Asia.

The criterion of relative advantage evidently should be applied also to cultural exchanges and to all travel on the China mainland. Permitting American correspondents and others to visit communist China would give the American public a certain amount of information in addition to the considerable volume already available from other sources, including objective individuals of various nationalities. It is improbable, however, that Americans would be permitted to learn appreciably more on the China mainland than European and Asian observers already there. A police state such as Red China has unrivaled means of controlling the movements of an individual and what he sees and hears, without being at all obvious about it.

Certainly the Peiping communists would never ask American correspondents and others to visit mainland China if they did not feel quite able to handle the situation to their own advantage. So far from reflecting on the objectivity of the Americans concerned, communist methods would capitalize on the genuineness of that objectivity. Thus the more experienced American observers would be expected to report both the good and what they were able to learn and send out of the bad, while others would be counted on to accept enough of what they were told to produce a total picture favorable to the Peiping regime.

Again, however, the immediate practical results of permitting American citizens to visit communist China would be less significant than the political or psychological effect throughout East Asia and elsewhere. As in the case of trade, relaxation of restrictions on travel to a country which practices the holding of American citizens as political hostages, and otherwise brazenly flouts the accepted rules of decent international conduct, would be hailed as evidence that United States policy had changed from firm confrontation to tacit accommodation. The encouragement thus given to the communists would be scarcely less damaging to United States interests than the concurrent disillusionment of its Asian friends and allies. . . .

Some day the international communist conspiracy will be exorcised. The Red menace in East Asia and elsewhere will disappear, whether by evolution, revolution, or war, piecemeal or otherwise. The only substantial alternative would be a free world surrender on the installment plan. The United States plans neither for defeat nor surrender, but for success and victory. By exploiting to the full all measures short of war, while maintaining a background of adequate military strength, there is a reasonable chance of eventual success without resort to armed conflict. Any significant yielding in this process by the free world in Asia, however, would suggest unwillingness or inability to learn from the endless record of communist perfidy and dedication to global conquest. If so, then the so-called free world would scarcely deserve to survive. The United States intends that it shall survive and that China, a quarter of mankind, shall have full opportunity to share in a better, freer future for humanity.

VI

Less than one month later, on May 24, 1957, the sacking of the American Embassy in Taipei took place. I was glad that my recent despatches on policy toward China had been completed and forwarded. In the weeks and months following the riot we were far too busy with other matters to prepare lengthy political reports. Moreover, the atmosphere for some time was not conducive to objective thought. By fall, however, we were once more functioning in our refurbished chancery. Despite our sobering experience, we could say in retrospect that the American effort in Free China had suffered no permanent damage. In fact, much good had been salvaged from what had seemed at the time an unholy mess. Our policy and strategy remained unchanged, and no significant modification of tactics had been required.

On September 12, Under Secretary of State Christian A. Herter, accompanied by Mrs. Herter and Ambassador (former Congressman) James P. Richards, arrived in Taipei for a visit of two days. The occasion was used to review the May 24 riot and its aftermath, as well as to discuss broader aspects of our effort in Free China. There was a useful conference with President Chiang. I thought that the visit went off very well indeed.

At this time our Consulate General in Hong Kong prepared a thoughtful paper on American policy toward that colony. My comments were put in a letter of September 15 to Consul Thomas P. Dillon:

Let me say that I find myself virtually in complete agreement with your strictures. Our policy toward Hong Kong has long been kept in the "too-hard file," for reasons which have never seemed valid to me. To consider Hong Kong as a problem apart from other areas in the "Near West" (which I much prefer to "Far East"), and to shy away from the mere mention of "colonialism," simply is not responsive to the situation.

Some years ago a British Foreign Secretary—I think it was Ernest Bevin—said that Hong Kong in due course should be reunited to a friendly, stable China. Doubtless the same thing has been said by others; it certainly is not far from our own view. Meanwhile, both the British and ourselves want to keep it out of communist hands, and in doing so we both recognize that there is no alternative to continued "colonial rule." The Chinese government here unquestionably feels the same way. The vote is unanimous!

As a corollary to the foregoing, I have long favored seeking agreement with the British on defense arrangements for Hong Kong, something which our military men, at least, also have come to recognize. To the extent necessary for practical purposes, the Chinese here can be brought into this picture. A couple of years ago President Chiang told me that he would be glad to help us, and with no political strings attached. In return, of course, we could ask the British to modify some of their other policies in this part of the world.

I hope that your paper will stimulate Washington thinking in a more positive direction.

VII

Pressure of duties in Taipei had prevented as much travel around the beautiful island of Taiwan as Pauline and I should have liked. In the course of more than seven years, however, we had been able to visit most of the principal points of interest at least once. But we had never been out to Green Island and Orchid Island, off the southeast coast of Taiwan. As our last year was drawing to a close, the Chinese Navy and the Peace Preservation Corps invited us to see them.

In addition to a small civilian population, Green Island contained a political reformatory for several hundred military personnel and civilians who had been convicted of illegal communist activity. There were no gates at the entrance of their spacious and immaculate camp, which we visited. Much of the inmates' time was spent attending lectures and other classes.

Orchid Island, farther south, had been called Death Island in earlier years because of a fever often contracted there. However, this had not prevented the primitive aborigines from maintaining themselves under Japanese and subsequently under Chinese rule. They continued to live in their simple houses, half underground, and to cherish various customs and superstitions. A few retained the handsome silver headdresses which they had inherited. Our efforts to buy one met with refusal on the grounds that it would be bad luck to sell. Meanwhile, the Chinese had opened a school on the island for the aboriginal children and were helping the population to improve both health and living standards.

On the return voyage from one of these islands, on board a destroyer, I was invited to the wardroom and confronted with a huge cake. Our hosts had learned that it was my fifty-ninth or, in Chinese terms, my sixtieth birthday. Again, in their terminology I had completed a "cycle."

Admiral Ingersoll was succeeded by Vice Admiral Austin K. Doyle, who carried on in the best Navy tradition and in closest cooperation with the Embassy. Major General Frank S. Bowen, Jr., continued in command of the Military Assistance Advisory Group, and Brigadier General Benjamin O. Davis, Jr., commanded our Air Task Force. Joseph L. Brent as director of our economic mission, and Ralph L. Powell as head of the United States Information Service, completed an exceptionally effective "country team." James B. Pilcher, my counselor and deputy at the Embassy, had proved himself one of our finest and ablest Foreign Service officers. Within a few months all of us were to be transferred elsewhere. Early in December word came that I would be appointed ambassador to Yugoslavia, and that I should arrive in Washington early in January before going on to my new post.

My successor as ambassador to China was to be Howard P. Jones, my former counselor. The Chinese were delighted with the selection. At the last moment, however, he was sent to Indonesia instead, and the Taipei post was filled by Everett F. Drumright, who had been Assistant Secretary Robertson's deputy in Washington and later consul general in Hong Kong. His extensive Far Eastern background and known sympathy for Free China's cause also made Drumright an excellent choice.

☆ *Policy*

The American University Club of Taipei invited me to address the membership at a dinner on December 18. This club was made up of several hundred Chinese and a number of Americans, all of whom had studied at colleges and universities in the United States. They included many of the most prominent Chinese in public life, and served as one more evidence that a great part of the "cream of China" was on Taiwan. My remarks were published some weeks later in the official Bulletin of the Department of State, thereby implying the Department's approval of what I had said as a statement of policy. The text follows:

Just over a year ago I had the privilege of addressing this distinguished body of Chinese and Americans who have shared the benefits of education at more than one hundred colleges and universities in the United States. At that time the entire world had been watching events in Hungary. The magnificent effort of the Hungarian people to regain their freedom had been ruthlessly suppressed by Russian troops. Yet we had seen new and unmistakable evidence of highly significant ferment behind the Iron Curtain. Here was reason for new hope that the evil power of international communism was indeed weakening from within. I concluded my remarks of last November by pointing out the overriding advantage enjoyed by China as compared to Hungary. That is, of course, the existence on this great island of Taiwan of a strong and progressive government, dedicated to bringing all of China, united in freedom, back into the family of free nations.

My time in China is coming to an end. It is nearly eight and a half years since I went to Canton and more then seven years since I arrived in Taiwan. It has been a period of trial, but also a time of accomplishment and hope. . . .

Today the Republic of China has come a long way from the dark days of 1950. Some mistakes were inevitable, both by Chinese and by their American friends and allies. But on balance we may take pride in what has been done in this great cooperative effort. I question whether, in general terms, a greater or more rapid advance in military, economic, social, political and international fields would have been humanly possible. The task ahead is to make the best use of this sound base to which so much effort has been devoted.

Now, let me say a few words about the future. For those whose interests are not directly involved there is always an attraction in accepting the *status quo*. It suggests peace, or at least the indefinite postponement of conflict. Many people ask, therefore, that we be "realistic" and "face the facts of life" by recognizing the Peiping regime. My reply to such proposals is that they overlook the real facts. Honest acceptance of the two Chinas concept is a political impossibility for any Chinese regime, whatever its political complexion. A great people like the Chinese will never acquiesce in the permanent dismemberment of their country; witness the history of Manchuria. But for the sake of argument, let us suppose that Peiping nevertheless should seem to agree to the existence of two Chinas. The government on Taiwan could only regard this as further evidence of communist duplicity, a move to gain tactical advantage in preparation for ultimate conquest. In any case, the government of the Republic of China cannot break faith with the Chinese people in such fashion.

Another question frequently asked in the name of "realism" is whether the government of the Republic of China genuinely believes in a "return to the mainland." My answer is yes. Since the conception of two Chinas in permanence must be excluded, there is no substantial alternative to reunion. However, many people both in China and abroad tend to regard this problem in purely military terms. They picture a huge amphibious operation, a great armed assault, with banners flying and bugles blowing. Now it might happen that way, but I would hope not. Military strength is essential in any event, but its optimum employment is to bring victory with a minimum of actual fighting. I need not describe the truly horrible character of full-scale modern war, for military and civilians on both sides. The Chinese people will fight for freedom if need be, no matter what the cost, but how much better if they can be spared at least some of the sufferings with which they are all too familiar!

I am confident that the Chinese Armed Forces will play a vital part in the eventual liberation of China, whether as a military force in being, or on the field of battle, or as forces of reoccupation and reconstruction. I believe also that political, economic, and social developments on Taiwan will be equally important with military strength in the redemption of China. And I am sure that the continued success of the Chinese government in maintaining friendships throughout the free world will contribute no less significantly to the same end. In these several ways, Free China today leads a crusade against the malignant influence of international communism which far transcends the conception of a purely military counter-attack against the mainland.

In his speech at San Francisco last June 28, Secretary Dulles predicted:

"We can confidently assume that international communism's rule of strict conformity is, in China as elsewhere, a passing and not a perpetual phase. We owe it to ourselves, our allies and the Chinese people to do all that we can to contribute to that passing."

And in conclusion he said:

"The capacity to change is an indispensable capacity. Equally indispensable is the capacity to hold fast that which is good. Given these qualities we can hopefully look forward to the day when those in Asia who are yet free can confidently remain free and when the people of China"—he referred, of course, to all Chinese—"and the people of America can resume their long history of cooperative friendship."

Free China is rich in leadership, in intelligence, in capacity for hard work, in patience, in determination, and in the capacity to hold fast that which is good. The Chinese government and people are engaged in an epic struggle to restore freedom and union in their country. The tyrants in Peiping leave no alternative to Free China but a policy of "we or they." All of the great qualities of the Chinese people are needed to bring success, and among these, patience and determination are indispensable. Persisting in the efforts which have accomplished so much, and never doubting the righteousness of Free China's cause, must lead to victory.

I leave with confidence in that victory.

On this occasion I was presented with a huge, yellow silk umbrella as a mark of honor. This was in accordance with old Chinese custom, I was told, but the audience enjoyed some fun at my expense when the question arose as to how I was to take it home, with the six-foot iron pipe which held the umbrella aloft. The pipe and various attachments had to be left behind.

IX

The Chinese were aware of our laws and regulations against acceptance of decorations or gifts having intrinsic value. As Pauline and I prepared to leave, we were deeply touched by many tokens of thoughtfulness from our Chinese friends. Instead of the decoration usually given to departing diplomats, President Chiang prepared for me a scroll in his own calligraphy, with the motto "Same boat, mutual aid." He presented it at a farewell luncheon, accompanied by some generous remarks. Chiang Kai-shek is a truly great man, and I had developed not only great respect for him but also warm affection. Pauline and I shared a similar regard for Madame Chiang.

Patriarchal Yu Yu-jen duplicated two scrolls he had written for me earlier and which had been lost in the riot. They contained the adjuration, "Bring light to our world. Sow good seed in the field." The flattering Chinese implication was that I had done these things. Most unusual of all was a book containing paintings and poems in calligraphy, which had been prepared for us by a number of leading Chinese artists and scholars.

I left Taipei for Washington on January 3, 1958. Pauline stayed on a few days longer before starting around the world in the opposite direction to meet me in Belgrade. Despite a steady drizzle, there was a sizable crowd to see me off at the airport, including cabinet ministers, generals, and many others. Among them was one whom I should miss particularly, Chao Shi-yu, who had looked after our household since Canton and Hong Kong days. We called him our steward rather than using the Chinese term "No. 1 boy," and more than that he was and is a good friend. A still larger crowd saw Pauline off some days later. Altogether, everything was quite different from our arrival seven and one-half years before. It was time to go, but I left with great regret.

☆ *Policy*

Whatever we at the Embassy had been able to accomplish in the preceding years had been due very largely to the splendid leadership and support, together with the exercise of almost infinite patience, which Secretary Dulles and Assistant Secretary Robertson had demonstrated. It is with special gratitude, therefore, that I quote the letters which they wrote on my departure from China:

January 31, 1958

Dear Karl:

As you leave for your new post in Belgrade I wish to express my deep appreciation for your outstanding services as Ambassador in Taipei during the past seven and one-half years. Your performance in this position during a troubled and momentous period in our relations with China has been in the highest tradition of American diplomacy.

In a very real sense you have symbolized in your performance as Ambassador in Taipei the constancy of United States policy and the traditional desire of the American people to put principle before expediency. In your actions and statements you have unfailingly demonstrated the determination of the United States not to permit Communist imperialism to engulf any more free peoples. You can feel justifiable pride in such a record.

After five years of close and warm association with you it is with deep regret that I see you leave the Far East. I will sorely miss your able and loyal support. My best wishes and those of your many colleagues in FE go with you on your new assignment. I am confident that your service in this important and demanding post will redound to your credit as fully as your exemplary performance in Taipei.

Sincerely yours,
WALTER S. ROBERTSON

February 7, 1958

Dear Mr. Ambassador:

The success of United States policy in assisting the growth of a strong Free China can in no small measure be attributed to the vision, skill and energy with which you carried out your duties during the seven and one-half years you served as Ambassador to the Republic of China. You may take satisfaction from the knowledge that in this way you have helped to curb Communist expansion in the Far East.

I wish you success in your new assignment.

Sincerely yours,

JOHN FOSTER DULLES

☆ ☆ ☆

Index

☆ *Index* ☆

☆ *Index* ☆